Donald Kennedy's
commencement speech coda
1981–1992

"Your days are short here;
this is the last of your springs.
And now in the serenity and
quiet of this lovely place, touch
the depths of truth, feel the hem
of Heaven. You will go away
with old, good friends.
And don't forget when you
leave why you came."

- Adlai Stevenson

Our family is touched and
honored by your presence today.

Robin Kennedy 10/24/21

Artwork by Donald Kennedy (2020)

A PLACE IN THE SUN

A PLACE IN THE SUN
A Memoir

DONALD KENNEDY

STANFORD UNIVERSITY LIBRARIES

Published by the Stanford University Libraries.

Copyright © 2017 by the Board of Trustees of the Leland Stanford Junior University.

No part of this book may be reproduced or transmitted in any form or by any means, electronic or mechanical, including photocopying and recording, or in any information storage or retrieval system without the prior written permission of the Stanford University Libraries.

Printed in the United States of America on acid-free, archival-quality paper.

Library of Congress Cataloging-in-Publication Data

Names: Kennedy, Donald, author.
Title: A place in the sun : a memoir / Donald Kennedy.
Description: Stanford, CA : Stanford University Libraries, 2017. | Includes bibliographical references and index.
Identifiers: LCCN 2017020153 | ISBN 9780911221596 (cloth : alk. paper)
Subjects: LCSH: Kennedy, Donald | Stanford University—Presidents—Biography. | Biologists—United States—Biography.
Classification: LCC LD3025.K46 A3 2017 | DDC 378.0092 [B] —dc23
LC record available at https://lccn.loc.gov/2017020153

ISBN 9780911221619 (e-book)

Designed by Bruce Lundquist

Typeset by Thompson Type in 10/14 Crimson Text

CONTENTS

Foreword   vii

Introduction: Steeples of Excellence   1

1. Long Journey West   15

2. Growing Pains: Early Career   27

3. Life on the Farm   43

4. Academic Freedom and Academic Duty:
    The Case of H. Bruce Franklin   61

5. Mr. Kennedy Goes to Washington   73

6. The Best Job in the World   89

7. The Rewards and Responsibilities of Leadership   123

8. Of Patents, Profits, and Their Ensuing Effects   143

9. Money Matters: The Indirect Costs of Doing University Business   151

10. Post Presidency: Picking Up the Pieces   163

11. Science: The Final Frontier   175

    Epilogue   201

    Robin's Epilogue   207

    Donald Kennedy: Memberships, Boards, and Directorships   209

    Sidebar Contributors   211

Notes   217

Donald Kennedy: Bibliography   221

Index   231

FOREWORD

I HAVE A PHOTO TAKEN at the end of my last game playing football for Stanford. Through miraculous circumstances that put us in field goal range, we had saved a loss to Cal (Stanford's archrival since 1892) with literally zero time on the clock. The sidelines erupted, and I turned around, and *there* was Don Kennedy. I hoisted him into the air and hugged him so hard that I could easily have broken a rib or two. Some photographer caught that picture, and I still treasure it (see p. 129). The irony is that within a couple of days I went from that height to the news that I wouldn't be playing football again. And then it was Don who hoisted *me*—academically, emotionally, spiritually.

I'd had a good year as a senior player and had another year of eligibility but was shocked when the coach told me that he was not inviting me back. I had planned to return for a master's degree but, without my athletic scholarship, I had no arrangements to pay for it. It pulled the rug from under me. Don heard about my situation and took it to heart, feeling that this was not the way my Stanford academic career should end. I was a good student, involved in public service; he went to bat for me with the coach, and I was able to keep my scholarship, although not allowed to play football. It was a difficult blow, the first time in my life that I confronted what I interpreted as failure. But Don helped me to reinterpret it as an opportunity, not only offering me a place to live in a cottage connected to his residence at Hoover House but also encouraging me to apply for a Rhodes scholarship, something I could not have done had I continued to play football.

What amazed me about Don, with all that was going on in the University, was the priority he gave to students, his interest in us as people, in the pulse on campus. He showed such joy and took such nourishment from his connections with students and his engagement in issues. We all stand on the foundations of our younger years. We owe debts to people from the past that we can't repay. Those include people whose names we don't know, who fought for us in wars or the civil rights movement. But Don is someone who I do know, and who, at a tough time in my life, was such an important leader, friend, and mentor, the foundation of who I am. He lifted me at an inflection point in my youth and helped make me the person I am today. I'm deeply grateful to Don and Robin Kennedy, and I hope that the leadership I'm rendering now as an adult, as a U.S. senator and public servant, in some way pays forward the goodness, the kindness, the love that he and Robin gave to me during my college years.

To have a mentor with the wisdom he had gained leading Stanford in times of both triumph and challenge was a powerful moment in my past. I thank him for helping me understand that there was a larger plan for my life if only I embraced it. Living for a year in close proximity to Don at a very impressionable age was one of the great gifts of my academic career. To watch him leading through the indirect cost crisis, through professional and personal attacks, under tremendous stress and strain, with clouds amassed over his head and challenges raining down on him, was a study in leadership, character, and discipline, always better shown in times of crisis than when all is going well.

While this memoir recounts some of those encounters, it more importantly chronicles the extraordinary achievements of an exemplary life—one of innovation, discovery, and deep devotion to public service. Behind the mentor, teacher, chairman, commissioner, editor, and president, was always the brilliant, insightful, and discerning mind, a man of intellect, compassion, and balance in all endeavors.

—Senator Cory Booker

A PLACE IN THE SUN

INTRODUCTION
Steeples of Excellence

IN 1960, when I arrived as an assistant professor on "the Farm"—a name Stanford takes from its nineteenth-century beginnings on Leland Stanford's Palo Alto Stock Farm—the University was a respected regional institution but certainly not the international leader in higher education that it became in the ensuing half-century. Little did I know that Stanford, where I would spend nearly all my professional life, was poised at that moment on the threshold of profound transition, rising from its rural past to sow the seeds of a global future, one that would transform the nature of human society. The roots of the digital revolution reach deep into Stanford history.

The rise of the American West and the life of Leland Stanford were synergistic, setting in motion a chain of events that would revolutionize the means by which we conduct our lives. As a California governor, U.S. senator, and one of the Big Four who built the western leg of the transcontinental railroad, Stanford's final gesture was to found a university on the far edge of the last West, one that would not only come to lead the world in higher education but would ultimately spawn a revolution in technology comparable to the advent of writing, printing, or electric power.

At first, the new University suffered financial difficulties in the wake of Stanford's death and the Panic of 1893. To keep the school going, his widow Jane pawned her jewelry and sold her railroad stock. A few years later, the 1906 earthquake leveled many campus structures, bringing new financial woes. Yet innovations by Stanford scientists and engineers were already anticipating the link with local companies that would one day make Stanford the incubator of new technology. Within three years of the devastating quake, a young Stanford graduate started Federal Telegraph in Palo Alto, producing radios and making the region a leader in the development of vacuum tubes. David Starr Jordan, the University's first president, was an investor. California's dependence on the East for electrical equipment impelled a number of faculty members to invest in electrical start-ups launched by Stanford graduates. In 1912 they backed Lee de Forest's work on amplification, a key step in the birth of electronics. But the process by which

Stanford would become a wellspring of innovation and an entrepreneurial epicenter awaited a Stanford graduate named Frederick Terman, who returned to
the University as an electrical engineering professor in 1925, destined to become
the father of Silicon Valley.

THE PIONEER ETHOS

When Frederick Terman arrived at Stanford in 1924, the Valley was a stretch of
small rural communities connected by a railroad and a highway along which cows
grazed on green fields.

As a young member of Stanford's engineering faculty in the 1930s, Terman
was concerned with the lack of job opportunities for engineering graduates in
the area, so he urged them to start local companies near the University, and he
personally invested in many of them. In 1939, he encouraged two of his students,
William Hewlett and David Packard, to establish a small electronics company in a
Palo Alto garage, helping them with technical development, financing, and patent
rights. He provided similar support to other start-ups during the thirties, most of
them launched by Stanford graduates. Some, such as Varian Associates and Litton
Industries, grew into major electronics firms. Russell and Sigurd Varian, working
without pay in an unoccupied lab at Stanford, developed the klystron tube that
gave Allied radar the edge in World War II.

Very early
representation
of Stanford
University; plan
by Frederick Law
Olmstead, 1920.

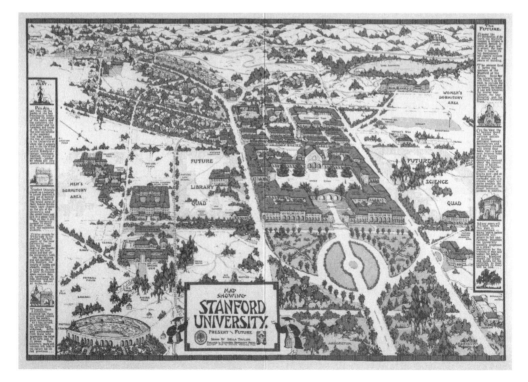

Encouraged by Terman, William Shockley, coinventor of the transistor, returned to his hometown of Palo Alto in 1956 and established the Shockley Transistor Laboratory. Eight members of his staff left to start Fairchild Semiconductor, the company that would develop the planar transistor and the integrated circuit—the seeds of Silicon Valley. Two of the eight went on to launch Intel, developing the microprocessor, which made possible the home computer, the Internet, and the digital revolution on which nearly all technologies now rest. By the late sixties, the area had become the center of American innovation, turning the rural valley into a sprawling electronic hub, transforming the modern world.

Terman saw the government's growing support of research as a major opportunity to build what he called "steeples of excellence"—academic fields of national importance that would attract federal patronage. Having headed a big defense project at Harvard developing radar countermeasures, his government contacts helped him lure federal funding to Stanford. He focused on attracting top professors in science and engineering who could then win government grants and contracts and teach students about recent developments in the field. The grants helped pay salaries, allowing the University to expand the faculty. Prodding scientists in local industry to learn how research occurring at Stanford might help their business, Terman initiated the Honors Cooperative Program, whereby engineers at local companies could take Stanford courses. In exchange for an annual contribution, corporations in partnerships with Stanford could have access to research results, sponsor joint projects with faculty and students, participate in conferences and workshops, recruit talented students, and retain faculty as consultants.

To finance the University's rapid postwar growth, Terman capitalized on the fact that the University had abundant land—8,180 acres, much of it pasture. With the help of President Wallace Sterling and David Packard, he created the Stanford Industrial Park in 1951, leasing land to tech firms such as Varian, Hewlett-Packard, Eastman Kodak, General Electric, Lockheed, and Syntex. Xerox's Palo Alto Research Center allowed graduate students and faculty to participate in research projects, developing the underlying technologies for the personal computer—windows, word processors, graphic displays, icons, drop-down menus, image processing, and laser printers. The park—now known as the Stanford Research Park—is currently home to about 150 companies.

As provost from 1955 to 1965, Terman greatly expanded the science, statistics, and engineering departments, encouraging interdisciplinary approaches by which physics, chemistry, and math could contribute to engineering advances. The resulting research grants, along with the entrepreneurial culture Terman had created between Stanford and tech companies in the area, put Silicon Valley at the epicenter of technological innovation, catapulting Stanford to the top of the world's educational institutions.

Over the last half-century, Stanford faculty, staff, and graduates have launched some 1,200 companies. It is estimated that they have generated revenues of $2.7 trillion annually and created 5.4 million jobs. A country composed only of Stanford entrepreneurs would rank as the world's tenth largest economy. Nearly 5,000 companies can trace their roots to Stanford, including Hewlett-Packard, Fairchild Semiconductor, Cisco Systems, and Sun Microsystems. In the 1990s, alumni Jerry Yang and David Filo founded Yahoo, while Sergey Brin and Larry Page developed their page rank algorithm as graduate students and started Google. It is no surprise that one-third of all Turing Awards—the so-called Nobel Prize in computer science—have gone to twenty-two Stanford recipients.

Research and development in solid-state technology at Stanford followed the four major waves of innovation in Silicon Valley: microwave electronics (1950s), semiconductors and integrated circuits (1960s), the shift from mainframe to desktop computing (1980s), and the rise of the Internet (1990s). Stanford has been a major engine driving the tech industry, with a constant injection of new people and new ideas. The entrepreneurial ecosystem resulting from cross-pollination between Stanford and Silicon Valley has owed much not only to collaboration with industry and abundant capital and government support but also to a university culture that rewards risk taking, a spirit of team collaboration, and students who are not experts in just one area but are also broadly educated.

The partnership between Stanford and Silicon Valley has redefined our daily lives, launching a technological and social transformation that will be seen in centuries to come as an epochal turning point in human evolution, a legacy to stand with that of the Nile Valley, the voyages of exploration, and the scientific revolution.

THE STATE OF THE ARTS

As one might expect, Stanford is sometimes accused of overemphasis on training for the job market at the expense of the humanities and a liberal education. In truth, study of the humanities has declined in colleges worldwide. The drop has been largest in the top universities, particularly the Ivy League. Concern dates from the sixties, with humanities majors in American universities falling from 14 percent in 1964 to 7 percent in 2014, while the sciences have grown steadily. Yet 16 percent of the majors at Stanford are in the humanities, twice the national average.

In fact, Stanford ranked number one in *Times Higher Education*'s 2015–2016 World University Rankings in arts and humanities programs. Nearly half of Stanford's faculty, in contrast to the 16 percent of its students, are in humanities, and English, history, and psychology remain among the top ten majors. Thus any lack of balance lies not in the University but in student preferences. I have worried that some of my faculty colleagues and the students with whom they work may be too ready to sacrifice long-term benefit for short-term gain, starting a new technology company or pursuing an athletic career in lieu of completing their education. These preferences can jeopardize a larger perspective—students' intellectual ability to evaluate global issues, the long-range needs of society, and how they might contribute.

To insure a broader education, Stanford instituted new undergraduate requirements, including eleven courses in eight subject areas and such joint programs as computer science and English or computer science and music. Engineers are required to take humanities requirements, while English majors must fulfill an engineering credit. In addition, about one-third of undergraduates study for one or two academic quarters at one of Stanford's thirteen overseas centers—"mini-Stanfords"—with faculty in residence at campuses on six continents. Admissions to the Stanford Graduate School of Business place heavy preference on humanities and social sciences, with nearly half of the incoming class majoring in those fields, higher than at Wharton, Sloan, or Harvard.

Recent decades have also seen the growth of Stanford's interdisciplinary programs. As chairman of the biology department in the late sixties, I joined a group of faculty from both biology and medicine to initiate an interdisciplinary, interdepartmental, undergraduate Program in Human Biology, the idea being to provide students with strong backgrounds in both biology and the social sciences, a combination essential, for example, to many careers in law, government, health, and public policy. Following the spectacular success of that program, Human Biology became Stanford's most popular major. Numerous other interdisciplinary programs have since emerged, most significantly the interdepartmental Program in Earth Systems, focusing on the planet's most pressing environmental problems.

DREAM COLLEGE

Stanford opened in 1891 to 555 students and a teaching staff of about thirty-five. It has since grown to more than 7,000 undergraduates, 9,000 graduate students, and 2,000 faculty, including thirty-one Nobel laureates, twenty recipients of the National Medal of Science, two of the National Medal of Technology, three of the National Humanities Medal, five winners of the Pulitzer Prize, and three of the Presidential Medal of Freedom.

More than 5,300 projects were externally sponsored throughout the University during 2014–2015, with a total budget of $1.33 billion. As a national center for research, Stanford is home to more than 120 research facilities, including the Stanford Linear Accelerator, the longest in the world at two miles on 426 acres; Hopkins Marine Station for marine biology in Pacific Grove; Jasper Ridge, a 1,200-acre wildlife biological preserve located south of the main campus; the "Dish," a 150-foot-diameter radio antenna in the foothills; the Stanford Institute for Economic Policy Research; the Institute for International Studies; and the Stanford Humanities Center. Adjacent to the Stanford Medical Center, which is one of the top teaching hospitals in the country, the world's largest research

ness in South Africa. Our divestment of holdings in a number of companies did not, however, prevent a number of campus demonstrations and arrests. Unlike protests in the 1960s, when some scholars lost vital work to arsonists, student demonstrations in ensuing years were essentially peaceful, though a low point occurred when fifty-five students, demanding more minority faculty and a freeze on tuition, were arrested while occupying my office.

Speaking to incoming freshmen the following September, I addressed the pernicious national habit of single-issue, special-interest politics, noting that the great issues with which we grapple are seldom confrontations between good and evil but are almost invariably collisions between competing goods. Certainly the debate over the Western Culture program was such. Our intention was simply to broaden the course in Western civilization to include non-Western cultures. But a national media circus ensued, polarized between those who viewed the change as a "trashing" of Western culture and those who saw our balanced efforts as a racist refusal to go the distance.

Our decision to expand the Western Culture requirements to the more inclusive "Cultures, Ideas, and Values" was but one facet of a larger multicultural movement during my presidency. A focus on minority hiring and student diversity in the mid- to late 1980s led to more African American, Hispanic, and Native American students in the freshman classes. We created culturally based "theme houses" in which half the residents belonged to an ethnic group and the other half were those interested in learning about them. In response to an unfortunate racial incident in Ujamaa, the African American theme house, I published an essay in the *Stanford Daily*, warning against extremities on both sides. The incident led ultimately to a vanguard model for change, a 244-page report recommending ethnic innovations in courses, faculty, admissions, and financial aid (Chapter 6).

But, in retrospect, what would come to define my twelve years as president were less the ground-shaking incidents than groundbreaking developments and transformations. High among my priorities was a commitment to encourage public service, stressing the obligation students have to live up to the responsibility inherent in their advantaged opportunities—to make a difference in a world encumbered with so many aching needs. To that end we developed the Haas Center for Public Service, sponsoring a host of programs involving hundreds of students, along with a Haas Centennial Professorship of Public Service, public service fellowships for students, and release time allowing staff members to do public service (Chapter 6).

I also sought to rebalance the emphasis given to teaching and research in favor of the former, calling on faculty members to renew their commitment to teaching as "first among our labors." Speaking at an alumni conference, I noted the "continuing ambivalence in America between the utilitarian function of education and one more closely related to the traditional purposes of liberal learning."[1]

Education, I suggested, should generate a capacity to analyze and communicate adequately, if not beautifully. It should promote an understanding of our heterogeneous culture and its multiple origins, of the natural world and its laws. It should instill a respect for knowledge and for the process of acquiring knowledge in a way that leaves one not only open to its lifelong pursuit but insistent on that pursuit. Among efforts to achieve those ends, we created the Stanford Humanities Center, expanded interdisciplinary studies, and unveiled a $7 million package of new programs to improve undergraduate education.

Those same years saw spectacular growth and expansion at Stanford. We added overseas campuses in Kyoto, Japan, and Oxford, England; announced plans for another in Berlin; and created the Institute for International Studies to coordinate Stanford's international efforts. In 1988 we launched the Stanford-in-Washington campus, an idea I had entertained after returning from two years as Commissioner of the Food and Drug Administration (Chapter 5). The construction of facilities critically needed for research, teaching, housing, administration, and athletics doubled the value of Stanford's physical plant. The Medical School was augmented with the addition of the Lucille Salter Packard Children's Hospital and the Beckman Center for Molecular and Genetic Medicine. In 1983, the Center for the Study of Language and Information was founded, a major institution for the development of integrated theories of language, information, and computation, and ground was broken for the Center for Integrated Systems, a joint venture between twenty industry sponsors and Stanford faculty and students. The completion of several large student residence complexes included Governor's Corner, Sterling Quad, the Suites, Rains Houses, Kimball Hall, and Manzanita II, with two more planned. Among other projects were the construction of the Tennis Stadium, the Ford Center, Sweet Hall, Littlefield Center at the Business School, Braun Music Center, and the Rodin Sculpture Garden.

Our five-year Centennial Campaign, which raised almost $1.3 billion for everything from new equipment and buildings to endowed professorships and student financial aid, was at the time the most successful fund-raising endeavor in the history of higher education. Stanford's endowment tripled to almost $2 billion, another historic high.

Among the best of the many wonderful things about working and living at Stanford is the character of its student body. *Creative, compassionate,* and, of course, *intelligent* are adjectives that describe the many amazing students who have walked those shady arcades of sandstone and tile. During my twelve years as University president, I made a conscientious effort to carve out time to interact with these talented young people. Through teaching, advising, and cheering them on—whether on the field, in the classroom, on the stage, or in the biology labs—some of my very best Stanford experiences involved my interactions with undergraduates (Chapter 7).

He maximizes people through his own energy. For example, the Humanities Center was created because Kennedy thought it was a good idea and breathed energy into it.

—*Albert Hastorf*

Don Kennedy pushed hard for improvement in undergraduate teaching, for increasing opportunities for students to find ways to serve others less fortunate than they and to address significant society problems, for expanding international studies, and for increasing interdisciplinary research and teaching—efforts so fabulously driven by his successors, Gerhard Casper and John Hennessy. Don led in the restoration of the beauty of our campus and the addition of much needed academic, administrative and athletic facilities—an ambitious construction process his successors gleefully embraced!

—*Jim Gaither*

Incredibly, Don Kennedy, his predecessors, and his successors have been uniquely successful in bringing about extraordinary change without allowing Stanford to become rigid or bureaucratic. Don's eyes always lit up when considering interesting ideas and opportunities. As much as any start-up in the Silicon Valley, Don brought an entrepreneurial spirit to everything Stanford took on. That spirit still distinguishes Stanford from its peers.

—*Jim Gaither*

Kennedy's tenure was a period of enormous accomplishment. Probably no university in the United States has made as broad a level of contribution as Stanford has under Kennedy's presidency. I have a tremendously high opinion of what has been accomplished at Stanford in this decade.

—*Harold Shapiro, Princeton University President*

During my years as a Stanford student, Don was instrumental to helping me see a broader horizon and realize my potential. He knew my parents had wanted me to go to medical school, but he also knew I had other talents and passions, especially in public service. In my senior year, Don encouraged me to apply for a Rhodes Scholarship, and he wrote a very strong letter on my behalf. His support was undoubtedly one of the reasons I got the scholarship, and that alone was an incredible act of mentorship. Don went beyond that, however. When my parents were still a little unsure why I was not going straight to medical school after graduation, it fell to Don—the president of Stanford University—to call my parents to assure them that it was "okay" I was going to Oxford on a Rhodes. By his example, I learned how you can make an enormous difference in the lives of young people. He did that not only for me but for countless others, over and over again.

—*Goodwin Liu*

Don was one of those presidents who really related to the student body. He loved dealing with students, and he announced early on in his presidency that any student who really wanted to talk to him should just show up at the president's house at six AM and run the Dish with him.

—*Bob Freelen*

Don was beloved by the students and by the people who worked with him. He was a wonderful, upbeat, and forward-looking person to work with. And then this twisted attack came up near the end of his tenure as president, and that's what a lot of people remember, and that's a shame because it's not who Don was, not what his aura was like during the time he was president.

—*Mike Hudnall*

Don is such a positive human being, full of love and relentlessly optimistic. There's a twinkle in his eye—a knowing, an understanding that's telling you "you've got this." That gleam in his eye is the Stanford spirit, the belief in this group of people, this place, this mission. I think his faith in what people can do stems from his view of the university—both faculty and students—as having the horsepower to solve global challenges, and his belief that the privilege of being at Stanford involves a responsibility to make the very most of whatever skills you have.

—*Kai Anderson*

Smiling in the Quad arcade.

The relatively low barrier to accessing distinguished senior faculty—Nobel laureates, Pulitzer Prize winners, and MacArthur Fellowship (the "genius award") winners—creates an unusually open and easy atmosphere. And those faculty feel as privileged to be engaging with these gifted, funny, generous, young people as the students feel to sit with recipients of National Medals of Science, Technology, or Humanities, or a former Secretary of State. Thus, day-to-day life as a member of the Stanford community is quite extraordinary.

The many positive events and developments of my presidential years, which included visits by Mikhail Gorbachev and Queen Elizabeth II, dwarf the few negatives. Yet because my name had become somewhat tainted by my role in the indirect cost controversy, and despite full exoneration, it was clear to me that I could not be identified with the problem and remain a spokesman for its solution.

Following my consequent decision to resign, I was lucky in being offered some other rewarding and engaging opportunities. I was soon asked to return to teaching in the Program in Human Biology, which I had loved since my involvement in its inception in the early 1970s (Chapter 3). Almost immediately, I found a source of recovery and renewed inspiration from a teaching position at Stanford's campus in Washington, D.C. (Chapter 10), which brought me together with twenty-three bright and motivated undergraduates, many of whom maintain personal relationships with me. Much later, an invitation to serve on the David and Lucille Packard Foundation Board of Trustees offered an opportunity to learn about a new set of programs and initiatives in science, conservation, and population. Finally, in the year 2000, to my great surprise and pleasure, I was named editor-in-chief of *Science*, the weekly research and news journal of the American Association for the Advancement of Science (Chapter 11). All of these, along with my involvement in environmental politics, reawakened new possibilities in fields left behind by my presidency.

PUTTING THE PAST IN PERSPECTIVE

These welcome opportunities had unfolded serendipitously, lacking any master plan on my part. Also unforeseen, but surely unwelcome, was an increasing absentmindedness—leaving my eyeglasses about or forgetting my keys. My wife Robin frequently bore the brunt of these displacements; for my part, I found the stress of losing everyday items increasingly upsetting. The cumulative minor annoyances led to more anxiety and agitation until, finally, Robin found herself living with a person she had not known in more than two decades together.

In April of 2010, a battery of tests and a brain MRI at UCSF's Memory and Aging Center, along with a description of my change in temperament and loss of short-term memory, led to a diagnosis of undifferentiated dementia with mild cognitive disorder, information we kept to ourselves for several years. In subsequent years, the diagnosis was refined as a combination of Lewy Body Dementia and Alzheimer's disease.

In light of these recent events, I now see that my earlier assessment of the indirect cost controversy as the low point of my life was excessive. With maturity, one comes to understand that not all of the circumstances that affect one's pride or sense of self-worth arise from exogenous sources. Some happen because individuals themselves change: one ages, physical strength and health fail, attitudes evolve. The story of a life cannot be complete unless the account gives due weight to internal changes in the subject, not just those arising from external events—thus my attempt in these memoirs to put my past in perspective.

What has happened to me involves loss of the very capacities that allowed me to succeed in earlier roles for which I am now receiving belated honors. Now I find myself in the unsettling position of being memorialized for past accomplishments I could not possibly achieve today. My dementia results in fluctuating cognition, especially recurring difficulties with short-term memory and a certain loss of executive function. I find I have challenges sustaining a conversation with a knowledgeable person on a scientific, technical, or political topic. Lecturing, even to a small and somewhat sympathetic audience, is something I have learned to avoid. Small computations and number sequences, and even telling time, are problematic for me.

To say that I am unhappy about the lost capacity is true enough, but I am hardly miserable. Most of my friends and colleagues are aware of my difficulties and, to my joy and deep appreciation, they have been supportive and forgiving. Some, in fact, have offered their recollections and reflections in the sidebars that punctuate these chapters,

Finally, I could not begin to imagine my life without my wife, Robin. At every turn she has been there to support, comfort, and help me. Without her, my worst days would be intolerable. She is loving, capable, compassionate, resilient, and patient. With her, I continue to find happiness in the simple pleasure of time spent together. Robin is my champion. I dedicate this book to her.

CHAPTER 1

LONG JOURNEY WEST

A BOY'S FORMATIVE YEARS mold the man he will become. In that regard, I supposed during my youth that my trajectory did not differ much from most others. What is perhaps atypical, though I hardly realized it at the time, was a family life I experienced as disorienting, confusing, and even bewildering. In retrospect, there were three aspects of my young life that I now recognize as having been out of the ordinary: One is that our family moved a great deal—by my count at least five or six times before I reached the age of fifteen. The second was the number of years I spent living away from home. Third, and foremost, was my younger brother, Dorsey.

When I was born, on August 18, 1931, my father was employed as a writer at J. Walter Thompson, the advertising giant in New York City, where, a year earlier, he had encountered Barbara Bean, who turned up in his office looking for work. The rest of that story, of course, is history, and once the two of them started their family, Father commuted to New York City from the caretaker's house we rented on the Decker estate in Greenwich, Connecticut. It was a beautiful slice of New England ecology, forested, with a stream and a pond—a young naturalist's paradise, and I was given the run of the place, catching brook trout.

My first school was Greenwich Country Day School, where I was disastrously promoted midyear from the second grade to the third, leaving me all but friendless. Those I left behind in the second grade were resentful, hostile, and envious, and those whom I joined in the third thought me to be a precocious and annoying little kid. I suppose that someone has since done a serious study of midyear grade promotion and what happens emotionally to the children on both ends of that transaction. For me, it was not a happy outcome. To take my mind off it, I was allowed to tap the maple trees on the Decker property and even persuaded my mother that the sap could be boiled off to make what I thought was pretty good maple syrup. The Decker estate attracted birds in abundance, and I was given a copy of *Birds of America*. So natural history was an early part of my life.

Very small
Donny, 1934.

MY BROTHER'S KEEPER

Dorsey was born in New York City on October 31, 1938, in the immediate aftermath of the New England hurricane of that year, still recorded as among the most damaging storms to unfurl fury on the eastern seaboard. On September 21, 1938, the hurricane hit with such ferocity that it is estimated to have taken some 800 lives, damaging or destroying 57,000 homes, and causing property losses of $300 million in the currency of the time, the equivalent of $4.7 billion in 2015. New Englanders still bear the scars of the damage—the forest devastation in Connecticut and Massachusetts, the changed aquatic landscape, and a rich memory bank full of averted damage and heroic saviors. As my parents and

I would soon discover, Dorsey would unleash his own brand of turmoil, emerging from the womb a month after the hurricane, accompanied by significant emotional and psychological anguish, only much later diagnosed as childhood schizophrenia.

Dorsey's diagnosis was not known for many years. My parents and I experienced a rash of inexplicable and seemingly unrelated symptoms. I recall he was required, around age three, to wear a patch over one eye—the conventional treatment for amblyopia, more commonly known as a "lazy eye." Whether a result of his troubles, or simply a function of his early age and temperament, Dorsey clearly objected to wearing the eye patch and, as fast as it was in place, he ripped it off, again and again. My mother, wanting to do right by him, took him back to the pediatrician, who prescribed a set of splints for the poor boy's arms, restricting

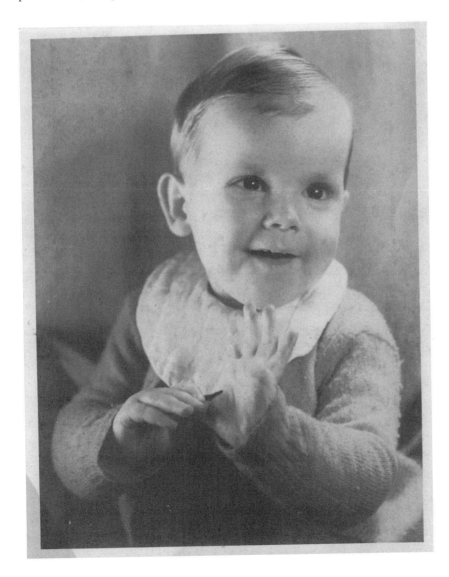

Baby Dorsey.

his ability to reach his face. It was barbaric. My mother and her circle of friends were horrified. Many years later, when we lived in Deerfield, Massachusetts, Dorsey fell off a swing and injured his arm. Once again, he was required to wear a splint, generating painful memories for our family.

I recall vacationing with my mother and Dorsey in Port Franks, Ontario, a rustic retreat near the sandy beaches of Lake Huron, with a nearby river and inland ponds surrounded by mixed forests full of interesting flora and fauna. In the post–World War I period, Port Franks had become a haven for suburbanites hungry for a wilderness escape, as well as a year-round home for a small community of braver souls, one of whom sometimes allowed us the use of his little fishing boat. On one occasion, Dorsey dropped a piece of fishing tackle off the boat, and it became my responsibility, as it usually was, to recover it. I don't recall any feelings of resentment arising from such repeated demands on me to rectify problems that Dorsey created, but I still wonder how I managed to sublimate them enough to avoid turning on my brother directly.

Times spent with Dorsey are powerful memories for me. At first, Dorsey's behavior was not so much dangerous as disruptive. He seemed to crave our parents' attention, and even, to some degree, my own. To get it, he engaged in general mischief making that would evolve into troublemaking. Pulling the patch off his eye was understandable enough, though explicitly against the rules. Other times he would sneak up behind me, sometimes from the backseat of the car—I generally rode up front with our father while Dorsey and my mother occupied the backseat. Dorsey would draw near and sneer in my ear, "I put a dirty thing in your hair"—a blatant attempt, as any child psychologist would confirm, to capture the attention of those he looked up to, namely, our parents and, to a lesser extent, me. My parents' Manhattan landlady, Mrs. Voight, expressed continual lament over Dorsey and his potential effect on her sprinklers. Dorsey's attention seeking later progressed to breaking glass. Once he threw a glass at me while I was in the bathtub!

It was not until decades later that I was able to acknowledge to myself what a toll Dorsey took on my childhood.

DEERFIELD

Before Dorsey was born, my parents and I made a number of moves from one bedroom community to another, all within range of my father's work. Soon after Dorsey was born, we settled down in one place, which turned out to be Deerfield, Massachusetts. My father would take the train to Manhattan every Monday morning and return every Friday night.

At age eight I became a boarder at the Bement School, where my mother was working. Bement was a school founded in 1925 after educator Grace "Menty" Bement agreed to a request by the headmaster of Deerfield Academy that she tutor one of his students. As word of her successful educational approach spread, more and more students came her way, giving rise to the founding of the school, which focused on the individual child—a revolutionary concept for its time.

Our home, a short walk from the school, was a historic seventeenth-century farmhouse called the Allen House, which had survived the famous Bloody Brook Massacre, an Indian ambush that killed fifty colonists during King Philip's War in September 1675. Its horribly drafty rooms were so uncomfortable that I didn't mind being sent to live in the school dormitory. I don't recall feeling any home-sickness, probably because of its proximity and my mother being a teacher at the school. (I do recall my relationship with my mother being more like student-to-teacher than child-to-parent.) Nor did it seem out of the ordinary that I wasn't sleeping in my own bed or sharing meals with my parents and my baby brother. I don't recall ever experiencing it as rejection. In hindsight, I wonder what prompted my removal from the family home—whether it arose from my parents' concern over Dorsey's affect on me or from my mother's maternal limitations.

Our family mobility was attributable largely to my father's professional life. In the spring of 1945, at the end of my time at Bement and our family's three-year stay in Deerfield, my father's persistent quest for military employment succeeded with his appointment to the Strategic Air Command at the Air Force School of Applied Tactics just outside of Orlando near Winter Park. I don't remember objecting to the uprooting or being dissatisfied in any way, but I was recurrently confused about the sequence of how I got from there to here, and whether life was characteristically this bewildering.

FLORIDA

Our family lived in base housing, and I attended Winter Park High School for about half a year, the only Yankee in the freshman class. During that time, my first cousin Ellie, daughter of my mother's older sister, was sent to live with us due to her own mother's mental illness and inability to care for her and her brother. She was three years my senior and we attended high school together, which made that period tolerable for me. When our family moved off the Air Force base to an area called Windermere, I was homeschooled by my mother for the rest of the school year. Like my midyear promotion from second to third grade, my homeschooling was another disastrous educational experiment.

As Dorsey's elder by seven years, I was occasionally charged with his care-taking. While in Orlando, I took him to a park in the middle of which stood an immense enclosure displaying a beautiful Brazilian macaw. Subsisting on a diet consisting primarily of nuts, the macaw is known for its powerful beak, strong enough to penetrate seed casings, nut casings, and even coconuts. Dorsey, then around seven years of age, was fascinated, as any youngster would be. Fingers wiggling—his characteristic expression of excitement—he squirmed out of my hold and pressed a pudgy digit into the cage with the hope, I suppose, of petting the colorful creature. The screams of pain still ring in my ear.

Don's father, Bill, was quiet and reserved. He had worked in advertising at J. Walter Thompson when they lived in Greenwich, Connecticut, and hated it. According to Don, one morning he stood waiting for the train to New York City and literally could not get on it. He turned out to be suffering from what was then called a "nervous breakdown." Bill actually served in both world wars. In the Second World War, he joined the OSS, and Don was taken by his mother to the Bement School in Massachusetts, at which she and two of his aunts were teachers. Later the family moved to Virginia. Don planted a vegetable garden there and was excited to be in a place long enough to be able to reap his harvest. Sadly, his father got transferred one more time, and Don never saw it come to fruition.

Don's parents were intellectual and liberal. His mother, "Babbie," short for Barbara, was the fourth of six Bean girls. She was the daughter of a Maine guide and a schoolteacher. She grew up in Berlin, New Hampshire. The paper mill there was run by Orton Brown and his wife, who sponsored the Bean girls and gave them many things that made their lives easier, including money for college. Babbie was a great raconteur and fascinated people with her tales. She was very interested in psychiatry and was in therapy

Barbara Bean at her Wellesley commencement, 1921

for most of her adult life. After Bill retired, they moved to Zurich, Switzerland, and attended a school for Jungian psychologists. Babbie had a great many hobbies. She built the first tongue-and-groove steel house in America in their house in Winter Park, Florida. She actually sold her engagement ring in order to buy a printing press at one point, but Bill gave her a huge zircon which she loved to flash.

Babbie was not maternal and wasn't at all interested in grandchildren. She was interested in the idea but not their actuality. When Page was an infant, she told me that she would never baby-sit and I shouldn't expect it. On the other hand, after Julia was born, Babbie sent Page a beautiful wardrobe from Saks Fifth Avenue. Bill, on the other hand, though quiet and reserved, was always the one who wanted to visit us. He came regularly. I remember he once said that, even though they were small, Page and Julia took up a lot of psychic space. Babbie was writing a book—somewhere in the sixties I think that started—and she would not come out to see us, using the excuse of having to write the book. Babbie did not see Page and Julia for eight years until we brought them to Maine. Babbie later got one of the worst and most long-lived cases of Alzheimer's. But Bill's mind was bright and clear into his nineties.

—*Jeanne Kennedy*

A mere boy of fourteen myself, what was I to do with the child, now shrieking at the top of his lungs, his bloody finger extended as a badge of his suffering? What I did was flag down a passing motorist, a nice woman who asked how she could help. I asked her to take us to a nearby doctor, and two youngsters, one of them bloodied and bawling, climbed into a stranger's car, trustingly headed off to a destination unknown. But that kindhearted woman delivered us to the safety of her own doctor's office. For reasons still difficult to understand, I did not experience my mother's absence from that scene as out of the ordinary.

LIFE WITH MOTHER

Looking back now on my relationship with my mother, I recognize that life must have been difficult for her. She was ambitious, hopeful of doing good things, and yet, as a woman, a wife, and a mother in mid-twentieth century, she was limited in what she could accomplish.

She was born Barbara Bean on January 12, 1898, in Berlin, New Hampshire, one of six sisters to whom she was known as Babbie. After a childhood in a town dominated by the Brown Paper Company, she went off to Wellesley College. After graduation, she began a career as a journalist with her sister Dorothy, writing stories for the *Springfield Republican* and another paper in Boston, while Dorothy took the photographs.

Wanderlust took hold of the two sisters, and they moved to Los Angeles, where they both obtained teaching positions at the prestigious Marlborough School. My mother donned what was then described as a "full Princeton" attitude, keeping up with the best of them, but eventually returned to the East. Both her writing and her teaching would contribute considerably to the course of her life.

Disappointments over her limited professional prospects, her husband's later infidelity, and the tragedy of a damaged child limited my mother's ability to be a fully present parent. As a young adult she had suffered from breast cancer and undergone a mastectomy. Sadly, Dorsey and his considerable needs devastated and paralyzed my mother for much of her adult life. In hindsight, I believe that I too suffered from her neglect, so focused was she on herself and a hoped-for career that never materialized.

My mother was not happy after we left Deerfield. Again, she found herself frustrated with her professional prospects. At one point she purchased a large heating press that would produce huge amounts of pressure designed to fuse patent leather and vinyl, thinking it might make an excellent material for shoes. But she was disappointed by the response of the company she approached with her inventive idea, regarding their dismissive reply as maltreatment. She was not very available to me during that period. Perhaps our generally easy relationship was due partly to the fact that we spent little time under the same roof.

NEW HAMPSHIRE: ON MY OWN

In the autumn of 1946, I was awarded a scholarship to the Dublin School, a small college preparatory school located near Mount Monadnock, with a panoramic view of the hills of southwestern New Hampshire. I left behind a large public high school with about 400 ninth graders for a tenth-grade class with only a dozen other students.

The move to the Dublin School meant that, except for an occasional summer, I would spend only one year of my childhood after the age of eight living with my parents and my brother. My memories of the time at home include arguments at the family dinner table, usually involving my mother's views—about politics, psychology, or Dorsey—and my father trying to understand but often differing with her. At other times, my mother would pose a problem, and I would offer the solution as though there were only one right answer. One night, in frustration, my father slammed a book on the table and shouted at me, "Donny, you will learn far more from people and journals than you will ever learn from books!" I don't remember any out-and-out fights, but there were frequent differences and flares of temper, and I was not shielded from them. Perhaps this early training provided a good model for learning to disagree without being disagreeable.

A year after I moved to the Dublin School, my family moved to Detroit. The war had ended, and my father had yet another new job. As Director of Publications at the Ford Motor Company, he qualified to live in corporate housing, and the family had a nice place on Southfield Road on land that had once been soybean farms. If one liked natural history, as my father and I did, there was plenty to do in the surrounding area. When I came "home" during traditional breaks from school, I was able to invite Dublin classmates to visit. Soon after our arrival, which inevitably triggered the Dorsey issue, as Dorsey needed to be attended to, introduced, and explained. But before long a visiting classmate and I would be off fishing a Northern Michigan river, which meant an enjoyable week and an end to any awkward family situations. I am discomfited to admit that I was sometimes embarrassed by my brother, especially when my friends came around.

In Dublin I met Ernest B. "Ebbie" Dane, who went on to Harvard with me. Like me, he was a devoted outdoor explorer and avid skier, and we often went off in the woods to hike, fish, or watch birds together. During a break in our junior year in Dublin, Ebbie came to visit in the family's barnlike residence on Southfield Road. As coresidents of the dorms at Dublin, and later Harvard, I was slow to understand the world Ebbie came from. His stepfather was named Sturtevant, and the whole family was part of an upper-class society on the coast of Rhode Island. His mother was an extraordinarily lovely and well-appointed woman, and his two brothers, Ben and Roger, joined us at school when their time came—a family tradition, whereas my enrollment at Dublin depended on scholarship support.

Ebbie was extremely popular and a member of Harvard's elite Porcellian Club, the iconic social club often bracketed with Yale's Skull and Bones, Princeton's Ivy

Club, and Oxford's Gridiron Club. An urban legend intimates that if members of the Porcellian do not earn their first million dollars before they turn forty, the club will give it to them. Ebbie's was the only wedding reception I ever attended after which the groomsmen and newly married husband drank to the health of the bride and threw their champagne glasses into the Harvard Club fireplace.

DORSEY LEAVES HOME

As Dorsey's behavior became increasingly erratic and unpredictable, my father turned his attention to obtaining a diagnosis. Although Dorsey strenuously resisted being with strangers, let alone a physician laser-focused on him, my father persisted and was ultimately told that Dorsey suffered from childhood schizophrenia, a diagnosis that never changed throughout Dorsey's life, though advances in the field now recognize that the label was in many cases a misinterpretation of traits lying on the newly discovered autistic spectrum. The need to identify and secure a suitable place for Dorsey, an institution or school that would care for him professionally, compassionately, and in a way that allowed him to be as productive as possible within the considerable limitations of his disability, quickly became my father's highest priority. He took to researching this with some care. Balancing his need to support a young family with the responsibility for mapping a care strategy for a damaged child could not have been a simple matter. At some point during my three years at the Dublin School, Dorsey was sent to the Devereux School in Goleta, near Santa Barbara, California.

From that point on, Dorsey and I led separate lives. After Devereux, he was relocated to Spring Lake Ranch, a licensed therapeutic community outside Rutland, Vermont. Dorsey eventually became an outpatient, living in his own small apartment in town and receiving daily visits from a Spring Lake Ranch social worker. He earned a bit of pin money from fixing old televisions and radios and spent it on candy.

Ironically, Dorsey moved away from California a few years before I left the East Coast for Stanford. Both emotionally and geographically, he was outside my ken and, for many decades, out of my reach.

FATHER KNOWS BEST

I am a little ashamed to admit that while my father was still alive, I forged ahead without much thought to Dorsey and his circumstances. I viewed my father as enormously capable and placed great trust in him. We enjoyed a warm relationship, based in part on our mutual interest in nature and fishing and his ability to impart valuable lessons. When he noticed that I was serious about making a contribution in his area of interest, he would take me on trips to fish, watch birds, and explore.

Born William Dorsey Kennedy on September 9, 1894, Father was raised in Cleveland, Ohio, the son of a Presbyterian minister who had a penchant for playing the stock market successfully—so much so, in fact, that for a balmy week or two each year he hosted his congregants on an annual trip south to escape the Ohio winters. Father attended the prestigious Asheville School in North Carolina, the Southeast's elite boarding school, and went on to graduate from Williams College in 1917. Realizing that he had a military obligation, he enlisted in the Army. Early in his enlistment he won a pistol-shooting contest at Fort Chillicothe in Ohio, which was noticed by the higher-ups and eventually led to his assignment to Officers' Candidate School. Before long, Father was a first lieutenant leading an artillery battalion in Southern France.

After his discharge, Father resumed his Harvard connection. He earned his master's in business administration in 1919, served as an occasional assistant to faculty in Cambridge, and was an assistant dean of the business school, a role he continued until early 1926.

His next journey was to assume the editorship of a literary magazine, *The Writer*, an endeavor that was supported by what he later referred to as a patrimony—a sum of money provided by his father to assure his ambitions would be realized. Eventually, though, the patrimony ran out. Because *The Writer* had no advertising to support its production, my father folded the publication and moved to New York, where he was hired to assist Henry Luce in founding a new magazine that became *Time*.

Left to right: Don's uncle Fuzz, grandfather Rev. Finley Kennedy, and father Bill Kennedy, 1910.

Don and Dorsey at Spring Lake Ranch, Rutland, Vermont, in the early 1980s.

Bill and Babbie, Don's parents, in Damariscotta, Maine.

Father's ethical code was strong, if not occasionally misplaced. For example, while a senior at the Dublin School, I was awarded the merit-based Pepsi-Cola Scholarship, comparable to today's National Merit Scholarship, an honor awarded to just two students in each state. Rather than rejoice in my accomplishment, my father insisted I decline the award: Why should we accept this scholarship when he was prepared to manage the expense of my college education just fine? He wrote to the Pepsi-Cola Company, saying we were grateful, but the scholarship should be awarded to a needy student.

Years later, when my mother was living in a memory unit at Miles Hospital, a victim of Alzheimer's disease, Father visited her every day. It reflected the kind of care he characteristically took of her and of others in the course of his life. He had indulged her keen interest in Jungian psychology, even moving with her to Switzerland in later adulthood to facilitate her study and engage in his own. I think he had an unusual sense of responsibility for the welfare of others and for not disappointing those he cared about. My mother's death in 1991 was fully anticipated. According to her wishes, her ashes were sprinkled on her sister Margaret's garden in Damariscotta, Maine, a charming town that three of the Bean sisters made their last home.

On my father's death in 1989, I became the trustee of a small trust he had left for my brother, which I believed would be sufficient to support Dorsey's needs throughout the rest of his life. The imposition of financial responsibilities required that I focus on Dorsey's care. My wife Robin, a person as dedicated to family as anyone I have known, convinced me to take her to visit Dorsey, and we made several visits together to Rutland. Within a few years of my father's death, the trust was depleted, so Robin and I assumed financial responsibility for him. As his health worsened in later years, I was appointed his conservator with respect to medical decisions as well. But Dorsey rejected all medical care, including medications that might have helped with his schizophrenic symptoms. Having lost the ability to regulate his diet, he grew morbidly obese—over 300 pounds—and developed diabetes. Every so often he would fall, and the fire department would have to be called to get him up from the floor. Sadly, the frequency of his falls eventually rendered him unable to live the independent life he cherished.

Ultimately, Dorsey chose the time and means of his own death when, during a bout of serious pneumonia, he declined antibiotics with full knowledge that he would not survive. In occasional moments of reflection, I have struggled with passing judgment on myself over the moral and ethical terrain of sharing a childhood with Dorsey and yet not sharing it fully. My final responsibility to my brother was to honor his wish that his remains be delivered to Goleta, California, to the Devereux School where he had felt most accepted and valued. I was pleased to be able to honor this final request of my brother Dorsey, whose path diverged so distinctly from mine, but whose life so deeply affected me.

CHAPTER 2

GROWING PAINS
Early Career

THE NATURAL WORLD has been a passion of mine from childhood, foraging in the New England woods with my father, tapping tree sap, and watching birds of every variety. To this day, every time I glimpse a bird or hear a bird call, I stop in my tracks, searching for an identification, hoping to see a new bird.

The summer after my junior year at the Dublin School, I was given an opportunity (I suspect due to a touch of nepotism via my father) to spend a summer outdoors. During that summer, I was privileged to work on what might be characterized as a dude ranch. Stanley Resor, my father's friend from his days in New York advertising, was the proprietor of the Snake River Ranch in Wyoming. My father somehow persuaded him that I might make an able summer ranch hand, so I shipped West by train to help with chores, handle guests' baggage, and chase an occasional mink from the swimming pool. My days started early, at 5:30 AM, with duties that included going cabin to cabin igniting the soft-coal boilers beneath each one so the guests would have hot water for their morning showers. On occasion, I was permitted to take a guest or two fishing.

The situation was likely reminiscent of my father's own sojourn in the West, leading a cowboy's life for a time before embarking on his military career. Family legend has it that Father was struck by a taxi in Harvard Square just as he was proposing to start his graduate work at the Harvard Business School. The accident put him in a coma for a short time, and by some arrangement, either his own or his father's, he was sent West to work with a crew of people who may have been hunting or doing natural surveys. So for a short while he led a rather rustic, rugged life. I think he enjoyed it immensely, and it may have prompted him to seek a similar opportunity for me.

Occasionally I was able to make use of the fishing skill my father had imparted and encouraged, taking ranch guests out to the streams, suggesting prime casting spots, and teaching them something about managing a hooked fish. There were wonderful trout streams nearby, and it was possible to catch all four major species of trout in the little tributaries of the Snake River. It was a good introduction for a sixteen-year-old, both to trout fishing and to various chores on an interesting ranch in the Tetons. I suspect it was that summer experience that launched my lifetime love of the American West.

At the end of the summer, I returned to New Hampshire to complete high school and rejoin a wide circle of friends that included Ebbie Dane, my roommate Henry Horner, and his family friend, Jeanne Dewey, who attended a nearby, rather tony prep school. Among our social activities, we enjoyed traveling to neighboring communities like Peterborough and Jaffrey to attend square dances. If one were reasonably good at square dancing, there were plenty of girls to entertain, though none were dating affairs. But by this time I had come to know Jeanne, and we started a relationship that deepened during our first years in college.

HARVARD COLLEGE

Jeanne eventually went off to Smith College in Northampton, Massachusetts, and I matriculated at Harvard. She occasionally commuted to Cambridge to take a class useful for her major in mathematics, which for a time eased the strain on our long-distance romance. Smith had a wonderful tradition called Mountain Day, in which Smith undergraduates were encouraged to travel to some other place, and of course they traveled to where the boys were! She would use the occasion to come to Cambridge, giving us a chance to be together. In the end, she may have thought she picked the wrong "sister" of the Seven Sisters colleges—the elite all-women's liberal arts colleges then comprising Barnard, Bryn Mawr, Mount Holyoke, Radcliffe, Smith, Vassar, and Wellesley. It would have been easier for us had she been at Radcliffe; nonetheless, our relationship endured.

During a visit at her parents' home in Worcester, Massachusetts, she helped me assemble a paper I'd written with my Harvard classmate, Bill Warren, on water policy in New England and the Connecticut River. It was like a senior thesis, an important project; thus my panic when a breeze kicked up, sending the papers flying around the room—and I hoped not out the window! We laughed as we scurried to gather them up and collate them in order. We had that kind of fun together during our courtship, and a year after we graduated from college we were married at her family home in Worcester.

Our wedding took place during a huge tornado that did widespread damage and injured a great many people. The Worcester tornado was in fact a historic milestone, striking the area over a three-day period from June 6 to June 9, 1953, the precise dates of our wedding festivities. The storm traveled forty-eight miles across Central Massachusetts, spewing baseball-size hail across twenty communities. In all, ninety-four people were killed, ranking it the twenty-first most deadly tornado in U.S. history. In addition to the fatalities, some 1,300 people were injured and 4,000 buildings were damaged. The tally of 10,000 homeless stood as a record unchallenged for twenty-six years. The tornado caused $52 million in damage—about $350 million adjusted for inflation. Jokesters in our wedding party, composed of our many mutual friends, would later describe it as "the year of the big blow."

MAJOR DECISIONS

Despite my interest in the natural world, early in my undergraduate career at Harvard I thought to pursue an English degree. I considered myself a pretty good writer, thanks in large part to the thoughtful attention of William North, my high school teacher at Dublin. Excused from Harvard's freshman English requirement, I took an upper division course in creative writing. I liked writing; my father was a writer; and I really hadn't considered that interests in maple trees, trout fishing, and bird watching could provide a career focus and life trajectory, whereas my father's experience demonstrated that writing could. But the words of a respected Harvard faculty member dramatically changed the course of my life.

English "C" was taught in sections and intended for people who had already published or hoped to do so. Taught by Ed Gwynne and John Ciardi, a respected poet, the assignments involved pieces on one's aims and experiences with the best papers read aloud. Celebrated novelist Rona Jaffe was in the class, a frequently touted student. My own work was met with mixed reviews, sometimes taken seriously and other times missing the mark. I am forever scarred by receipt of a C on one assignment, the only C on my academic record!

The course final was a 5,000-word paper over which I labored intensely. The paper was returned with an A and an invitation to visit Professor Gwynne in his faculty apartment at Adams House, along with an instruction to bring the paper with me. He poured me a glass of sherry, made some pleasantries, including compliments for my paper, and then said, "Tell me, Don. What *else* interests you?"

Surprised by the question, I gathered my wits and responded, "Well, biology and natural history, I guess."

"Biology," he said. "That sounds like a wonderful choice."

Perhaps he feared what many in the humanities find concerning—that the professional opportunities for liberal arts majors are not as obvious or abundant as they are in the sciences and engineering. Whatever the reason, Gwynne's was an enthusiastic endorsement of biology, although it was clear to me that my idea of biology differed from that offered at Harvard. While my interests were in organisms (critters) and animal behavior, the coursework available was centered on molecular biology and genetics.

During my time at Dublin, I had gained a passion for skiing and was good enough to join the men's ski team as a Harvard freshman, competing for two years, traveling the circuit to the eastern college ski meets. I was never a top-ten scorer or a first- or second-place skier, even within our mediocre team. Nevertheless, I had fun, went to many different places, raced against rather good people, and wasn't good enough to be disappointed that I didn't excel. While pursuing my PhD at Harvard, I was given the unlikely position of coach of the men's ski team. With a thesis and so many other things to complete and a career to plan, it was probably silly to take this on, but I enjoyed it, and in the end it did not distract me from my path.

When I went to Harvard I thought I wanted to be a forest ranger and rebelled against biochemistry, so was driven to every course they had that dealt with real plants and animals. I majored in biology, but I took most of the required courses with a sullenness that stayed just on the borderline of rebellion. This was only partly because they interfered with my skiing career. I was also an authentic zoologist, captivated by butterflies and birds and hopelessly hooked on fish. Two events rescued me from the inevitable conclusion to this beginning. The first was John Welsh's course in comparative physiology, which I took in my senior year. It was everything an academic experience should be: demanding, exciting, an opening-up of totally new prospects. The second happened when Harvard persuaded Don Griffin to move to Cambridge from Cornell. Griffin, an animal behavior specialist, soon convinced me that you could, after all, have it both ways, that it was possible to retain a focus on the whole animal in its natural state and yet do an analysis at a deep level on some physiological process. I also learned from him the joys of expeditionary biology, and I regret not having made better subsequent use of that lesson. The expeditionary ventures provided the side benefit of a lot of personal instruction. I learned that teaching and research are kingdoms with poorly mapped boundaries. Most of all, I learned from Don a respect for diversity, for the instructive power of the odd mechanism or the chance solution—in short, the lesson that evolutionary opportunism provides the investigator with a great natural laboratory.

I was lucky to have a couple of mentors at Harvard. I worked on vision and visual physiology with George Wald, who later won a Nobel Prize for his work with pigments in the retina. As I was engaged with graduate work in a research project on fish behavior, the Fish & Wildlife Service invited me to Woods Hole Oceanographic Institution, the world's largest private nonprofit oceanographic research institution and a global leader in the study and exploration of the ocean. It was the first of several opportunities I would have to conduct research at Woods Hole, and I was privileged to do some of it with Griffin. He invited me to work with him on bats and how they navigate. His later celebrated work in the echolocation of bats began with the two of us filling big tubs with water and placing hydrophones under the water to see what sounds were produced by the bats as they cruised over the water's surface. The idea was that the hydrophones would detect whether the bats' sonar penetrated the water.

I liked working with Griffin. I recall with delight an encounter in the summer of 1953, in a small boat navigating uncertainly through a fog on Buzzards Bay off of Cape Cod. Griffin, then a professor of biology at Cornell, was the pilot. The passengers included an assortment of graduate students and others with a common interest in animal behavior and physiology, along with a susceptibility to the lure of Griffin's often rather harrowing expeditionary schemes. Our goal was a small island at the end of the Elizabeth chain where we intended to trap terns, take them inland, and release them to see whether they could find their way home. What I remember best about the trip was a growing uncertainty, out there in the fog, that *we* would be able to find our way home! Later, the sun broke through and we made our landing on a lonely, rubble-strewn island that contained the nests of thousands of circling, screaming terns. A group of ruined buildings added to the desolation. This chunk of terminal moraine, deposited by some glacier off the coast of Cape Cod, looked as though it might once have been a bombing range—and indeed, it had been.

We trapped our birds, explored a little, ate lunch, and headed back for Woods Hole. We put a dozen resentful terns into light-tight boxes with internal illumination set to mimic false times of day so that we could evaluate whether the birds were using the sun for navigation. Then we drove them north in an old station wagon in a bad-weather odyssey through New Hampshire and Vermont, releasing them from one small-town airport after another. Our routine was to set each bird loose and to have two widely-spaced observers follow it through binoculars mounted on alidades; in that way the final heading could be approximated by triangulation. The results were surprising only if you were as bound up in the preliminary hypotheses as we were. From a tern's point of view, they made perfect sense. Irrespective of internal "time" or location, all of the released birds flew southeast. If you nest on the New England coast and you are lost inland over unfamiliar territory, that is exactly what you ought to do.

The other explorers dropped out in Boston toward the end of this exercise, and I found myself alone with Griffin driving southeast on Route 28. It was a marvelous opportunity. Griffin was on his way from Cornell to Harvard, where I was a first-year graduate student in the process of transitioning my focus from ecology to animal behavior. He had developed an extraordinary reputation for his work on echolocation in bats and on the migratory navigation of birds. We talked that night about the puzzle the terns had given us, and then about behavior and physiology more generally. I remember an explanation of the cochlear microphonic potential, with a crude diagram drawn on a dusty dashboard. It was a scientific watershed for me. I later became Griffin's graduate student and went into caves with him after bats and released other birds in other places. My PhD dissertation focused on neurophysiology with an emphasis on vision, studying the electrical signals generated by the retina and what they revealed about the nature of its visual pigment. However, once I assumed my first faculty post, I turned my attention to neuromuscular systems in crayfish, studying how systems of single nerve cells are assembled and how they are then activated to produce a coordinated motor response.

INTRODUCTION TO TEACHING

Also during my graduate work at Harvard I worked as a teaching fellow for a young faculty member I much admired, Bill Drury, with whom I did some work in the field. He let me give one or two lectures in his Natural Science course and

The first year of our marriage, while I was finishing college, Don's parents gave us $200 a month while my parents paid all my college expenses. When I finished, his parents wanted to keep on giving us the money. We said no, because Don was earning $1,800 a year as a teaching assistant and I had gotten a job for $200 a month. Our budget was $15 a week for groceries, and our rent was $75 for a modern studio apartment.

—Jeanne Kennedy

When I was at Harvard with Don, we were invited by a cousin of his to a costume ball up in Boston. Our brainstorm was to convert an inverted garbage can into a top hat in which Don would crouch dressed in a rabbit suit, and from which I—as a top-hatted magician with an oversized mustache—would cause him to suddenly emerge. It turned out to be a very staid affair and somehow our act didn't win any plaudits. So we headed home, smelling like a brewery, in the robin's-egg-blue Model A Ford we had bought jointly for $100. It was freezing cold with the top down, and the top wouldn't go up. It was so cold that I put my magician's hat on and Don struggled into the rabbit suit. Driving through town, the sole car on the road in those wee hours, we became aware, over chattering teeth, of an inopportune siren. Spotting a robin's-egg-blue Model A, driven by a magician in top hat and mustache with a giant rabbit in the passenger seat, they pulled us over. Apparently a store had been robbed, and we were the only car in sight. Held at gunpoint, we ended up offering our story in the police station. In the end, we were given two baseball caps and sent on our way. Those were the days when even a liquor-scented guy in a rabbit suit could have a friendly exchange with a cop and end up heading home in a new Red Sox cap.

—Bill Warren

At the time of graduation from Harvard, 1952.

At Harvard, Don and I signed up for the first course ever in environmental studies. It was a landmark course on a topic of little concern in the postwar era. Don was an outdoors person, and we took on a very large project, planning to canoe down the length of the Connecticut River. But realizing that 400 miles was a sizeable canoe trip, we ended up walking and driving along a partial segment, sometimes by bus, studying problems relating to pollution and fish population. I believe this may have been a seminal point in Don's lifelong concern for the environment.

—Bill Warren

We had Don's professor and his wife, Don and Ruth Griffin, for dinner early on. We wanted to have it be a "grown-up" dinner so we served them the first martinis we had ever made. Since I was inexperienced, it took me a long while to cook the dinner and Don kept pouring the martinis. I was making veal in wine and the wine caught fire in a whoosh of flame. Don came in to help me put it out and we finally served the meal. As soon as it was put on the table, poor Ruth passed out with her head in her plate.

—Jeanne Kennedy

Griffin wanted to know if the birds knew which direction to fly to get home when they were released in a strange place. We now know that various cues are involved, including the earth's magnetic field, but we knew very little then. We thought if we could recover the birds quickly after determining the direction, we could do more experiments. We rowed out in middle of the pond in a small row boat with Don's fishing gear (Don was a keen fly fisherman). We tied the bird's foot on the end of the fishing line and tossed it into the air to see in which direction it would fly. As the line played out, it got too heavy and the bird fell into the water. We rowed frantically to get to bird before it succumbed, with Don trying to reel in the line. As soon as we got the bird back in the boat, Griffin was on the shore calling "Try it again, try it again." We tried it once more. The bird fluttered around the boat for a moment, then settled down on the transom and refused to budge. The bird was smarter than the professor.

—Tim Goldsmith

Don has a way of making you feel important while teaching you at the same time. He wouldn't coddle you, nor would he give you a C to teach you a lesson. He was never vindictive. He helped you get to the point where you were doing your best work in such a supportive and confidence-building way. There are not many people of his stature who see all of the good and all of the potential in their students and recognize that sometimes the carrot is a better motivator than the stick.

—Kai Anderson

Don was my mentor. He supported me even when I moved away from his field of interest. He sought out people to help me and made Stanford feel like home to me. He was warm and casual, and he was always interesting, with broad observations, even outside his areas of expertise.

—Josephine Chen

Only a week or so into the quarter in a multi-hundred-person lecture class, Don was calling on everyone by their first name. I was just one of those hundreds, but he saw me walking out of the library and shouted, "Great job on that test!" He just knew everyone, very quickly.

—Deborah Zarin

Don's lectures were unmatched. His ability to tell stories and then fuse things with clarity, enthusiasm, and passion was brilliant. Speaking in public, he combined data and information from many walks of life, explaining very complicated things in what appeared to be unwritten talks, sometimes in areas that were not his central domain.

—Deborah Zarin

lead groups of students out to do fieldwork, see new places, and examine natural history. It was a pivotal experience, and I learned how to teach.

What I learned was that a lecture should not be too perfect. Rather, it should be provocative; it should arouse questions. Lectures ought to be something a little bit hard to swallow, or something that generates introspective analysis. A great lecture should not go down slick as an oyster. I often wished I could know what students were thinking as I lectured to them, but you cannot learn that simply from watching faces. You can judge it better from the questions they ask. And you can improve as a teacher by responding to those questions, finding out what worked and what didn't, and collecting student reactions. Teaching, unlike presenting, is an interactive activity in which both teacher and student learn from each other.

Decades later, speaking at Harvard on the subject of education, I observed how little effort is made in the direction of teaching how to teach, noting that "most preceptors in the scholarly disciplines believe in some version of the old saw that teachers are born, not made; at least most of them doubt that there is any useful body of theory that could be deployed to help convert young people from adept learners to skillful teachers. Yet that is a difficult and challenging transition at which many members of the professoriate fail ignobly. And what about personal obligation to one's students? What kind of human attention do faculty members owe their students when there is obvious personal distress and emotional need? To what extent is it appropriate to use the classroom for promulgating personal views of the subject matter? I find few teachers who have wrestled seriously with such questions."[1] The response to the first question is often that "intellectual and not personal development is the faculty's responsibility. The second usually generates a quick assertion about academic freedom, as though that infinitely elastic concept could cover just about any degree of professional bias or idiosyncrasy." An extreme example was the case of Stanford English Professor H. Bruce Franklin (see Chapter 4).

In *Academic Duty*, I suggested that teaching, though it is our profession—an activity vital to ourselves, our students, and our public—seems mysteriously absent from our professional discourse, "as though it has no data base, lacks a history, and offers no innovative challenges. We are seldom focused on the vital classroom kinds of teaching, such as advising. In contrast to the popular view, students do not believe that they are pulling into an intellectual service station. Occupational preparation is not what they're after; they hope for meaningful contact with thoughtful elders—faculty members who can help them develop as individuals. We know that such experiences are best generated through close contact. No one, of course, should suppose that it is a faculty member's obligation to nurture each student's ego; indeed, strong and even harsh criticism may be called for. But it must be given with respect for the exercise and for the student's feelings, and with the clear purpose of bringing about improvement." A marginal note such as "This reads as though it had been written by a sophomore in high school" will likely result in a mixture of resentment and discouragement.

"To be a teacher is to be many things: a communicator of fact, a coach for skill improvement, an inspirer of creative insight or a thoughtful guide to analytical thought, a professional mentor, and many more. In making lists like this we tend to emphasize the things that happen in the classroom, but if we ask young people about their lives as students, and in particular if we trouble to inquire about the influences that were important to them, they usually tell us about one or a very few special teachers who made a difference in their lives. More often than not these accounts are deeply personal. If we ask, in short, about the influence of teachers rather than about what they do, we realize that in many cases they are functioning as role models and moral teachers, influencing the way students choose to conduct their lives."[2]

As postscript to the subject, I should add that we pay our elementary and high school teachers far less than we pay other professionals; worse, we treat them not like doctors or lawyers but like hourly wage earners. If only we behaved as though teaching really were a profession, half the problems of the schools would be solved overnight.

SERENDIPITY STRIKES: SYRACUSE UNIVERSITY

As I was finishing my PhD at Harvard, a situation arose that I could not have predicted, the first in a series of serendipitous events that have characterized my rather fortuitous career. I had decided to do more work on vision through a position at Walter Reed Army Medical Center Hospital in Washington, D.C., which would have entailed a four-year appointment as a second lieutenant in the medical service corps. It was a long term of service for a first job out of school, but it became impossibly unrealistic when I learned that the position would not be available for another year, and that in the meantime I would have to find something else to occupy my time and produce an income.

Although the military draft was in effect at the time, I was unlikely to be conscripted due to the wonderful news that Jeanne was expecting our first child. With the initial appointment stretching ahead for five years, we decided to consider other alternatives. And as luck would have it, one of my close colleagues in Cambridge, Roger Milkman, who had been scheduled to take an assistant professorship at Syracuse University, had just received an amazing offer to go to Paris and study with a distinguished group of geneticists. When he learned of my disappointing situation with Walter Reed, he wrote to the people who had proposed to hire him at Syracuse and suggested that I would be a fine alternative. I was soon invited to give a seminar in Syracuse. It went well, and they seemed to like it. In short order, Jeanne and I were en route to upstate New York.

Syracuse marked a very rewarding phase of my life. During our years there from 1956 to 1960, the birth of our daughter Page was an extraordinary passage, made all the more so by my close involvement with her in nighttime feedings and diaper changes. Unfortunately, Jeanne had suffered a hemorrhage during childbirth—not life threatening—but rendering her less able to care for the baby in the early months while she healed. We hired a nurse during the day while I was at work, but in the evenings the baby was my responsibility at a time when fathers were typically less involved than they are today. I have no doubt that the wonderfully close relationship I enjoy with my daughter Page is in part due to that bonding time.

We lived in an out-of-town apartment until Page was born and then found a home on Westmoreland Drive, a neighborhood populated by many faculty colleagues with whom we built an enjoyable social life. Among our friends was a neurophysiologist on the State University of New York (SUNY) medical center faculty, James Preston, who became a significant friend and colleague.

I was hired to teach two large lecture courses at Syracuse—an introduction to zoology in the Department of Zoology, and a general biology course in the School of Forestry, which was part of SUNY. The Forestry School is in an unusual situation in that it is half public and half private, neither fish nor fowl. But as a young and ambitious junior faculty member, I was happy enough to learn to teach through my large lecture classes. Nor did teaching inhibit my research interests, which had evolved from my dissertation on vision to the nervous systems of invertebrates.

CRUSTACEANS AND COMMAND CELLS: EARLY RESEARCH INTERESTS

My new friend Preston studied cats and other mammals, examining spinal reflex relationships concerned with behavior, gait, and so on. I suggested that pursuing the same kinds of questions using the simpler organisms that I was studying might reveal even more about the fundamentals of neural organization than working with a neural-rich organism like a cat. With crayfish, for example, one could identify most of the individual cells instead of just groups of them, as in the case of a complex mammal. That idea captured Preston's attention, and we embarked on an exploration that eventually produced a series of published papers on patterns of neural action in crayfish.

One of the interesting things about the central nervous system in crayfish is that many of the neurons also happen to be light sensitive, prompting questions about their biology. We were unable to show that their light sensitivity played a role in any natural behavior. But the light sensitivity made it easy to identify particular nerve cells in the nervous system and to begin to document their other features. It became clear that some single cells were able, when stimulated, to initiate important reflexes: some would produce an extension of the abdomen whereas another would connect with a circuit of very large cells to produce a violent tail flip that could make the animal swim backwards. Together with Preston, I was able to work out some of these single-cell properties. In perhaps the most arresting finding, made later at Stanford, it was found that some single neurons could produce a complex, fixed-action pattern of locomotory behavior. We began to call neurons with this property "command" neurons. What we did in the crayfish was to demonstrate some of the connection principles among nerve cells that impose the sequences underlying the behavioral event.]

When the work with Preston was prepared for publication, my status improved considerably in the Department of Zoology. It was an interesting period in neurophysiology, and I was gratified by the recognition our publications received. In my third year at Syracuse, I was rewarded with tenure. Although this was early by most academic time frames, I did not think of my new status as particularly accelerated at the time.

I enjoyed a friendly and constructive relationship with my department chairman, Verner Wulff, with whom I collaborated on the chemistry of visual pigments. My inner circle also included George Holtz from the school of medicine, a fellow fisherman and a great microbiologist. He was probably the closest faculty friend I had. He did excellent work and probably had more and better PhD students than anyone in the department.

I also had some splendid relationships with students. Syracuse was the first-choice university for some students from upstate New York and even for some from New York City's selective public schools who could not gain admission to Ivy League schools, due in some cases to religion quotas. Thus some of my students were from Midwood High School's Medical Science Institute and Stuyvesant High School—both exceptional, highly selective public secondary schools—and in that regard we at Syracuse were the beneficiary of some other institution's foolishness. I had one stunningly brilliant student named Merle Bruno who published two papers with me when she was still an undergraduate. She went on to do her PhD at Harvard and spent much of the last part of her career as Dean of Natural Science at Hampshire College, where my daughter Page would find herself enrolled some two decades hence. We still correspond, and Merle has been a wonderful friend.

WORK AND FAMILY

Although there is not much built-in reward at a university like Syracuse, it was interesting to teach there. I was teaching a lot—the chairman *expected* me to teach a lot—and gaining valuable experience. I enjoyed my research collaboration with James Preston, and many of my faculty colleagues became our friends. Though the winters were bitter in Syracuse, the university was located near interesting ski areas, and I often went off with a graduate student to run gates and enjoy an afternoon in the snow. It was great fishing country as well, with nearby fishing spots less than an hour away. So in the spring, Holtz, Preston, and I could leave the lab at a reasonable time and enjoy ourselves in good trout water, where we'd

His teaching was something that I tried to emulate all of my years as a professor at Stanford and Berkeley. He would tell a story and take it to an end—almost like an opera or great symphony. I watched him do that. He was an amazing teacher. He made neuroscience come alive.

—*Corey Goodman*

Dear Don: When I ventured into your office just prior to my sophomore year I was unhappy, alienated, and generally confused. You always reassured me that your office door was open to me if I encountered any new problems or if I just needed to bend someone's ear—and for that I am most appreciative. I am indebted to you for having helped nudge me along the often frightening road of self-discovery. I cannot begin to thank you adequately for all the assistance, guidance, and recommendations you have offered me. I will never forget what a big help you have been to me.

—*Jonathan Holloway [letter, 1989]*

Don saw and implemented a lot of educational reforms, but he wasn't credited for them, nor would he want to be because he did them *en passant*. He was being innovative without needing to say, "This is an innovation." He did many things before their time.

—*Ron Hoy*

An aspect of Don's teaching was his warmth and personal interest in individual students; there was always time to talk and listen to students and to respond to their needs. From the day of his first lecture in Biology 1, Don set teaching as a highest personal priority and led many of the other new biology faculty to do the same. The effect spread as a number of Don's PhD students learned from his example and have been recognized at other major universities and colleges for their excellent teaching, proving that highly successful researchers could also be caring, accomplished teachers.   —*Norm Wessells*

Don was never a high-tech neurophysiologist, but he got his results through the brilliant execution of classical, traditional skills. He was blessed with great hands—a great "wet-hand" neurophysiologist, one of the best I have ever known.   —*Ron Hoy*

The first in my family to go to college, I went to Syracuse in 1957, ostensibly to train for a job, meaning science, and ended up in Don's course. After missing two weeks of class with Asian flu, I returned to discover that there would be an exam the next day. I asked Don what to study in the text but was told that the book didn't relate to what he had talked about. The situation seemed hopeless. Then he said, "You can use my lecture notes." He never used notes; he just moved around, talked, and drew on board. But it turned out that the notes were almost verbatim, including the board drawings. Looking at those notes and drawings, I became enthralled and ended up with an A.

Taking that course with Don completely changed my life. He opened doors to me that I hadn't imagined existed, encouraging me to apply for grants and to go to graduate school at Harvard, which seemed a pipe dream at the time. My whole approach to teaching came from Don. He was excited by young minds, and he read the audience very well. You really felt like he was talking to you. He remained a touchstone throughout my career.

—*Merle Bruno*

There are a lot of brilliant people on this campus, including Don Kennedy, but he has style, which is unusual here. He is respected, admired, and envied by opponents. Everyone acknowledges his outstanding qualities, including his political opponents. I wish he weren't so gifted.

—*Professor Alphonse Juilland*

For me, Don is a living embodiment of Stanford—he's intellectually progressive, he's substantively distinguished, he's passionate and fun, but all in a balanced way, if you can be balanced without ever taking your foot off the accelerator.

—*Kai Anderson*

One-on-one teaching of an undergraduate.

find bats and watch cedar waxwings snatching insects from the air. It was a great zoological recreation area, rich in fish and their patterns of feeding, as well as various birds and bugs that contributed to streamside ecology. Yet in the back of my mind I wondered whether the possibilities were limited at a university with an annual budget that exceeded its total endowment.

In our fourth year at Syracuse our second daughter, Julia, was born. With the addition of another baby, winters became even more challenging. In each of our last two winters there, we endured more than eleven feet of snow! The weather systems moved west to east, and winters were grim. They generally started with southerly wind and rain that changed to snow. Then, as the storm crossed the Great Lakes it picked up more water and began snowing almost horizontally. Even today, from a distance of six decades and 3,000 miles, I can still visualize those appalling winters. And I was an adult! Imagine such winters for a small child in Syracuse—snow suits on, snow suits off, crackers and milk, and a host of weather protections that could become a full-time job for a loving parent, as Jeanne certainly was for our two girls.

DECISIONS, DECISIONS

In 1959 I received a call from Stanford with an offer that was, in truth, not very good. I hardly considered it, instead referring the department chairman to a colleague from graduate school at Harvard—Tim Goldsmith, of whom I thought highly. (Victor Twitty, the chairman of the Department of Biological Sciences, asked me—to my astonishment and distress—whether Tim was Jewish, explaining that his reason for asking was that the Department had already added a Jewish professor that year. That brief conversation resounded for me decades later when I met Robin, a Jew who had then and still does devote much of her Stanford volunteering to improve Jewish life on campus.) Goldsmith also rejected the position, instead spending most of his career at Yale.

A year later, I was again offered a position at Stanford. It was only marginally better—an assistant professorship teaching large lecture courses, and no tenure. But it seemed to me that the stars had aligned and the gods were smiling on Stanford. The medical school had just moved from San Francisco to the main campus, many new faculty in the basic sciences were coming on board, and chemists and biologists were expressing excitement about the contributions they could make through collaboration. Given such powerful events, it struck me that Stanford was the place to be, poised for transition to greatness.

The Stanford opportunity now before me presented a chance to start anew. My marriage with Jeanne was evolving in a very sweet way, and she was fully engaged with raising our children. I laugh now when I think of the colleague who wrote to me, incredulous that I was giving up tenure at Syracuse to go to Stanford, as if my decision were an affront to the profession! I actually considered that my decision to move on created advancement opportunities for others at

Syracuse. So for many reasons the time seemed right, after four years, to take a chance. Jeanne was supportive and had had her fill of the snow. So in 1960 we made a leap of faith, packing up Page and Julia and motoring across the continent, stopping where we could to feed and water the children, heading out west to the Farm.

CHAPTER 3

LIFE ON THE FARM

AS I WAS GROWING UP, and certainly as a student at Harvard, I had a vision in mind. It entailed working toward a teaching position in a small New England liberal arts college—a place like Bowdoin, Bates, Middlebury, or Williams College—my father's alma mater. I pictured membership in the professoriate as an opportunity to mingle with thoughtful people who were interested in the future of their institutions and were engaged in teaching and communicating to eager undergraduates.

My serendipitous appointment at Syracuse did not stain that vision. Although my primary purpose there was teaching, I was able to pursue some interesting research on nervous systems, which advanced my standing in my own department of zoology by a notch or two. In the process, I became excited not only about disseminating knowledge but about creating it.

It turns out that teaching large lecture classes was good experience, and Stanford's primary interest in me was my ability to do it as well as I had at Syracuse. But in coming to Stanford, I had also expressed an interest in continuing my research on the nervous system of lower animals. The latter, it turned out, would take some time and doing. I was hired primarily to teach Biology 1, 2, 3—a large lecture course for undergraduates who had not taken biology in high school. (I doubt that any undergraduate is admitted to Stanford today without having taken a high school course in basic biology, if not more advanced study.)

THE TERMAN FACTOR
Despite the temporary postponement of my research efforts, the offer to leave Syracuse for Stanford was an extraordinary opportunity for a huge career step, though at the time it was unquestionably a leap of faith—one that turned out to yield a future I could not possibly have expected, for Stanford was on the brink of remarkable things.

I was privileged to be part of a wave of faculty hiring launched as part of Provost Frederick Terman's vision. He personally recruited the brilliant Arthur Kornberg to the new department of biochemistry. Kornberg, in turn, brought

Lecturing, 1960s.

on a young scientist named Paul Berg. Kornberg, Berg, and later Kornberg's son, Roger, brought honor to Stanford when they each won a Nobel Prize.

An early dramatic example of the rapid and stunning growth in quality and stature of Stanford in higher education produced by the collaboration between Terman and President J. E. Wallace Sterling was their approval of the project now known as the Stanford Linear Accelerator Center, or SLAC. It involved the commitment of enormous financial, faculty, and land resources, with no explicit understanding of what might result. Technically, this venture was a GOCO—an acronym for "government owned, corporation operated." That leap of faith—an early public–private partnership—has been rewarded handsomely, drawing renowned physicists from the world over and developing into one of the world's most robust instruments for physics research and discovery. SLAC thrives to this day.

The other development, nearer my heart, was the decision to move Stanford's School of Medicine from San Francisco to the main campus in Palo Alto, which would, I hoped, facilitate collaboration across disciplines like the one I had enjoyed with James Preston in Syracuse. The move attracted some extraordinary new faculty, notably a brilliant set of microbiologists hired from Washington University in St. Louis. The medical school faculty, along with several of us in the School of Humanities and Sciences, collaborated much later to spawn the interdisciplinary Program in Human Biology, of which I was one of the founding faculty. The shift toward basic medical research helped physicists, chemists, and clinicians to become even more excited about contributions they could make by collaborating with colleagues in the basic biological sciences. Those were powerful and persuasive events.

Initially, I had to put my enthusiasm for the interdisciplinary opportunity on the back burner. It proved a bit of a struggle to resume my research career when colleagues viewed my primary utility as a teacher of large undergraduate lecture courses. I focused on trying to be a good lecturer to students who might have preferred to be anywhere but in biology class. My usual colleagues were David Regnery and, much later, Chuck Baxter, who would continue to be a strong and valuable fixture at Stanford's Hopkins Marine Station in Pacific Grove. With large enrollments of hundreds of students, lectures in Biology 1, 2, 3 were held in Memorial Auditorium, a 1,700-seat hall that doubled in those days as main stage for the Drama Department. Every so often I arrived at class, only to find the podium situated on the stage setting of a play. There I would be, delivering my lecture beside a rumpled bed reminding the students perhaps of the amorous activities of the romantic leads in the current show, or situated in a seventeenth-century castle paced the previous night by a tortured undergraduate Hamlet.

To make biology a little more realistic than the usual mode of lecturing, we had regular laboratory sessions led by graduate teaching assistants. For more variety, I occasionally took students out on Stanford's man-made Lake Lagunita in the fall to do some fieldwork, trolling for algae and insects in an aluminum boat. That adventure involved an undergraduate named Jean Doble, still a good friend, who now recalls the unexpected diversity of the creatures we were able to collect. Lagunita is a model "vernal pond," but, decades later, California's drought left it empty. The opportunity to venture out on the lake, a welcome respite from administrative duties, put me in closer association with students I came to admire and respect.

THE PURSUIT OF NEUROPHYSIOLOGY

At the same time that I was organizing my Biology 1, 2, 3 lectures, I also began to prepare a course in neurophysiology and behavior that would introduce students—graduate and some undergraduate—to experimental methods. I approached several manufacturers of scientific equipment, including Hewlett-Packard and Tektronix, to provide equipment so that I could outfit a laboratory with stations for the students who would enroll in the course. It was my aim to have a complete electrophysiology apparatus for each student. Although my efforts to secure in-kind gifts were successful, and I am grateful to those donors, two students would occasionally have to share one experimental set-up.

It was the practice in my lab to ensure that those who did the work received or shared the credit, and there were enough interesting projects that every student who wanted to could have a primary role on one of them. Three or four undergraduates finished their degrees with their names on published papers—along with me, or with one or more postdoctoral fellows, and a graduate student or two. This practice was a bit unusual for the time, making it a priority that we avoid any appearance of favoritism. As I explained in *Academic Duty*, "The rapid

When Don came to Stanford, he expected to have his lab all ready for him and to be responsible for the big freshman biology course. Unfortunately, his lab wasn't ready, and he had to teach the course under David Regnery. It was six months before the lab was ready for him do research, and he was very unhappy not to be in charge of what was being taught. It was a tough time for him. Once his lab opened, he began his research and taught his own courses. But it was quite a shock at first to find out what he was actually hired for.

—Jeanne Kennedy

In linking the medical school with the rest of the university, moving it from San Francisco to Palo Alto, Don not only had contagious enthusiasm, but very good ideas about how to proceed.

Don's role in creating the human biology program contributed to a higher level of student interest and a broader range of components for what became a "major." Now, in its forty-fifth year, it is surely one of the most successful majors Stanford has ever had and indeed has had worldwide recognition.

—David Hamburg

The course was all Don and everything in it was interesting. I'm sure his personal taste was largely responsible for the illusion that all neurophysiology is interesting. The fact that there was a brilliant teacher and some remarkable material really made neuroscience happen at Stanford, and just about everyone wanted to work with Don.

—Howard Fields

When Don was a young associate professor, we were in an old laboratory suite with wooden floors and plaster walls. There were three or four rooms, and his office was unfortunately right in the middle of it, so that everyone walking back and forth would pass by his desk. He had no privacy at all with telephone calls or conversations. We had a preparation going with a recording system in the back room that amplified the activity in the nervous system and fed into a loudspeaker so you could listen to the cell spikes, the action potentials, and there was one cell in particular that gave very large spikes, and Don referred to it as "Big Bertha." When we heard the cell popping Don would go to the wall and say, "Speak to me, Baby! Speak to me, Bertha!" It was a mechanoreceptor, so when he banged on the wall it would respond to his knocking. We had so much fun. We would all get together for parties.

—DeForest Mellon

He set an example for us all by being a superb teacher in the classroom, by maintaining a stimulating research atmosphere in his lab, and by staying on top of each project there. Don also ran terrific seminars, which were held in "facilitative" locales, like Rossotti's, where we discussed motor control over endless pitchers of beer. But his lab was the best environment I've ever seen for nurturing the human side of science. It was not only a place for scientific apprenticeship, it was also, frankly, a place for some of us to grow up. The tone and style of a lab is set from the top, and it was a privilege to have been part of the Kennedy lab in the 1960s.

—Ron Hoy

increase of multiple authorship, especially in the sciences, has given rise to the problem of 'complimentary authorship,' whereby a person not really meriting a place in the list of authors is given one anyhow. The motives vary; some of them stem from a misguided form of good will—a professor wanting to help a student's career, for example. Whatever the motive, it puts both the included author and the scientific enterprise at risk.

"Complimentary authorship is one by-product of today's highly competitive academic scene. Jobs are hard to get. Although faculty members often want to help their students for the best of reasons, it is important to remember that they also gain prestige when their students do well. Thus this is a more common transgression than one might suppose, and it is a serious one, not at all mitigated by the elements of good will that sometimes motivate it. Complimentary authorship not only distorts the historical record of who did what, and allocates credit to those who may not deserve any, but also may negatively affect the innocent coauthor if the work turns out to be tainted.

"One would not, however, want this argument to be mobilized against the impulse to allocate credit generously. Those who took part in the work ought to be included in the list of authors. But because they share responsibility for the quality and truthfulness of the work, they need to have been real—and knowing—participants, and to be fully involved in the decision when and where the work should be published."[1]

When our lab was moved from Stanford's Inner Quad to the new Herrin Hall in the developing research area devoted to experimental science, our facili-

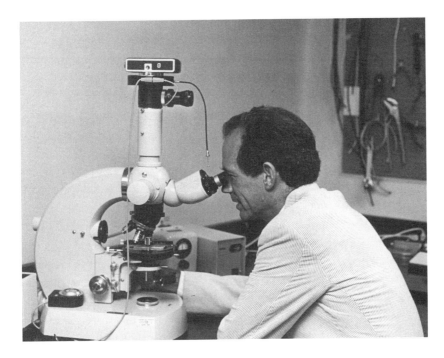

At the microscope in the Kennedy lab.

In the Kennedy
lab, 1960s.

ties improved substantially and we were able to do more serious work in neurophysiology. My relationships with increasingly talented graduate students and postdoctoral fellows grew, and some of them became academic stars with whom I was proud to collaborate—and later to follow as their talents took them beyond our lab at Stanford.

In teaching that first course, I got to know Howard Fields, then a medical student, and we formed a closer association as he undertook advanced work. Until much later Stanford did not offer a combined MD/PhD program; Howard essentially invented one by doing coursework and subsequently writing a dissertation in his "spare time"! We sought grants together and explored ways to explain how nerve cells may be organized to produce stereotyped behaviors in which an entire pattern is generated by stimulating a single nerve cell. Fields, who now serves on the faculty at the University of California at San Francisco, wondered whether there was a way to retain the pain-relieving effect of opiates while avoiding the addictive quality. A tangible result is the use of naloxone in emergency overdose treatment of those who battle substance abuse.

Fields went on to do brilliant work on pain and addiction, identifying the "placebo effect" in pain management and showing that it could be blocked by naloxone. He and his colleague, Jon Levine, found that if both morphine and naloxone are taken simultaneously, a patient will receive the necessary analgesic effect of the morphine but avoid the potential for addiction. The focus of Howard's work is now on opioid addiction and the neurological cause of alcohol dependency. Howard remains among the closest of my academic friends.

LEADERSHIP TRANSITION

When I arrived at the department of Biological Sciences at Stanford, it was blessed with abundant resources. The Carnegie Institution of Washington, D.C., had established a biology lab on campus. Based on the good relationships and results coming out of the lab, they established an additional program in global ecology, facilitating a number of new faculty appointments between 1964 and 1975, including a neurobiologist, a geneticist, and a physiologist. Among the superbly capable colleagues joining the Stanford faculty at that time were Don Wilson, Marc Feldman, Craig Heller, and Chris Field.

Notwithstanding the growth and energy in the department, Chairman Victor Twitty was deeply unhappy about his own life and the status of the department; no one quite knew the depth of his struggle or how to help. Sadly, in 1967, Twitty took his own life, and I was called to the scene to witness what had happened. It appeared he had used potassium cyanide to cut his life short at the age of sixty-five.

Confusion over the future of the department ensued, and the question of leadership and direction was explored by a committee composed of both Stanford and non-Stanford faculty. In the department were powerful leaders in molecular biology and the emerging field of genetics—Charles Yanofsky, who narrowly missed a Nobel Prize, and Paul Ehrlich, an expert in ecology and evolutionary biology. Clifford Grobstein appeared to be the "chairman in waiting," but at the time of Twitty's unexpected demise he had already begun a serious negotiation with the University of California at San Diego to become chairman of its biology department. To my surprise, after a period of evaluation, with seven years under my belt at Stanford, I was appointed to succeed Twitty in the post then titled "Executive Head." With that sign on my door, it was surprising how many walked in expecting to find the bathroom!

I was a somewhat reluctant enlistee. I was of course interested in getting along well with my colleagues, many of whom were older and viewed me as teaching faculty only. Our distinguished older faculty was a great asset, but we also needed to prepare a succession plan based on a collective vision of what the department should become, an issue on which the faculty was split. My sense was that we could emphasize two foci, molecular biology and ecology/evolutionary biology. But that was not a decision to be made unilaterally, least of all by the untested and relatively young new chairman. Fortunately, most in the department came

Young professor Don, 1960s.

around to a unified view on the dual mission. We were blessed with two academic leaders who respected one another so deeply that there was more collaboration and support than competition. I doubt we could have developed two active research divisions in biology without the leadership of Charles Yanofsky and Paul Ehrlich.

Yanofsky was a brilliant scientist who first demonstrated that changes in DNA sequence can produce changes in protein sequence at corresponding positions—the so-called one gene, one protein theory. His fundamental observation helped determine the genetic code, one of the great scientific breakthroughs of the last century.

A butterfly expert by training, Ehrlich made his mark through his dire warnings about population and limited resources. He became

In the fifty-three years that I've known Don, he's been nothing but supportive of me and of everyone else who passed through his lab. Don always seemed to be more interested in fostering the scientific and personal development of his students than in harnessing their efforts to the pursuit of his own scientific goals. He had remarkable breadth as a biologist and remarkable depth as a neurobiologist. He was full of ideas for undergraduate, graduate, and postdoctoral research projects that had obvious connections to his special interests, but he also encouraged students to follow their own interests even though they were tangential to or quite far removed from his.

—*Richard Roth*

Don recognized the importance of encouraging students who were facing a much more challenging era than he had. Rather than saying, "It was hard for me; I made it; you can do it, too," it was more like, "It was actually less hard for me; you have a more difficult challenge, and I'm going to cheer you on in any way I can."

—*George Karlin-Neumann*

He was a role model. His knowledge of the literature was a talent that I aspired to. It seemed like he had read every paper and knew them all in great detail. The lab was in Jordan Hall, and his office was the passage to the back room and was not very private, but he was never at his desk. Nor did I ever see him in the library. When he wasn't teaching or on committees he was doing experiments with that infectious enthusiasm. To this day I don't know how he found time to read the literature, write grants, or review manuscripts.

I don't think I've ever known anyone to be so uniformly positive and enthusiastic and supportive. That was huge because you internalize it—that sense of confidence and enthusiasm—it became part of my personality. If something didn't work out, the idea was that you would figure it out, you would make it work.

—*Howard Fields*

Don ran a really lively cutting-edge laboratory, full of enthusiastic graduate students and postdocs, who loved him and loved being in the lab. He invited all of his lab students to his house for parties. Don really enjoyed himself. He was by no means a chaperone; he was a full-on participant. He loved to dance—he was just totally full of life. I've never known anyone else who could find everything so enjoyable. I never heard him seriously complain about things; sometimes you'd hear an edge, but he was never one to go to the deep end and wallow in "woe is me." That was never Don. He was always one to think of a solution.

It's so hard for senior scientists to do bench work these days, and I know very few who successfully do it. But Don was a master multitasker. On top of all his later commitments, he would still come into the lab every Saturday morning, roll up his sleeves, and dissect a crayfish with his postdocs. To really be at the bench—in spite of all his involvements—he came in every Saturday morning, virtually without fail, and spent those four hours. He didn't stay the whole day because he wanted to spend part of the weekend with his family. He was great with his kids, a really affectionate father.

Don was a mentor forty years before that term was applied as part of a senior academic's job description. He did everything then that a good mentor by today's standards is supposed to do. But he did that genuinely out of his heart. There were no rules for what a good mentor does. Don just did it naturally. He was an extravert; he loved people. In my own career, I often ask myself what would Don have done. and then I realize if I could do 20 percent of that it would be great.

—Ron Hoy

Don was the youngest chairman of a department at Stanford. He became chair of the Biology Department in 1965 as an associate professor, which was unusual. We then had to do a lot of recruiting. We had a Rangpur lime tree right outside the dining room window, and the candidate would watch us lean out to pick a lime in the dead of winter for the gin and tonic. We called it our recruiting tree.

—Jeanne Kennedy

There was a time when university presidents were very influential, and Don was perhaps the last of the great university presidents who were public intellectual figures.

—Paul Ehrlich

I was defending my thesis, and one particular faculty member was giving me an especially difficult time. I had labored over the thesis for months and was really at the end of my rope. I presented my argument and tried to rebut the points he was making, but it seemed lost. I would have to go back and readdress what were fundamental concerns. But at that moment Don spoke up and came to my defense. He repackaged the arguments I had made but in a more coherent fashion, helping me navigate through that moment in a way that allowed everyone involved to save face. He had taken the faculty member's comments and the rebuttals I had presented, harmonized them, explicated the differences, and made it evident that they were not fundamentally incompatible, that they were just different ways of looking at the same problem. It was an amazing moment of academic and intellectual diplomacy, and I learned a lot from it.

—Thomas Butler

While I was working as a research assistant in Don's lab, he was also paying me to help write the renewal grant for the Human Bio program. I didn't understand what it really was or how to do it, but he gave me some materials, and I submitted a draft of a section. We met in his office after he'd gone over it, and I remember walking out feeling *really good* about myself—euphoric. But I got about 200 feet into the Quad when it began to dawn on me that he had basically told me to rewrite the whole thing—totally marked it up, completely changed everything—yet I still felt on top of the world. That ability to make you feel great while telling you to start completely over must have played out everywhere he worked—one of many reasons why his staff was so loyal to him.

—Deborah Zarin

well-known after the publication of his 1968 book, *The Population Bomb*, which sounded alarm bells over issues related to rates of population growth, food production, and food distribution. At Stanford he had established a research program looking at natural populations of a checker-spot butterfly and its preferred food plant. He was able to follow local shifts in both, and to measure population of plants and insects also at the Rocky Mountain Biological Laboratory, of which Paul was an original founder and where he continues to contribute to conservation biology.

That these two distinguished scholars each respected and recognized the importance of the other was a huge boon. I was able to avoid the potential for polarization precisely because Ehrlich and Yanofsky were great peacemakers. I applauded and encouraged the respect that they had for each other, which helped to offset the kinds of instincts that sometimes occur in competitive academic departments, with separate factions defined by separate disciplines. I needed to ensure that the Department of Biological Sciences remained a single unit, that it did not split in two because some thought they would receive more favorable attention from the provost if they stepped away from the unified whole. With Yanofsky's and Ehrlich's collaboration, I was able to chart a new course in the biological sciences at Stanford.

As a young academic leader there was a lot for me to learn. Provost Fred Terman was enormously influential in demonstrating how to staff a department with faculty at various stages of their careers, how to interact successfully with the dean of humanities and sciences, and how to work well with the provost, who serves as the university's chief academic officer. To build a department that was diverse, interesting, and covered the field well, we aimed toward a three-tiered hiring policy, bringing in senior faculty, midcareer faculty, and some very promising younger faculty. Our goal was to attract very good scientists with powerful interests in one discipline, which would give them the status to attract other faculty of similar quality.

INTERDISCIPLINARY, INTERDEPARTMENTAL INNOVATION

A couple of years into my chairmanship of the Department of Biological Sciences, I was part of a group of faculty from both that department and the School of Medicine who were eager to initiate an interdisciplinary and interdepartmental undergraduate Program in Human Biology. The aim was to fuse the social and natural sciences, providing educational background that might serve students interested in policy, nonprofit, and government service pertaining to health.

Those energized around this effort were a stellar bunch from both the School of Humanities and Sciences and the School of Medicine: Paul Ehrlich, biology; David Hamburg, psychiatry; Craig Heller, physiology; Norm Kretchmer, pediatrics; Josh Lederberg, genetics; Sandy Dornbusch, sociology; Al Hastorf, psychology; and Herant Katchadourian, psychiatry. We were blessed by generous funding from a Ford Foundation grant that allowed us to secure a deeply engaged faculty. Combined with individual contributions from alumni, the program was off to a stable start. Very often, foundation support provides short-range program support and a precipitous drop-off when the grant period ends. Leveraging the Ford Foundation grant, we were able to hedge against this cliff, attracting private funds for named chairs and senior faculty who took turns leading the development of the Human Biology core curriculum.

The Program gave medical school faculty the opportunity to teach Stanford undergraduates, who were given the chance to learn from professors to whom they would otherwise not have had access. As an interdisciplinary, interschool, interdepartmental program, the collective faculty was determined to blend the social and biological sciences. This collaboration had the amusing effect of producing rather unusual class projects. I recall, for example, small musicals and other artistic expressions created to demonstrate a particular biology principle, with lyrics—often quite funny—devised to illustrate the serious point effectively in a fun-loving spirit.

The idea of the Program was to produce scholars with strong backgrounds in biology as well as in the social sciences, essential for aspects of law, government, health and medical policy development, and other careers where presentation skills as well as intellectual ownership of the scientific material were essential.

The Program, now nearly a half-century in operation, succeeded beyond anyone's imagination. Undergraduate alumni of the Program have found terrific career opportunities, demonstrating that a doctorate is not always necessary. In working closely with students in the Program, I made an early assessment that perhaps half the students would go on to law school and the other half to medical school. But in fact they have pursued careers across a much broader swath, many in nongovernmental and nonprofit organizations, as well as state and federal posts.

The first course in the Program, Introduction to Human Biology, was taught by Colin Pittendrigh, who had studied infectious diseases in Trinidad. Recruited from Princeton, where he had served as dean of the graduate division, he was a much-admired, colorful lecturer, a master of the old-fashioned lecture style. Pittendrigh was persuaded to come west in part by the proximity of excellent fishing waters in Montana and Wyoming! He later became director of Stanford's Hopkins Marine Station in Pacific Grove. A postscript is that decades later Pittendrigh was an overnight guest at Hoover House, the residence of the Stanford president. His visit was in anticipation of surgery, scheduled the next morning at Stanford Hospital. But the 6.9 Loma Prieta earthquake struck that afternoon, and Robin, who rushed home from her campus office fearing for the safety of our daughter, our houseguest, and the staff, sought out Colin in his guestroom, suggesting that it might not be safe to remain inside. Colin told Robin he would be glad to sit in the driveway in front of the house so long as he had a comfortable chair, an ottoman, a bucket of ice, a glass, and a bottle of good scotch. There he sat, contentedly drinking for hours until the Stanford officials declared it safe to reenter!

In addition to an all-star faculty, the success of the Program in Human Biology depended in large part on the integration of what we called the "A-side," which was primarily biology, and the "B-side," which comprised the social sciences. The letter designations refer to the succession of lecture topics the faculty originally proposed for the core curriculum in Human Biology: "A" and "B" side lectures were presented back-to-back, in that order, making it possible for faculty teaching partners to hear their colleagues. Such careful planning between the two sides has been an important element of the program's success and survival.

It has always seemed to me that the prestigious Lloyd W. Dinkelspiel Award for Outstanding Service to Undergraduate Education, which I received at commencement in 1976 for my involvement in Human Biology, should have included as recipients all my colleagues who developed and devoted themselves to the Program in Human Biology. I was happy to credit my colleagues in accepting the award.

Since the inception of the Program, nearly forty other interdisciplinary, interdepartmental programs have been established at Stanford. The Program in Earth Systems has been one spectacular addition. Students learn about and independently investigate complex environmental problems caused by human activities in interaction with natural changes in the Earth system. Earth Systems majors become skilled in those areas of science, economics, and policy needed to tackle the globe's most pressing environmental problems, becoming part of a generation of scientists, professionals, and citizens who approach and solve problems in a systematic, interdisciplinary way. Other universities have developed programs resembling Human Biology: Oxford University, for example, has developed a "Human Sciences Honors School," and a few of our own Human biology students have continued their studies there.

The autonomy of a department chair at Stanford differs from that at Harvard, for example, where the university president reserves the right to serve on ad hoc committees regarding academic appointments. The president of Stanford has no such right. Conversations take place between deans and department chairs about how they propose to develop a department, but rarely are specific appointments discussed. My knowledge of Harvard is based on eight years as an undergraduate and doctoral degree candidate and later as an elected member of the Harvard Board of Overseers. The differences in governance, management, and style between Stanford and Harvard merit comment. Whereas the Board of Trustees at Stanford is the sole source of fiduciary authority, the Harvard arrangement is bicameral: the legal entity of Harvard is the president and fellows, comprising talented, successful, self-succeeding (and often generous) alumni. Harvard overseers have no role in governance but are often individually affiliated in helpful ways with one or another Harvard school or department (in my case, the School of Public Health and Biology).

With respect to differences between these institutions of higher education, Harvard's organization is often (and perhaps unfairly) characterized as "every tub on its own bottom." One might take this to mean a certain independence of the schools (law, medicine, arts and sciences, and so on) with respect to budgets, fund raising, and policy. In fact, however, there is a difference in the way power is allocated. As seen in the premature end of Larry Summers's Harvard presidency, it was a vote by the Faculty of Arts and Sciences that led to his dismissal. When this news came to Stanford, its faculty expressed widespread astonishment: Where was the law school faculty? Where was earth sciences, or education, or business? Decisions pertaining to the university as a whole entail a much broader collective of key stakeholders than one would assume to be concentrated in just one school. Another difference is the involvement in Stanford's Academic Senate of elected representatives of all seven schools. On a regular basis, the university president and provost report and then to respond to questions from the assembled faculty. I know of no such arrangement in other leading universities. It's likely that the communitarian sensibilities of the Stanford administration seeped into the undergraduate sensibility, which, as I discuss in Chapter 4, has always been characterized by cooperation rather than competition.

Harvard commencement, 1971; Don as overseer.

THE UNEXPECTED: WHAT HAPPENS WHEN YOU ARE MAKING PLANS

Amid all the academic planning, team building, and department development, it is difficult to predict the surprises that might come one's way. Victor Twitty's suicide was certainly an example, as was the case with one of my recruits to the Department, Don Wilson from Berkeley, a man with strong politically progressive attitudes who also liked to go rock climbing and river rafting throughout the West. He was a pivotal figure in the emergence of neuroethology as a discipline, and in the use of invertebrate "simple systems" for neurobehavioral research in the 1960s. But in June of 1970, while on a whitewater rafting trip in Idaho, Wilson drowned. I was called to come to Idaho to retrieve the body—an unanticipated responsibility arising from yet another colleague's untimely death.

In May of 1975, I found myself in the middle of another unpredictable situation that made international headlines. Armed rebels kidnapped three Stanford students who had gone with Dr. Jane Goodall to observe chimpanzee behavior on the Gombe Stream Reserve primate research center in Tanzania. Two were seniors in Human Biology and directly under my supervision—Carrie Jane Hunter and Kenneth Stephen Smith; the third was PhD candidate Barbara Smuts, a graduate student in neurological and behavioral sciences. The three students and a fourth hostage, a Dutch researcher named Emilie van Zinnicq Bergmann, were taken across Lake Tanganyika and held hostage for weeks in cold mud huts alongside African civilians seized by members of Zaire's People's Revolutionary Party (PRP) and forced into slave labor. PRP leader Laurent Kabila eventually took over the Zairian government in 1996 and was assassinated in January 2001.

The PRP had perpetrated the kidnapping as a tactic designed to focus global attention on Zaire and to gain concessions from Tanzania. A week after the hostages were seized, our graduate student, Barbara Smuts, was released. She carried with her ransom notes threatening to kill the other two students if the raiders' demands to the Tanzanian government—$460,000 ransom, arms and ammunition, and the release of PRP prisoners in Tanzania—were not met. Human Biology cofounder David Hamburg, who was Stanford's chief liaison with the Gombe facility, immediately traveled to Tanzania and joined an international team negotiating for the release of the students. He was assisted by graduating Human Biology student Michelle Trudeau and others who had also been at Gombe and understood the lay of the land. Eventually, the families of the kidnapped victims raised over $460,000 to pay Kabila's ransom. After two months of anguished suspense and difficult negotiation, the students were released unharmed. By coincidence, my one-time Harvard roommate Herb Levin was the U.S. Foreign Service officer in the region. His efforts, in stealthy collaboration with the Israeli government, provided transport across Lake Tanganyika for the remaining hostages.

When the students returned to Stanford, I did my best to provide guidance as they reentered academic life. After the kidnapping incident, Gombe was deemed too dangerous, and the Human Biology fieldwork program there was discontinued.

FAMILY MATTERS

During this period early in my Stanford career, as I was learning how to be an effective chairman of the Department of Biological Sciences, I received an editorship of sorts with a textbook publisher, W. H. Freeman Company, which had proposed to produce a series of collected scientific works. I worked with Bill Kaufmann, my good friend from Syracuse days, to develop and publish several collections designed to summarize the state of particular research areas. Examples were *Selected Topics in Development*, *Animal Behavior*, and *The Biology of Organisms*, with regular commentary on developmental biology and patterns of animal behavior. The work involved assembling short but influential papers to include in these collections, a few of which I wrote myself, and writing general introductions to each topic to help contextualize it, primarily for undergraduate readers. The collections proved useful in teaching each topic.

As it was primarily a summer pursuit, the work for W. H. Freeman connects to a family story. By this time, Jeanne, Page, Julia, and I, sometimes accompanied by a friend of one or both of the children, developed a tradition of renting a cabin for several weeks each summer near a fall on Glen Alpine Creek, just above Stanford Sierra Camp, which borders Fallen Leaf Lake, a tributary of Lake Tahoe.

The cabin was owned by Stanford professor Margaret Yates. We all loved the place and were invited to connect with the many activities and alumni families at the camp, where I had first been invited to lecture in 1961. The children explored enthusiastically and eventually could identify the species of hummingbirds that frequented the feeder at the cabin. While they were having some woodland adventure or hiking the trails, I often had a typewriter out on the deck in the mornings, trying to create one or another Freeman booklet.

Julia was fascinated with nature in a great variety of ways, including one too intimate by her father's assessment: She would occasionally bestow a quick kiss on a bumblebee or toad. She discovered patches of wild onion in interesting spots and thoroughly explored the streams. Both Page and Julia were quite independent at camp, with many adults available to watch the camp children from afar. Jeanne and I were permissive parents, letting the girls explore and learn. We shared the same convictions about good things for the children and approached our parenting in similar style, though Jeanne was unquestionably the primary parent.

We were serious hikers, sometimes scaling Mount Tallac, with and without our children. Jeanne and I got interested in the natural history of the region, so she was a good companion on hikes and trout fishing expeditions. Page and Julia were often left to find friends or interesting forms of nature, and both grew into a love of the place, which persists some fifty years later. On occasion, we entertained a visitor at the cabin. My former colleague Tim Goldsmith and his children visited, hiking with us, and our children got a sense of other people in our lives who seemed in some way to serve as extended family. For my part, I regularly ventured down to camp and enjoyed playing volleyball with the alumni guests. Julie and her husband Ted continue to rent the Yates cabin, and after Robin and I married, our blended family attended Sierra Camp Week Four for several years, an opportunity for all our grandchildren to bond and band together. All in all, the summers at Stanford Sierra Camp have been a steady, stabilizing element of our family life.

Don remained very cool during the kidnapping, while being pressured to pay for the Stanford student and abandon the other two, or to demand we send in the marines. Student delegations were demonstrating. He instinctively understood that out in the middle of the African jungle, coordinating with the British, Dutch, Tanzanians, and these crazy Zaire kidnappers, that this was not the time to kibitz or micromanage from California. He had good political instincts, and we ended up negotiating and getting all three students out safely.

—Herbert Levin

Don and I both arrived at Stanford in August of 1960. Our families became close, and the two girls and three boys grew up together through those early Stanford years. We spent innumerable Sundays at Pescadero or other beach spots, throwing frisbees, tossing footballs, hiking, even swimming. I saw a loving, caring Don, who gave Julia and Page the fondness and attention and encouragement that means so much in the development of happy and successful adults. They are living examples of the benefits of such a parent.

—Norm Wessells

Don opened to me a whole new arena of intellectual thought and academic excellence in which I felt at home. Inveterate explorer of the natural world, his fascination with animal behavior (especially birds), oceans, mountains, and deserts increased and enhanced my own inclinations. He never cared about money or material possessions, but he did care profoundly about science, Stanford, and sports. Often referred to as a Renaissance man, Don excelled in the academic triumvirate of teaching, research, and administration. He was intense, definitely type A, driven, charismatic, and incredibly articulate in the spoken and written word. His ability to quickly assess people and reflect back to them their best selves made them feel totally understood. My life has been enriched by our marriage and our friendship. Because of the opportunities he provided, I achieved far more in my life than I had ever dreamed.

—Jeanne Kennedy

When I came to Stanford as the first non-Christian university chaplain, it wasn't entirely clear what my tasks would be or how to pull it off. My position was a bit tenuous in that I was the first rabbi on campus who was not hired by the Jewish community. So there was a great deal of suspicion—"Who *is* this person that we didn't invite?" But Don was my booster from the get-go. As someone who is not himself religious at all, he really had a sense of appreciation and translation, of the importance of translating religious language to a secular sphere in which community and meaning and purpose are essential. Though he didn't start from a religious place, he understood the value of what I was attempting to bring and has always been incredibly supportive and made me feel like my work matters, and I think that's probably true of every person in the university who worked with him.

—Patricia Karlin-Neumann

I was addicted to Bob Dylan and would spout phrases from his songs. There was one called the "Memphis Blues," and whenever anything went wrong I would say, "Oh Mama, can this really be the end to be stuck inside of (something) with the (something) blues again," modifying the lyric to the situation. I was kind of a flaky kid at the time, and Don would try to impress upon me this incredible focus that he had. We were doing an experiment, and I had to leave, and he said "Come on, we're just about to get this cell, I know it's there; we're going to get it!" The cell that we were looking for was interneuron C, but we called it "biff-bam" because when you listened to the electrical activity of this neuron on the audio monitor, it sounded like biff-bam. I promised I'd be back in two hours, and I returned to find the electrodes still in place, still inside biff-bam, and a note that said "Oh Mama, can this really be the end, to be stuck inside of biff-bam with the shifting zones again." He'd picked up on my little Bob Dylan quirk. It was whimsical but also chiding me for not riding through on it. That had a big impact on me.   —*Ronald Calabrese*

I was a weak student from a torn background with no real balance and no idea how to navigate this new terrain. Don helped me find a balance among the numerous directions that interested me. He would review assignments with me before and after grades, teaching me where and how to make the words do the work. I got smarter just walking in and saying hello. He was parental—firm but understanding—treating me as though I were just like the others. He made me believe that I could make a difference in people's lives. I became a teacher, and I raised my sons to appreciate the kind of critical thinking that I had learned and practiced with Don.   —*Vaughn Williams*

His advice to me as a student was to focus on the research and scholarship, on the science, and do really great teaching, but don't get involved in university politics or get yourself on all kinds of committees. When you're young, knock it out of the park, build your scholarship and scientific reputation, also your reputation as a teacher and communicator, and your chance to do public service and all those things will be much more effective later on. I modeled myself after that. It was always Don's voice in the back of my head, in a kind of fatherly way, giving me the blueprint on how to have a successful career, how to set yourself up to have the biggest impact on society. He was spot on.

—*Corey Goodman*

The reason Don was so well liked was that he genuinely liked people. He enjoyed what he was doing and the people he was working with. He was a terrific teacher. He liked students and was always willing to talk to them. It was the same with staff members. Some people go to a political reception because they have to. They do the best they can and can't wait to get out. But Don *liked* everything he went to; he *liked* raising money; he *liked* development; but he also liked the political process and the people in it. He wanted to talk to people and they wanted to talk to him—it was that boundless enthusiasm.

—*Larry Horton*

At home in Palo Alto, Page and Julia attended Walter Hays Elementary School and Palo Alto High School, or "Paly" as it is known locally. After Paly, Page attended Humboldt State, and after a time up there beyond the redwood curtain, she came back for a critical year, 1977, during which Jeanne and I were contemplating an offer to go to Washington, where I would head the Food and Drug Administration. Page's experience at Humboldt delivered her some singularly unproductive prospects, and I spent much time after that running and exercising with her, praising her to raise her spirits, and telling her that all would be well, as it turned out to be.

Still, I feel I left a lot undone with respect to parenting and parental relationships. It's possible I picked up an incorrect signal from my mother, who seemed unable to engage with any childhood difficulty. I remember a visit from my mother to our young family in Syracuse. Page ran to greet her, stumbled, and hit her eye on the corner of a metal sofa, producing a good deal of blood. My mother could not cope with the temporary emergency, the mess, and what to do next. A bit of chaos ensued but was eventually resolved. Although I am not reflective by nature, I have given some thought in recent years to the parenting that I received and how it might have influenced the parent I became.

CHAPTER 4

ACADEMIC FREEDOM
AND ACADEMIC DUTY
The Case of H. Bruce Franklin

THERE IS PERHAPS NO SINGLE VALUE more respected in higher education than academic freedom. We cherish the tenet that freedom of inquiry by faculty members is essential to the mission of the academy and that scholars should have the freedom to teach or communicate ideas or facts—including those inconvenient or uncomfortable to external political groups or authorities—without being targeted for retaliation, job loss, or imprisonment. Over a long career, I treasured the value of academic freedom, which deserves stout protection, as well as its corollary, academic duty.[1] The balance between freedom and duty is a hallmark of every great university.

In the fall of 1971, eleven years after my arrival at Stanford, I found myself weighing the responsibilities of academic duty as well as the standard of academic freedom as I presided over a hearing concerning the proposed ouster of a tenured faculty member, H. Bruce Franklin. On the one hand, as Chairman of the Faculty Advisory Board of the Academic Council, it was my duty to manage inquiries regarding the roles and responsibilities of faculty members. At the same time, the University upheld the rights of faculty to speak out on issues of importance. Among the most important issues of the day was the Vietnam War.

CAMPUS TURMOIL

The late sixties and early seventies were years of turmoil on the Stanford campus. As Herbert L. Packer, then Jackson Eli Reynolds Professor of Law, described in *Commentary*:

> "Trashing" or window-breaking cost the University about a quarter of a million [1972] dollars. There were at least five sit-ins during the period, which disrupted the lives of the community. There were numerous incidents of arson, including destructive fires in which scholars lost irreplaceable papers. A staff member had his house fire-bombed. Another was shot at through the front window of his living room. The president's office was destroyed by arson. On occasion, faculty, staff, and students stood round-the-clock fire

watches. Throughout this period [Professor H. Bruce] Franklin was in the forefront, accelerating the coercion and violence through his charisma as a tenured professor, and urging impressionable young people on to ever more activity.[2]

Franklin was a renowned authority on the work of Herman Melville, the author best known for *Moby Dick*. A tenured professor in the Department of English, Franklin campaigned strongly in the community and on campus against the Vietnam War. In his passionate opposition, he was far from alone. I and many among the faculty, as well as students and members of the Stanford and Palo Alto communities, opposed the war. But according to charges brought by Stanford President Richard Lyman in connection with four campus incidents, Franklin had crossed the line from free speech to incitement. Lyman had recommended Franklin's dismissal from the faculty, and it was the role of the Advisory Board to hear the University's charges and Franklin's defense and render a verdict. There was no question about where my primary obligation lay. It was to ensure, in my role as a sitting judge, that the highest standards of procedure would be followed in reviewing the charges against Professor Franklin.

President Lyman was a historian specializing in recent British history and had served as correspondent for the *Economist* on American affairs. A Democrat by party affiliation, he consistently opposed the war in Vietnam, helping to organize what may have been the first teach-in on the war. He was also a faculty-oriented president. As Franklin's acts escalated, it fell to Lyman to initiate action against him, a responsibility he undertook with great care. The charges, prompted by incidents early in 1971, were based on Stanford's 1967 Statement of Policy on Appointment and Tenure, which provided that a faculty member shall not be dismissed without a finding of "substantial and manifest neglect of duty" or "personal conduct substantially impairing the individual's performance of his appropriate functions within the University community."[3] The Advisory Board was designated by the Tenure Statement to hear cases in which a faculty member chooses to have a hearing before he can be subjected to sanctions. President Lyman's specific charges against Franklin were four:

- On January 11, 1971, Professor Franklin intentionally participated in, and significantly contributed to, the disruption of a scheduled speech by Ambassador Henry Cabot Lodge, presented by the Hoover Institution on War, Revolution and Peace. Such conduct prevented Ambassador Lodge from speaking, forced cancellation of the meeting, and denied others their rights to hear and be heard.
- On February 10, 1971, a war protest rally was held in White Plaza, the campus "town square" bordered by the student union, a U.S. Post Office branch, and the Stanford Bookstore. Professor Franklin urged the audience away from tactics aimed at influencing government policy off cam-

pus. Instead, he urged and incited students and others to disrupt University functions by shutting down the Computation Center. Subsequently, a shut-down was achieved through an unlawful occupation of the Center.

- Following that illegal occupation, Professor Franklin significantly inter-fered with police orders to disperse, intentionally urging and inciting stu-dents and others to disobey them.
- Following these events, during an evening rally in the Old Union Court-yard, Professor Franklin intentionally urged and incited students and oth-ers to engage in disruptive conduct, or "people's war," which threatened injury to individuals and property. Acts of violence followed.

THE "TRIAL"

The Franklin "trial" took place in the Physics Tank, a large lecture hall normally reserved for introductory courses in the physical sciences and extensively modi-fied for this event. The hearing room setup included a table for the University "prosecution," capably represented by attorney Ray Fisher, a recent graduate of the Stanford Law School then practicing in Los Angeles; a table for the "defense," from which Franklin represented himself with help from such notable "friends" as Harvard Law School Professor Alan Dershowitz and his assistant, Joel Klein, both visiting fellows that fall at Stanford's Center for Advanced Study in the Be-havioral Sciences. (Klein went on to become Superintendent of New York City Schools). There were also a number of talented amateur volunteer lawyers. The dais was occupied by my six Advisory Board colleagues, our counsel Jan Vetter (a professor at the University of California Boalt School of Law), and me. We played to a packed house of some 200 observers six hours a day, six days a week, for six weeks, from September 8, 1971, to November 5, 1971. Our proceedings were televised live over closed-circuit TV across the campus and broadcast on the campus radio station, KZSU. (On football Saturdays, the student broadcaster in the KZSU radio booth would flash me the game score. I have been a die-hard fan from my first days on the Farm.)

Over the defense table, Franklin draped a large sheet of white paper on which the number of Vietnam casualties was updated each day. Behind it, im-ages of Chairman Mao Zedong and Joseph Stalin were posted prominently. A self-described revolutionary, Franklin traced his ideological evolution to Chair-man Mao, through Stalin and Vladimir Lenin, to Karl Marx. During lulls in the testimony, Franklin would flip through his *Little Red Book* of Mao's quotations, perhaps to underscore his doctrinal roots.

Our panel, elected by a vote of the faculty, agreed rather quickly that no find-ings should be made on the basis of the first charge—disruption of the Henry Cabot Lodge speech. The Advisory Board held unanimously that conflicts in tes-timony left the University unable to prove the charge based on the Lodge inci-dent. Although Franklin may well have been a ringleader among those loudly and substantially disrupting Ambassador Lodge's remarks in Dinkelspiel Auditorium, we concluded that political discourse, however impolite or inhospitable, was not off limits.

On the remaining three charges, the Advisory Board heard no fewer than 111 witnesses, generating more than a million words over thirty-three days of testimony. The resulting transcript ran over 5,000 pages. Witness after witness paraded to the stand to claim their beliefs as their own in an effort to dispel the notion that Franklin was a campus zealot directing the thoughts and actions of others. Sometimes witnesses would approach the stand in costume, and our hearings were occasionally interrupted by unscheduled acts of guerilla theater, in which large groups descended on the proceedings wearing combat fatigues or dressed as fascist "pigs." To say a circuslike atmosphere prevailed is an understatement. Although we had the benefit of legal counsel, there was no bailiff or sergeant at arms in our "court." When such interruptions occurred we had no choice but to recess the proceedings temporarily until the room could be cleared and decorum reestablished.

Due in part to the courtroom theatrics, my six Advisory Board colleagues and I privately took solace in a bit of humor, nicknaming ourselves the Seven Dwarfs. We dubbed our capable administrative assistant, Sally Freelen, Snow White. Her organization of the entire process was an enormous help to all of us. I found humor, too, in an article Dershowitz wrote some time afterwards, in which he described the Chairman of the Advisory Board (me) as a "crab scientist," referring to my early research on crustaceans or perhaps to my personal demeanor during the proceedings,

At the conclusion of the testimony, Dershowitz approached me with an offer to write a summary of the whole proceedings for the University record, a responsibility he was well aware fell to the Advisory Board. Although my three-word response was "Thank you, no," I did suggest that either party—the University or Franklin—could agree to have him speak for them and thus represent them. Neither party did.

INCITING STUDENTS

"See, now, what we're asking," said Franklin, concluding his February speech in White Plaza, "is for people to make that little tiny gesture to show that we're willing to inconvenience ourselves a little bit and to begin to shut down the most obvious machinery of war, such as, and I think it is a good target, that Computation Center" (applause and shouts of "Right on!").[4] The Advisory Board held unanimously that in this instance Franklin had incited students and others to forcibly shut down the Computation Center, which they did immediately following the assembly. We concluded that Franklin must have reasonably expected that his advocacy of "shut down" would be interpreted by at least a substantial portion of the audience as calling for forceful disruption of the Center.

The third charge against Franklin was the one I found most serious—that he had incited the crowd to disregard a police order to disperse. As the White Plaza crowd moved toward the Computation Center, the University administration closed the building. Demonstrators then broke into the building and shut down the power for the IBM 360 computer, interrupting work in progress for university departments, Stanford Hospital, and the many individuals whose research depended on that computer. The police were called, and the Computation Center building was cleared of protesters. A large crowd milled around outside the building, and when the police ordered it to disperse, Franklin urged the crowd to disobey. Several individuals refusing to disperse were injured, and four were arrested. The Advisory Board held that Franklin had pressed the crowd to disregard the police order although knowing that he was substantially increasing the risk of injuries.

The fourth charge concerned a pair of speeches that Franklin gave later that night at another rally, this one held in the courtyard of the Old Union, a handsome mission-style building that was once the student union. Using what could be described as "code language," he called for the students to "make people's war" against the University in protest of "campus police occupation."[5] My sense during the hearing was that he had been encouraging troublemaking to distract and detain campus police—throwing rocks, setting fires, and assembling late into the night. Later that night, a number of windows were broken, several fires were started, and two young men were wounded by gunfire.

Though nothing of this sort was an official charge against Franklin, I was troubled by what I considered Franklin's only really serious *academic* transgression—his propensity for moving his Melville class from a classroom in the Main Quadrangle, where English classes were regularly held, to the site of the next demonstration, such as the Computation Center, where he did not discuss the topic of the class but rather his views on the University's "unconscionable" service in support of U.S. military action.

AN ALL-STAR CAST

Franklin's clownlike antics were mainstays in the hearing room, creating a carnival atmosphere that might have been humorous had matters not been so momentous. He was often assisted by the very competent Joel Klein. Choosing to represent himself at the hearing, Franklin questioned the witnesses, doing so as though he were teaching a class, pacing back and forth, pausing for dramatic effect, and making motions suggestive of the fictional television lawyer Perry Mason.

The University appointed to the Advisory Board an extremely capable and helpful lawyer, Jan Vetter. During the hearings, Vetter sat at my side and often guided me as to whether to grant a motion or deny a request. On one occasion, I was absorbed in the proceedings and didn't fully hear the motion Franklin made.

Fortunately, Vetter did, and he whispered in my ear that I should go ahead and let him have it.

"Overruled!" I shouted to some surprise in the gallery. The request had been fairly innocuous and Vetter had recommended granting it, but his choice of words, "Let him have it," made me think I was to throw the book at him!

At the end of most hearing days, which ran from 1:00 PM to 7:00 PM, Vetter would join me at my house in Palo Alto to review the day and enjoy a short scotch. His participation made an otherwise difficult situation more bearable. Advisory Board member Pief Panofsky's humor, in particular, was a bright spot. When we had disruptions—activists, for example, parading through the hearing room in costume—he would make a very amusing joke of it, considerably easing the palpable tension that was always present in the hearing room. Pief built a little enjoyment into the process. I'm also grateful to David Hamburg for his contributions, particularly the depth of his professional understanding of human behavior and motivation.

RENDERING A VERDICT

In the end, we found that Franklin did, in fact, urge the students to wage a "people's war" against Stanford, to disrupt classes and lectures, and to close down university facilities involved in research that might have some relation to military applications. Violence ensued, and reasonable people could find, as the Advisory Board did, that the violence was caused at least in part by Franklin's inflammatory speeches.

The ultimate responsibility of our Advisory Board was to impose sentence on Franklin. President Lyman had recommended dismissal—in my view a potentially draconian precedent when applied to a tenured professor. Neither I nor my colleague, Robert McAfee Brown, Professor of Religious Studies, felt that such a severe consequence was warranted, and we recommended a one- or two-quarter suspension without pay. Brown and I thought the intent of speech and freedom of speech were both important elements of the case. And, frankly, I didn't think the evidence of damage to the institutional culture was quite as powerful as it could have been.

But Professor Brown and I were outvoted by our fellow panelists—David A. Hamburg, Vice Chairman of the Advisory Board, Chairman of the Department of Psychiatry; G. L. Bach, Frank E. Buck Professor in the Graduate School of Business and Professor of Economics; Sanford M. Dornbusch, Professor of Sociology; David M. Mason, Chairman of the Department of Chemical Engineering; and Wolfgang K. H. "Pief" Panofsky, Director and Professor, Stanford Linear Accelerator Center—all of whom participated collectively in writing the 157-page majority report recommending dismissal.

Personally, I felt well supported throughout the Franklin hearings. My chairmanship of the Advisory Board came about in part due to the Franklin case itself:

My board colleagues felt that I could be somewhat relaxed about the matter and could supply an occasional sense of humor to what would undoubtedly be a very difficult, complicated, and potentially embarrassing situation.

Service on the Advisory Board is perhaps the most significant civic duty that can be bestowed on a faculty member by his or her colleagues. My fellow board members were good natured, thoughtful, and able partners in what was, inarguably, difficult work—assessing the future of a tenured colleague. It posed a significant challenge to the University to form a group that would deliver a just and fair conclusion to the president's recommendation that Franklin be discharged or subjected to other penalties.

My colleagues in the Program in Human Biology, in which I was then teaching, were wonderful about backfilling for me, ensuring that the work of the fledgling program would move forward as I carried out my academic duty to the University by chairing the Advisory Board. My wife, Jeanne, was present in the hearing room almost every day. Her calming presence and show of support was important to me during that trying time.

Franklin had argued that his urging of various actions against the University was in fact constitutionally protected speech. The Advisory Board held to the contrary, finding that under the most liberal Supreme Court standard Franklin's speech constituted incitement in that it increased the risk of imminent lawless action and injury to others. In its 157-page report, the majority statement of the Advisory Board held that Franklin had "exceeded the permissible bounds" of free speech, and that he could not "encourage violent and coercive action as he did without risking his position." "Tolerance of such attacks on the freedom of others, under the guise of protecting Professor Franklin's freedom to act as he wishes," said the report, "would be subversion, not support, of true academic freedom and individual rights."[6]

As it turned out, neither Stanford nor Franklin seem to have been harmed in the process. The Board's responsibility to hear Franklin's case and make a recommendation to the president as to the suitability of the penalty was certainly out of the ordinary. No panel of successors has faced such duty in the ensuing near-half-century. My sense is that we carried out our academic responsibility in a careful and fair fashion that not only avoided lasting damage to Stanford but enhanced the University's reputation for undertaking a balanced approach to a difficult matter, one that would have challenged many other places

APPEAL AND AFTERMATH

Never one to be complacent, Franklin challenged his dismissal from Stanford in the California courts with the help of the American Civil Liberties Union (ACLU). After a tortuous eight years of decision and appeal, during which every ruling went against the ACLU, the case was finally decided in the University's favor. To be part of the process that removed a tenured colleague from his post was

At those sometimes raucous hearings, when Franklin would quote Chairman Mao Tse-Tung to prove a point, Kennedy, without hesitation, would throw back a different Mao quote in refutation.

—Andy Doty

Don should have received an honorary law degree for his role in the Franklin hearing. He handled it with the professionalism of a judge, and when he dissented from the decision to dismiss Franklin, no one could doubt the fairness of the proceedings under his guidance.

—Paul Brest

The kitchen staff was going to go on strike while I was a faculty resident in Flo Mo [the Florence Moore dormitory], and Don came to dinner, sitting with me and the students. At one point he turned to me and said, "I don't understand why they're going on strike." And I said, "I'll tell you one reason, you have never gone in and talked to them where they work." He got up from the table and went into the kitchen. He talked with them at length, and they remembered it for a long time. It was the first time he or any president I'd known had gone into the kitchen. Word got around quickly, and it probably had something to do with them not going on strike. A few years later I was walking by Flo Mo and one of the kitchen workers called out: "Hey, Professor! You remember that day the president came to talk to us in the kitchen?" It made a huge impression. Don had the common touch.

—Mark Mancall

Presiding over the Franklin hearings, 1971.

personally painful, but it was the view of almost everyone knowledgeable about the events that Franklin had crossed a line and gone too far. Most observers, both within and outside the University, saw our process as a responsible exercise, and most accepted the judgment. Weighing the possible damage to Stanford's reputation for dismissing Franklin against the potential damage that would ensue if he were permitted to remain on campus and continue to incite violence, I felt we had reached a legally defensible and ethically justifiable conclusion.

Franklin sued the University, calling for Stanford to reinstate him. And he wrote a scathing public attack, "Where All Freedoms but Stanford's Are Academic," published in June 1972, protesting that his academic freedom had been violated. Though he was unable to find widespread sympathy in the Stanford community, Franklin landed on his feet.

As Lyman later explained:

[Franklin] became the most conspicuous leader of the radical anti-Vietnam movement on campus, and he became eventually a self-declared Maoist, which wouldn't have got him fired, although he sometimes said later it was because he was a Maoist. That isn't the case. He was fired because he had, in fact, to use ordinary layman's language, incited people to riot. And that is a crime if you can prove it, and we proved it to the satisfaction of the faculty advisory board and then in the courts later.[7]

But, far from derailing his academic career, Franklin parlayed his activism to great success. He went on to become a visiting lecturer at Yale and Wesleyan University and, in 1975, joined the faculty at Rutgers, where he has spent the balance of his career. In 1987 he was appointed to an endowed chair, becoming the John Cotton Dana Professor at Rutgers.

Of tangential interest to me was Franklin's newfound interest in a matter of natural science. He wrote a fabulous book called *The Most Important Fish in the Sea*, about the threat that continued capture of the menhaden posed to the oceanic ecosystem. Caught in large numbers to serve as a source of fish oil, the reduction in the menhaden population threatened striped bass and bluefish, common targets of sport anglers, as menhaden is a favorite food of these species. Ever the radical, Franklin finds corporate misconduct in fishers of the menhaden, who created a marketing phenomenon about the value of fish oils for good health and longevity.

I wish him both.

RIGHTS AND RESPONSIBILITY

In my presidential inaugural, a decade after the Franklin case, I spoke about the challenge of "overcoming the emotional scars" from the campus turmoil of the sixties and the "aftermath of mistrust"[8] that hung over us. Two and a half student "generations" had come and gone since 1970, but in 1980 over half the faculty remained from 1970, many still harboring a subtle sense of alienation. Participation in residential education, advising, and more casual, voluntary relationships with students were a frequent casualty of those troubled times. Certainly during the Franklin hearing it seemed to all of us as though the very fabric of academic life was under unbearable stress and that cases such as Franklin's would decide whether the great universities of this country could remain livable places.

Several years after the decision, I was asked how I felt about my own investment of time and energy in the case. I replied that I thought I had wasted half a year of my life. But in hindsight I now realize that the Franklin case was influential in reshaping the faculty's view of its own role, leading to a new Statement of Faculty Discipline in 1972, providing more precise definitions of sanctionable activities. As I later wrote, this case and others like it proved that "faculties can take hold of the values of their institutions, defend them successfully, and make a reality of the vision of the academy under even the most stressful challenges. The Franklin verdict, whether one agrees with it or not, represented a triumph of due process."[9]

Most of the arguments presented in the Franklin hearing dealt with the *rights* of faculty members. Largely ignored in the decision, because they were not pertinent to the specific charges, were even more significant issues in the area of *responsibilities*. A central purpose of teaching, as of scholarship, is to help students acquire a capacity for analytic detachment. Plainly, one of its enemies is too much passion for a particular point of view. Zealots who assign infinite worth to their favorite cause, and who seek to destroy all those conflicting, separating matters of intellect from those of community, are really insisting that we cannot lead examined lives. The truly hard choices are not between good and evil, but between competing goods. The worth of individuals or of programs or of governments is not to be sought in single dimensions or issues but in the full complexity of all their consequences.

The teacher brings formidable powers to the teacher–student relationship. The charismatic but careless professor, with a gaggle of adoring but uncritical followers, is a fairly uncommon but nonetheless troubling campus landmark. In the late sixties it was both more common and more troubling. The primary ethical test is the teacher's ability to put the student's interest first. Its basis is the presumption, which I believe is beyond argument, that members of the professoriate are following a calling in which the central purpose is generational improvement. Professors are agents for improving society, generation by generation.

There are important things that the tradition of academic freedom does not condone. It does not permit a faculty member to turn a course in the humanities or social sciences into a one-sided presentation of personal views. Another tradition is that good teaching carries a reasonable burden of objectivity, and our tradition of academic freedom should not protect bad teaching. Neither does the right to hold and express strong opinions extend to the right to coerce or disrupt those who hold different views. Two criteria should be met before a faculty member imposes personal convictions in the classroom. First, such persuasions should pass a germaneness test; there should be an arguable relationship between the professor's opinions and the subject matter of the course. Second, the professor should disclose any biases. Freedom of speech is important, but it is not to be confused with coercion, intimidation, or incitement, and we have a long and carefully crafted judicial tradition in this country to help us sort them out.

CHAPTER 5

MR. KENNEDY
GOES TO WASHINGTON

DURING THE LAST TWO YEARS of the Ford administration, I had been commuting from Stanford to Washington regularly, serving as Senior Consultant to Guyford Stever, Director of the Office of Science and Technology Policy. Stever had been mandated to appoint two assistant directors but lacked the time and inclination, knowing they would have to face congressional scrutiny and approval. So he opted instead to name two senior consultants—me and William Nierenberg, a physicist most closely identified with the Manhattan Project and with whose views I frequently differed.

The first person to talk to me about leaving Stanford for a stint at the Food and Drug Administration (FDA) was Jim Gaither, who later became my boss as chairman of Stanford's Board of Trustees during a portion of my term as the University's president. Recruited by Joseph Califano Jr., Secretary of Health, Education and Welfare, to line up nominees for various appointments in the new Carter administration, Gaither talked with me about becoming Assistant Secretary for Health.

But it didn't take long to figure out that nobody wanted an Assistant Secretary for Health who didn't have a medical degree, and when Califano came to the same conclusion our conversation shifted to the FDA, where it made sense to bring in a scientifically trained academic. The position appealed to my scientific interests and passion for public service. So at the end of the 1976 academic year, when the moment came for Jeanne and me to decide if we were going to move to Washington, the answer was a resounding "Yes!"

The years in Washington at the FDA, 1977 to 1979, were fascinating ones for our family. Almost immediately on our arrival, Jeanne reconnected with our friend and colleague from Stanford, David Hamburg, who was president of the Institute of Medicine. She was delighted with a position that David helped arrange for her in his office, as Director of Resources Development, and would come home with interesting stories of life at work. Every once in a while she would happen on a large pile of long-unanswered mail, to which she would have to devise diplomatic responses for the high-level officials to whom the letters were addressed: "To my utter horror, I have noticed that we promised that we would do so-and-so . . ." She was quite effective, ever polite and politic, successfully dodging otherwise tight and uncomfortable corners.

We lived on a steep side street below Sibley Hospital that led down to Mac-Arthur Boulevard. The mid-Atlantic winter took its toll, especially on rainy days and nights, but by and large we were happily engaged with our life inside the Beltway.

FDA CHALLENGES: SWEET(ENER) SORROW

The FDA is charged with accomplishing a remarkable range of things: assuring the safety and purity of the nation's food supply, validating the safety and effectiveness of drugs and medical devices as well as vaccines and biologic products, inspection and safety testing of such radiation-emitting products as X-ray ma-

Swearing in as FDA commissioner with Jeanne, Page, Julia, and HHS Secretary Joseph Califano, April 4, 1977.

DONALD KENNEDY

His Book

Don being sworn in as COMMISSIONER
U.S. FOOD AND DRUG ADMINISTRAT

chines and lasers, evaluating animal drugs and additives to livestock feed, and assessing the safety of cosmetics. These responsibilities added up to the regulation of nearly twenty-five cents out of every dollar of consumer expenditure in the United States.[1]

The work captured my attention from the first day on the job, when I was greeted with a data set and lobbying effort that sought an FDA ban on the artificial sweetener saccharin, alleged to cause bladder cancer in male rats. With the involvement of Deputy Commissioner Sherwin Gardner, early results of tests conducted in Canada showed that the response was dose dependent: A calculation by one of the scientists indicated that a human would have to consume several hundred cans of a product containing the sweetener before developing a problem. Nevertheless, Congress was bound by an earlier statute—one that included the Delaney Clause of the Food, Drug, and Cosmetic Act passed by Congress in 1958—prohibiting the use of all food additives found to be carcinogenic to humans or animals. So we had no choice but to propose the ban on saccharin. Though the public seemed often to assume that we were in a vacuum making arbitrary decisions, we were in fact operating under an array of laws and regulations.

Public outcry from the diabetic community pushed Congress to place a moratorium on the proposed ban for two years during which further tests could be conducted. Senator Ted Kennedy, who had made a name for himself in Congress as a serious-minded health advocate, told me that the outcry generated more mail in his office than the U.S. bombing of Cambodia in 1970. The implication seemed to be that cancer-causing products should be taken off the market except when people enjoy them.

In addition to the moratorium, a companion piece of compromise legislation was passed, the Saccharin Safety and Labeling Act, which required a warning label that the product may cause cancer but avoided the outright ban. At FDA, we regarded the labeling law as a springboard encouraging further study of the saccharin problem. And we held a series of hearings involving consumers concerned with artificial sweeteners in general.

In one of my first meetings I found myself surrounded by television cameras and a set of difficult questions. Opposition to the regulatory stance FDA was about to take with regard to saccharin was vested in an outfit called the "Calorie Control Council," a lobbying entity with strong involvement from Coca Cola and Pepsi Cola. The Council launched a media blitz, with full-page advertisements in many metropolitan newspapers expressing opposition to an FDA ban. I was astounded at the amount of money spent. Their campaign flooded the markets in which FDA measured public reactions to its proposed measures. They also supported meetings at which, for example, mothers complained that their children should have the opportunity to accompany their friends to cafes or drugstores to enjoy a companionable drink of a sweetened beverage without the sugar.

One might wonder why, despite the Congressional compromise, the industry's interest in the regulation of saccharin stayed intact and became even more aggressive. It turns out that it was costing the cola producers a bit more to produce the regular soda containing sugar than the diet soda containing saccharin. So the consumer choice to buy the diet product actually netted the cola companies a few pennies more per bottle or can. No wonder the Calorie Control Council continued the fight!

Interestingly, the testimony led to an unintended but beneficial market effect: The potential threat of losing saccharin, combined with the public outcry for artificial sweeteners, actually stimulated a hearty market response that much later resulted in the variety of sugar substitutes now available—Sweet 'N Low, Equal, NutraSweet, Sugar Twin, Truvia, stevia, aspartame, and the list goes on.

Also fascinating was the result of further scientific inquiry that arrived many months later. It turns out that the male rat is absolutely the wrong animal in which to study the carcinogenicity of a particular additive, in this case saccharin. The recurrence of cancer could not be replicated. A string of experiments persuaded the FDA to withdraw its 1977 ban, and eventually the warning label was withdrawn from the products containing it.

LAETRILE: HOPE OR HOAX?

The years 1977 to 1979 were headline-generators at FDA. In addition to the saccharin debate, many may remember the mania regarding a cancer "wonder drug" called Laetrile. Manufactured from apricot pits, it was purported to cure cancer. Americans were flocking to Mexico to acquire it and urging expedited FDA approval. Two hundred and eighty members of Congress supported a bill to make Laetrile available, while some states attempted to approve its manufacture and sale. Senator Kennedy was again inundated, this time by relentless Laetrile proponents, considered quacks by most scientists and doctors.

From the 1950s through the 1970s, Laetrile grew in popularity in the United States as an alternative treatment for cancer. For this reason, and despite the lack of scientific evidence that Laetrile was effective, the National Cancer Institute (NCI) studied it through a retrospective case review in 1978, inviting more than 400,000 doctors and other practitioners to submit positive results from cases involving Laetrile. Although an estimated 75,000 people in the United States had taken Laetrile, only ninety-three "positive" cases were submitted, and in only six of those was there evidence of significant tumor shrinkage.

A 1991 NCI review of the evidence of Laetrile's effectiveness reported that "scientific studies were conducted for more than 20 years, starting in the mid-1950s, looking for evidence of anti-tumor efficacy by Laetrile." "In no instance," the review concluded, "was evidence found that treatment with Laetrile results in any benefit against tumors in animals." Califano would later refer to the NCI review as "the first political clinical trial."[2]

ANTI-ANTIBIOTICS

Perhaps the most significant work we undertook during my time at FDA was an issue still brewing today—the use of antibiotics in the feed of healthy livestock. In addition to preventing disease, antibiotics have the ability to remodel the digestive tract flora of livestock animals, and with modified digestive systems the animals gain weight much faster, even on high-calorie diets. In fact, about 80 percent of the antibiotics sold in this country are intended for food animals, not people. But the practice also breeds antibiotic-resistant bacteria, which pose a serious risk to public health. According to the Centers for Disease Control, some two million Americans become infected each year with bacteria that are resistant to antibiotics, and at least 23,000 die as a direct result of these infections. Many more die from other conditions that are complicated by an antibiotic-resistant infection.

In 1977, the FDA's national advisory committee recommended that we ban routine feeding of low doses of antibiotics to healthy livestock, warning that such use was breeding drug-resistant bacteria that could infect people. The fear was that people consuming small but accumulating doses of the antibiotic in beef and pork would eventually develop a tolerance for the drug. In the case of cattle, antibiotics were being used not to prevent or cure disease but simply to make livestock a more profitable product. So I authored a federal register order to end the use of penicillin, chlortetracycline, and tetracycline to fatten livestock. At the FDA, we thought that the threat of antibiotic resistance would ultimately spread, transmitted especially to and through farm workers who handle the feed, developing a resistance to the very antibiotics they might one day need to fight disease or save their lives.

And yet, in the absence of a smoking gun about verifiable antibiotic resistance and the threat to public health, the register order failed, and any proposal to eliminate the use of antibiotics in livestock feed has been defeated again and again. The hearings we scheduled in the late 1970s to begin the process of curtailing the use of penicillin and other antibiotics for livestock production were halted by Congress before they began, opposed by the likes of the Texas Farm Bureau, the Mississippi Pork Producers Association, the National Broiler Council, and the National Turkey Federation.

In 2007, I wrote an editorial on this topic in *Science*, having testified before the House Oversight Committee with two other former FDA commissioners on the growing rate of antibiotic resistance and the need to improve monitoring on the safety of marketed drugs. The United States, I noted, lacks a system adequately tuned to detect adverse reactions. The measure requires a numerator and a denominator: the number of reported adverse events divided by the number of prescriptions issued. The FDA knows neither. And there is no national prescription record. The House, I suggested

> should make "orphan drug" provisions clearly available for developers of new
> drugs that confront antibiotic resistance. Its bill should be firm about requiring that all clinical trial results be available to the public and include muscu-

lar provisions for monitoring drug safety—a national database, for example, containing required reports of adverse drug reactions and provisions for a national prescription audit. Though the FDA now has a database on adverse reactions, the reports are voluntary. A prescription audit may be politically naïve, but why take essential needs off the table because they may not be politically popular?[3]

Today the science is even clearer that antibiotic overuse in agriculture is dangerous, and the very same risks persist. In September 2014 the President's Council of Advisors on Science and Technology declared that the problem of antibiotic resistance had become "dire," requires "urgent attention," is growing at an "alarming rate," and threatens medicine, economic growth, public health, agriculture, and national security.[4] Under the leadership of Commissioner Margaret Hamburg (daughter of the aforementioned David Hamburg), the FDA instituted a voluntary guideline known as Guidance 213, which instructs pharmaceutical companies to stop marketing certain antibiotics for the production of livestock. Compliance cannot come too soon.

While at the FDA, I also I favored giving consumers better information about generic drugs, about the fact that the same chemical, under different brand names, may sell at very different prices. The drug firms themselves claimed that there was a difference between brand names and generic drugs. We published a list of medically equivalent drugs to help consumers, doctors, and pharmacists choose the least expensive medications available. We urged Congress to enact the Drug Regulation Reform Bill of 1978, intended to encourage innovation in the drug industry in return for greater control over drugs once they reach the marketplace. We were defeated in both objectives. I commented at the time that industry needed to get over its perception of the world as a conspiracy between the public interest movement and the regulators.[5]

FOLLOWING THE RULES

My encounters at FDA included a wonderful story about ice cream. Federal rules require that everything characterized by a common or generic name, like ice cream, has to have a recipe listing its ingredients. Certain ingredients may be substituted one for others but the recipe is the mechanism by which a category of food retains its distinction.

In the manufacture of ice cream, two ingredients are mutually replaceable—nonfat dry milk solids and a variety of other products that are by-products of the manufacture of cheese. In ice cream, nonfat dry milk solids are far more prevalent than the cheese derivatives. So, as part of our official duty to certify the recipe for ice cream that includes both, the Department of Foods made up a batch of ice cream, replacing the nonfat dry milk solids with cheese derivatives. We tasted it and thought it was just fine and thus proposed that use of the cheese derivatives could save on the cost of the product without damaging ice cream's properties.

Don took a demoralized public agency beset by serious congressional and public relations problems and turned it into an effective agency with stronger congressional and public support. What impressed everyone was not only his high energy level but his constant testifying on controversial issues before Congress, where he was very persuasive and did a superb job. Don's stock in Washington and his reputation among other presidents and members on the hill was exceptionally high.

—Larry Horton

Mr. Kennedy is an exceptionally articulate as well as competent scientist. His predecessors at the FDA, all physicians, were less comfortable with the controversies of scientific testing. When Mr. Kennedy said some animal study was solid, or shaky, his judgment carried authority.

—New York Times, *July 2, 1979*

All along, as he [Kennedy} tackled one problem after another, he chatted about what he was doing. He was good press and he knew it, employing with great skill a breezy mixture of clarity and wit in order to advocate his policies and explain them to the public. While he made enemies, he did not let anyone make an enemy of him.

—John A. Owen Jr.

If we were to single out one special achievement that Donald Kennedy made, we would cite his "humanization" of the FDA. He met with countless groups, engaging them in the most lively and informal discussion and inspiring such a feeling of openness and credibility that he came to be nicknamed "The Visible Commissioner."

—Edward G. Feldman, "A Plea for FDA Stability."
Journal of Pharmaceutical Sciences, *68 (July 1979).*

Donald Kennedy saw the job of FDA Commissioner as one of an activist, an ombudsman for the concerns of the American consumer. He based every decision on the best available evidence. He never sidestepped appropriate action, even if announcing a new regulatory decision might prove controversial.

—Hon. Henry A. Waxman

The Food and Drug Administration has recently undergone a most surprising transformation, and the reason seems to lie in the brief but enlivening reign of its now departing commissioner, Donald Kennedy. His style produced an intangible change of great moment. He raised the esteem in which the agency was held by outsiders, and in doing so he transformed morale within. Kennedy also enjoyed an unusually cordial relationship with Congress, a body accustomed to batting the FDA commissioner about like a shuttlecock. Unlike Energy Secretary James Schlesinger, whose approach to hostile questions is to intellectually demolish the questioner, and thus lose the battle, Kennedy's style was to disarm his interrogators with charm and a direct but tactful answer. Somehow or other, he managed to gain the respect of all the FDA's constituencies, a group whose members do not invariably see eye to eye with each other.

—Nicholas Wade, Science, *1979*

It turns out that nonfat dry milk solids extracted from milk are stored in warehouses and released primarily for the manufacture of ice cream. So when we proposed to let ice cream makers use casein, a major by-product of cheese manufacture, in their mixes instead of nonfat dry milk solids, the dairy interests fought the measure on the grounds that it would reduce the nutritional quality of ice cream, their real motive being that it would have added to the already high political cost of the federal milk support program. We had strayed into the politics of protectionism. Most casein is imported from Europe, whereas nonfat dry milk solids are a domestic dairy surplus commodity, then subsidized by a rather cushy support price. Before I knew it, I was in a meeting with Pat Healy, head of the National Milk Producers Federation, unquestionably the most sinister-looking lobbyist I encountered during my time in Washington and the only person I know who could roll a cigar around his mouth while talking!

"What mischief are you planning?" he demanded to know.

In the end, he persuaded many congressional representatives from dairy states to raise questions that required my congressional testimony. It soon became clear to people following the case that the National Milk Producers Federation was attempting a ruse that would actually work against consumer interests, not to mention the annoyance of FDA. I thought I had answered the questions in the hearing satisfactorily, yet the headline in the *Washington Post* the next morning read, "FDA Plan Would Put Foreign Chemicals in Ice Cream."

An opinion piece in the *New York Times* recounted the entire story, suggesting that using substitutes for nonfat dry milk solids offered benefits—and did no harm—to the consumer. It concluded with an unforgettable sendoff to the lobbyists: "As for the National Milk Producers Federation, we wish them a rocky road."

A FAMILY AFFAIR

The FDA opportunity involved moving our entire family, finding a house, and much else. Our daughter Page, awaiting the upcoming fall semester when she would enroll at Hampshire College, got a job with Senator Ted Kennedy's Subcommittee on Health and Scientific Research—a post to which she returned during the summer of 1978. Our younger daughter Julia was still in high school—a difficult time to change schools, let alone move across the country. We identified what we thought was the ideal environment for a bright, athletic, and personable young woman—the Madeira School, a college preparatory academy for girls. She excelled in track and volleyball, and in her academic work as well. On graduation, she earned a spot at Stanford, a university she would make her own for a year before her parents' ultimate return.

Among our friends in Washington were Jeanne's colleagues from the Institute of Medicine and some of mine from the FDA. It turns out I sometimes liked the lawyers a bit better than I did the scientists, and I often turned to them first

when the need to draft policy arose. The FDA lawyers, Stuart Pape, Mike Taylor, Rich Cooper, and Dick Merrill, were interesting and smart, often intellectually well paired with their scientific colleagues. Merrill went on to become Dean of the University of Virginia Law School and later, with me, co-chaired the National Academy of Sciences's Committee on Science, Technology and Law.

With Congressman Paul Rogers, Senator Ted Kennedy, and HHS Secretary Joseph Califano, 1979.

One of the lawyers, William Vodra, was very thoughtful in his deliberations and proposed that the process by which drug companies attempt to gain approval of a new drug was overly elaborate and difficult. He persuaded many of us that efforts to simplify the process would be regarded as a welcome change and would result in no detrimental effects. Senator Kennedy supported the changes and held hearings in the Senate; Rep. Paul Rogers of Florida, who headed the House Health Committee, also supported the effort. Unfortunately, like the effort to eliminate the use of antibiotics in livestock feed, efforts to overhaul the drug approval process also went nowhere in my time at FDA.

BUILDING A NEW CONSTITUENCY
FOR AGRICULTURAL RESEARCH

Among the lasting friendships formed during this period was one with Tom Grumbly, whom I persuaded to come to FDA from the Department of Agriculture. While at FDA, Grumbly and I became aware of a need to support research in the agricultural arena. We embarked on an exploration of what might be done within the federal research system to improve opportunities for competitive, peer-reviewed agricultural science. At the time, the nation was expanding competitive opportunities for funding through the National Institutes of Health (NIH), the National Science Foundation (NSF), the National Aeronautics and Space Administration (NASA), and the Departments of Defense and Energy. In contrast, research funding at the Department of Agriculture (USDA) followed a different path, employing formula funding on a regional or commodity-focused basis, largely through public land-grant universities.

Although we respected what had been accomplished in the past, my colleagues and I believed that progress in fundamental science could provide powerful new tools for advancing agricultural research. Accordingly, we could not understand why a brilliant cellular physiologist, for example, had to go to NIH instead of the USDA for support. The science of how we grow food and use it was losing ground.

In the last budget cycle of the Ford administration, lobbying efforts were made to establish a new program at USDA that used a competitive, peer-reviewed process in the selection and funding of new agricultural research. But whereas the creation of a small program was successful, its survival in future budget cycles was consistently at risk.

Some thirty-five years later, we have at last begun to see a real revolution in agricultural research. It has brought new opportunities, new tools, and capacities that blend biochemistry, genetics, and cell biology. The challenge now is to apply these new technologies to the old task of feeding the world.

In 2006, William ("Bill") Danforth, chancellor emeritus of Washington University, reported in *Science* that a USDA task force was pressing for a modern approach in tackling this critical question. In response, Congress enacted legislation that created a National Institute of Food and Agriculture (NIFA) within the USDA to manage a new program of competitive, merit-based grants for fundamental agricultural research. Since then, NIFA's program has been funded in each subsequent year, one of the few federal research programs to grow over that time. Yet in spite of the opportunity presented, the level of funding is far short of the needs of American agriculture and, indeed, the rest of the world.

Arguments for the critical importance of agricultural research on a global scale are worth articulating: not only does the United States have a crucial role in feeding a global population due to reach nine billion by century's end, but the U.S. role is fundamental to world peace and stability. Agriculture research is essential to coping with climate change, to ensuring economic success, to preventing disease, and to promoting good health. Thus, in 2012, I was convinced to join with a group of eminent colleagues to create Supporters of Agriculture Research (SoAR), a nonpartisan, science-based coalition seeking sound research policies that encourage more of our best minds to focus on feeding America and the world. SoAR's board, once chaired by Bill Danforth, includes scientists, academics, and representatives of consumer and commodity groups. SoAR's first president is my old friend Tom Grumbly, my partner in pushing the need for agricultural research at FDA in the eighties.

SoAR believes the time is right to greatly increase funding for competitive grants, which encourage innovation by directing federal funds to the most promising proposals. Congress needs to fully fund the USDA's Agriculture and Food Research Initiative (AFRI), the only agriculture-oriented competitive grants program in the United States. As a nation, we need to take advantage of new scientific opportunities, engage the best scientists, and develop broad, interdisciplinary programs that propel agriculture forward. What we do today affects our later lives and future generations. Paraphrasing President John F. Kennedy, "If you are going to plant a tree, plant it now."

SOCIAL OBLIGATION: PUBLIC POLICY AND THE PARADOX OF DECISION

My decision to spend two years in Washington was rooted in my belief that scientists should regard government service as a routine part of their careers. I felt that the FDA was exactly the sort of place you ought to go if you want to put your money where your mouth is. The better scientists in academic life are lacking in respect for the regulatory process. They tend to stay outside the government and support political actions that they think will benefit science, or they provide advice through a multitude of advisory committees. What is unfortunately less common is the academic scientist taking time to lend policy leadership to organizations that are involved in regulatory decision making. My argument is that more significant science policy is made every day at the working interface between the regulatory agencies and Congress, which is where the contributions of people with the kinds of training that academic scientists have are much needed. Scientists who come from outside not only bring an analytic style but are often more forceful with far more credibility than those who fly into Washington to give some advice to government and then fly out again or than full-time resident career scientists who are seen as having an investment.

I sometimes wonder how we could have reached a point at which public service requires special pleading. One reason is that political rhetoric about the ills of big government and bureaucracy have congealed into a generalized mistrust of the public sector. Speaking to the graduating class of 1983 with my FDA experience in mind, I observed that "for experienced men and women who have something valuable to contribute to their government, it is not easy to give up the comfort, the financial advantage, and the personal freedom that private life provides. The reward for going into one of the visible, high-pressure government jobs has traditionally been a sense of fulfilled obligation and a measure of respect from one's fellow citizens—not immunity from criticism, but decent, humane respect. If that is allowed to disappear, we may some day wake up to discover that

Commissioner Kennedy is just the sort of person our federal government should be able to attract. His vigor, intellect, and integrity were admired by everyone with whom he worked. His contribution was to prove that government regulation is essential, is beneficial, is protective of public health. It is this very regulation which has made it possible for the United States to have the very highest standard for safety and efficiency of food and drug products.

—*Hon. Henry A. Waxman*

I was heartened by how often Kennedy put issues and disputes into the context of human beings. The best of the government's regulators possess that instinct. It is crucial because many offices of federal agencies are filled with listless and time-worn officials who have forgotten that it is men, women, and children they are being paid to protect, not bureaucratic turf, past policies or other abstractions of power.

—*Colman McCarthy, Congressional Record, July 13, 1979, quoting the* Washington Post

The Food and Drug Administration lost its best commissioner in a long time Friday when Donald Kennedy moved to Stanford University. When he came to Washington two years ago, the agency was torn by internal dissension and charges in Congress that it had become chummy with the industries it regulates. Morale has been raised and the FDA's reputation is decidedly one of independence. One measure of the respect that Mr. Kennedy won is that spokesmen for both consumer and industry groups, who seldom agree on anything, rate him equally high.

—New York Times, *July 2, 1979*

Your leadership of the FDA during the past two years has been a remarkable demonstration of the effect that an individual with great talent and commitment can have on an organization. Your own personal commitment to scientific excellence—as well as your efforts to support and build the quality of the FDA's scientific staff—have contributed greatly to establishing public confidence in he FDA's regulatory process. Beyond your significant achievements at the FDA, I count the counsel you have provided me on so many health and scientific matters over the course of the past two years as among the most valuable I received.

—*Joseph A. Califano Jr., Secretary of HEW*

public life at the top has become such a psychic hazard that only the insensitive will undertake it."[6]

During my stint at the FDA, I learned a great deal and gained a sense of the roles of all the different actors—the White House, Congress, the policy leadership as opposed to the career bureaucracy. I learned to respect the complexity of many things I had thought were comparatively simple. Most important, I gained invaluable insight into the problems that accompany any regulatory action. Regulation is an extremely important social device, making up for the sheer inadequacy of the market to accommodate the fact that we no longer live the localized life of the nineteenth century, that society—nationally, globally—is too interdependent, too abstract to protect the individual against impersonal events, natural, economic, or political. But regulators must also realize their limitations. They often have to do things on the basis of evidence that is less than hard. But that doesn't remove the need to decide. Regulators inevitably have to face that reality with respect to risk assessment. It was well summarized in a cartoon poster that the American Chemical Society once issued using a quotation from, of all people, me. In the poster, a rat approaches two alternate doors, behind which the viewer can see, but the rat cannot. On the left is a cat even nastier and more hostile than Garfield, and on the right a piece of delicious smelly-looking cheese. The caption, as I recall it, was taken from a moment of unaccustomed frankness that occurred in a piece of my congressional testimony: "Sometimes you have to decide, even when the data are not as good as you would like."

In those two years at the FDA, I had a lifetime exposure to the costs of non-decisions. In a commencement address to the Stanford class of 1987, I recalled that "there is nothing more corrosive, more discouraging to innovation, than the failure to choose in the arena of public policy. The costs fall everywhere, like a widespread drizzle, while we are permitted the illusion that it isn't really raining hard in any particular place. The very first head of the FDA, Harvey Wiley, put it well when he said: 'not to decide is to decide.' In fact, not to decide is the ultimate form of risk aversion."[7]

The great question in making these decisions is how to balance personal freedom against regulation—how to provide effective, responsive rules without trampling on individual and business rights. This was highlighted in the saccharine debate, where Americans were unready to give up their diet soda and sugar-free foods. To what degree may the state intervene in the private behavior of citizens in their own interest? The answer is not a simple formula, but our society probably would want to include these principles: First, risk-taking should be permitted as long as the risks are not spread to others, and as long as knowledge of the risk and its relation to the benefits gained is available to the risk-taker. Second, the state has special obligations to those exposed to risk wherever there is incentive to exploit; that is, wherever benefits accrue to the persons who generate the risk and where there is a purposive or commercial element in the addition of the risk. Third, that obligation is increased where the state has placed the risk-taker in a vulnerable position by the action of its other authorities.

Our regulatory agencies are at the confluence of great social forces—on one hand, the pressure to get innovations to the marketplace to improve people's lives, and on the other, the demand, particularly in the area of chemistry, that those innovations are proven safe. Preserving innovation and maintaining a technological flow of health benefits are as much matters of consumer protection as safeguarding against adverse drug reaction. One of the things this society has not yet worked out is the problem of how fast new technologies ought to diffuse. The government has the obligation to encourage and foster innovation in the private sector, while also protecting the public, particularly in critical things like food and drugs, from the untoward consequences of too rapid introduction.

TRAVELING HOME

Although I enjoyed my years at the FDA, I was less happy with the atmosphere in Health, Education and Welfare than I was with that at the FDA. After a couple of years in the post, I responded to a few entreaties from Stanford to return as vice president and provost. The provost is the dean of deans, primarily responsible for constructing Stanford's institutional budget. Page was now enrolled at Hampshire College, and Julia was already an undergraduate at Stanford, so it didn't take much to persuade Jeanne that a return to Stanford would be the right move.

Many will recall that 1979 was a time of chronic gasoline shortage. President Carter had repeatedly called out the structural difficulties in the U.S. energy system, and fueling stations in most major cities had cars waiting in lines around the block. So Jeanne and I decided to avoid those as much as possible by heading up to Canada and crossing the continent there. We proceeded west to Michigan and crossed in the Straits of Mackinac to access the Trans-Canada Highway north of Lake Superior.

The coulees and small ponds of Saskatchewan were full of bird life, the cities were friendly, and eventually we reached Alberta and explored the ice fields near Jasper and Lake Louise. As we wound our way south through the Kamloops country and eventually into Oregon, we were tuned as usual to any station that carried National Public Radio. We soon learned that Joe Califano was out, as I had feared likely. He was in some ways a hard taskmaster in the demands he made on his delegates. But he was a deeply principled, no-nonsense executive, and he relied to a considerable extent on a group of talented, super-smart lieutenants. The FDA had prospered during his term, and I didn't like to see him pushed out.

The fact that Califano was leaving meant that the environment in Washington was going to change, and I had no regrets over my decision to return to Stanford. My path was never to be a career government bureaucrat. I enjoyed my time in Washington and had learned from it, but I was ready to return home. I had some strong supporters at the FDA who gave me a memorable farewell party, at which one of the roast-and-toasters constructed a parting gift that harkened back to my earliest days in the agency, wheeling in 1,200 sodas to the laughter of all.[8]

THE BEST JOB IN THE WORLD

MY ROUTE TO THE STANFORD PRESIDENCY was neither planned nor calculated. Having enjoyed my career as commissioner of the Food and Drug Administration, I was recruited back to Stanford in 1979 to undertake the role of provost. I was aided in that position by the budget group, the primary instrument by which university spending is kept in order. In addition to the late Ray Bacchetti and Tim Warner, who served in that often stressful function, my closest colleagues were the other five vice presidents: John Schwartz, general counsel; William Massy, business and finance; Robert Rosenzweig, public affairs; Gerald Lieberman, vice provost and dean of graduate studies; and Joel Smith, development. We joined in supporting President Richard Lyman, whose main focus was rescuing the University from the turmoil of the late 1960s and 1970s. He did brilliantly at that, but none of us was aware during my one-year term as provost that Dick Lyman was engaged in negotiations with the Rockefeller Foundation to become its next president, though we noted he was occasionally distracted. I took the lead in collaborating with my fellow vice presidents to shield Dick from any criticism.

The University was strengthened by the recurring debate between Massy, a professor in the Graduate School of Business, and Lieberman, a professor of statistics and operations research. In our discussions of economic trends and how to budget accordingly, Massy relied on economic cases and Lieberman invariably invoked statistics. The two frequently challenged each other's figures and case studies. I liked Lieberman, a charming and engaging man, and thought his quantitative skills in these interactions generally won the day.

Schwartz was a remarkably sensitive and intelligent university citizen. When we proposed a measure of some kind, he wanted to be sure that it would not attract adverse commentary from our faculty members or government patrons. Concerned with maintaining the public trust, especially in issues related to trustee conflicts of interest, he regularly asked: "How would that look if everybody did it?"

Rosenzweig remained a friend and an interesting and thoughtful colleague in many matters. His job as head of public affairs entailed several kinds of relationships. One set involved local communities and boards, including some well-known conflicts between Stanford faculty and local doctors over access to hospital-based services. In addition to maintaining and improving our town–gown relationships, Rosenzweig's role involved the myriad ways in which Stanford and other universities must work with various entities of the federal government. Taxes and tax policy—including rules regarding deductions—are often key concerns. So are the nation's research budgets, which support university-based scientific endeavor. Indeed, Rosenzweig was so successful in this role that, during my presidency, he accepted an invitation to become president of the Association of American Universities.

Joel Smith, earlier Stanford's dean of students, was a handsome, well-presented, and thoughtful person. He wrote little memoranda in the most elegant handwriting, and they were invariably positive, flattering, and constructive. As vice president for development he had done very well for Stanford. So when we learned that he was profoundly depressed and suffering, a whole universe of Stanford people began regular visits to his campus home; we all wanted him back at work, employing his charismatic charm on the people we needed to love us.

It was Smith who would manage my presidential inauguration in 1980, though he called his involvement "nominal," so severe was his depression at the time. After he had taken leave from his role as vice president, I continued to assign him various projects, hoping he would engage with them and that his illness would improve. In 1981, I appointed him to the newly created position of Secretary to the Board of Trustees, a position with prestige, access, and intellectual challenge but without the consistent pressure to deliver that a development officer must withstand. Yet the work was not sufficiently interesting to rescue him from his situation, and his decline continued.

I dreaded having to tell Smith that he could not continue at Stanford, but in February of 1983, I did just that. To my surprise, he turned on me in an angry and very public way. Years later, after extensive treatment and out of respect, I believe, for the close partnership we once enjoyed, he sent me one of his elegant notes, expressing his regret for what had transpired. I replied at once in a friendly tone. In an article Joel subsequently wrote for *Stanford Magazine* ("Falling Apart" January/February 2000), he referred to this correspondence, describing his note to me as one of apology and regret, and expressed his pleasure in having made subsequent visits back to Stanford.

About halfway through my first year back on campus, President Lyman announced that he planned to accept the presidency of the Rockefeller Foundation, prompting his departure from Stanford and a search for his replacement. Although a number of people thought that I would be a leading candidate, I did nothing to encourage them. I was only six months into my job as provost, learning a great deal and feeling challenged. Encouraging the speculation would have been dangerously close to promoting one's own interest, something that is not done in academia. I supported a national search, tough criteria, and thorough assessment of the candidates.

I never thought I had a strong claim on the job, although at the senior administrative level we had not had particular success in making outside appointments, which may have been a factor in the presidential search. Thus, I found myself in the difficult position of being, but not seeming to be, the inside candidate for the Stanford presidency.

What happens to relationships among colleagues when one member of the group is elevated? My fellow vice presidents were very supportive, perhaps because none had any interest in the presidency. The search process was somewhat secretive. I am sure there was a faculty committee; I am less sure whether any of my colleagues at the VP level served on it. What is certain is that the year we spent together working in the provost's office set a promising trajectory for my tenure as president.

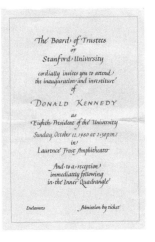

The invitation to Don's inauguration.

A university president has multiple constituencies and an extraordinarily broad job description. The constituencies include students and their parents, alumni, donors, athletic (particularly football) supporters, local municipalities and their residents, Congress and the federal agencies that fund research, the Board of Trustees, and, topping the list, the faculty.

The "buck," or, should I say, "all the bucks" stop with the president. The president is ultimately responsible—among other things—for the academic pro-

The inaugural march with Richard Lyman and Wallace Sterling, October 12, 1980.

A painting of Hoover House, the president's residence.

The entrance to Hoover House with Queen Elizabeth II, March 1983.

gram and mandatory curriculum for undergraduates; faculty recruitment and retention; campus facilities and services; fund raising; managing the endowment and multiple budgets; student life inside and outside the dormitories; admissions (everything from diversity issues to difficult conversations with angry alumni whose children or grandchildren were not admitted); alumni relations; campus safety and security; public affairs at federal, state, and local levels; compliance with government contracting and reporting requirements; defending lawsuits against the University; the hospital and its relationship with the medical school; greeting important visitors; religious life; ethnic and minority communities; press relations; speech making; and even faculty complaints about parking (on some days, the most unpleasant part of the job). Yet, and maybe because of this broad range of responsibilities, making each day of the job unique, I loved every minute of my presidency. At least once a day, I said to myself, "I have the best job in the world!"

BEING BOLD: THE CENTENNIAL CAMPAIGN

Stanford's Centennial Campaign, spanning 1985 to 1991, was at that time the most ambitious fund-raising campaign in higher education, with a goal of $1.1 billion. Among the first donors I approached was the late real estate developer Tom Ford, who wanted to create an endowed chair to be occupied by a free-market economist. My concern was that appointing of an economist with specific reference to market theory and political philosophy ran counter to academic freedom and our ability to attract the best and brightest faculty, regardless of their ideological orientation. So I made a counterproposal, to launch an economic policy research institute to be populated with scholars from various schools of thought that would strengthen Stanford's bona fides in economics. Ultimately, Ford agreed, and that was the beginning of the Center for Economic Policy Research, later renamed the Stanford Institute for Economic Policy Research (SIEPR).

The decision to announce a billion-dollar-plus goal was not one taken lightly. I took my first sabbatical since 1972, when I had been a fellow at the Center for the Advanced Study of the Behavioral Sciences at Stanford pursuing my interest in the problems of science and society. The purpose of my sabbatical in the winter quarter of 1986 was to work with an outstanding group of five young faculty and staff members on planning the Centennial Campaign, to be announced in a series of National Centennial Celebration events around the country from 1987 to 1989.

The panel also acted as a visioning group, imaging Stanford in the year 2010. We consulted widely with faculty, anticipating problems that Stanford might face, and presented our vision to the Board of Trustees during a retreat at Stanford Sierra Camp, engaging them in scenario-building exercises that augmented our work. Among other things, the report anticipated a Rose Bowl win, but no earthquakes! We could never have anticipated the technology revolution. In hindsight, although we had fun imagining Stanford's future, we were far off base on almost every aspect, which might tell us something about such future-scenario exercises. They may not be the best use of resources.

In the early stages of campaign planning, we visited thirty-one U.S. and four international cities. In Mexico City and Toronto, the host heads of state gave major addresses. We asked alumni and supporters their view of a billion-dollar fund-raising goal. Was it ambitious or obscene? Time and again, our alumni told us to be bold. When we spelled out the needs, the issues, buildings, professorships, and institution-strengthening activities proposed, we asked, "If we set a goal of $1 billion-plus, do you think you can represent Stanford's decision with respect to other people in higher education and succeed in making a plausible effort to exceed the goal?"

With our friend Joel Smith sidelined and the departure of his successor, Henry Riggs, we turned to John Ford, then director of development at Stanford's Medical School, to lead the campaign as vice president for development. It was a brilliant choice, He was treasured for his wisdom, his thoughtfulness, his persuasive manner, and his excellent management skill. He is a superb leader, and I owe him this: He never let me become afraid of fund raising.

Giving up resistance to early Stanford email, 1980s.

All of us who worked closely with him were envious of the fact that he could take a ten-minute nap in a congressman's office waiting for an appointment. He'd shut his eyes and be sound asleep. But as soon as you said, "Okay, we can go in now"—boom! He was on the game.

He was the consummate advocate for the university. He would testify in Sacramento and Washington, and he really understood that government relations and legislative processes don't wait for anyone. Legislators have a tendency to procrastinate to the last minute on difficult issues so you can be there until midnight or 2 AM. If you're involved you have to be able to get your CEO on the phone, even if you have to wake him up in the middle of the night to say, "Hey, this is what they're about to do, how do you want us to respond?" But Don never wavered. He could be at dinner, at a board meeting, or asleep. There was no penalty. He understood the process.   —*Bob Freelen*

He brings to the office many strong qualities: flair, imagination, a quick and agile mind, and great capacity to bring out the best in other people. We couldn't be in better hands.
                                                                                —*Richard Lyman*

Don came into the presidency with a burst of enthusiasm, affability, and collegiality. He was the right man for the job—energetic, outgoing, and jubilant about everything related to Stanford. He celebrated the institution and saw its many virtues. He liked being with undergraduates, seeing what they could do, and he loved everything athletic. He never seemed defeated, depressed, worried, or concerned. There was a buoyancy: "We're going to keep on going. People will understand."   —*Bill Chase*

Dear Don: This is a fan letter. I have seen you in action with large groups of alumni, small groups of people at your home, the press association in London, and in numerous other settings. You really do a great job. You manage to combine content with wit and with just the right touch for each audience. With warm personal regards, *George P. Shultz*

He's incredibly charismatic. I don't know anybody who's ever met him who wasn't immediately charmed.   —*Mark Wilson*

Don was so positive and energetic. He loved being out there meeting with people and talking about Stanford. We'd go to three different cities, three event-filled days and nights, and we'd all start to wear down, but he seemed to just get more and more energy. It just fed his energy; it was amazing.   —*Carolyn Manning*

The Centennial Campaign was made possible because Don is the kind of person he is. He thought about it early on—way back in '82 he was thinking about such campaign objectives as support for undergraduates, the humanities, the faculty, and science buildings. He had vision and was not only good at articulating it but was willing and able to go out and ask for large sums of money in a very persuasive, compelling, professional way. I think it's rare to find both these abilities resident in one person.   —*Richard Bennett*

Meeting with donors and learning their interests and priorities was actually a positive part of the job for me. It was clear that if the provost were permitted to determine the nature and allocation of contributions, he would put all of it in new faculty salaries and student recruitment, and we would become a cultural desert. To guarantee that we are as relevant and productive an academic institution as possible, Stanford depends on the quality of its faculty and the capacity to support graduate and undergraduate students. So when a donor indicates an interest in sculpture, for example, or athletic facilities, the provost might wonder why we couldn't persuade this friend to appreciate and fund our academic priorities instead. But I found that learning to respect the diversity of donor interests, within reason, advanced our institution substantially. Although some gifts are whimsical, and not every whim should be satisfied, an institution has to be open minded and respectful of what each donor wants to support.

For example, the well-known, yet controversial sculpture by George Segal known as "Gay Liberation" advanced the Stanford community's dialogue on issues pertaining to gay rights, tolerance, hate crimes, and the purposes of public art. The piece, initially commissioned for installation in New York City, proved so divisive there that in 1980 it was offered on long-term loan to Stanford, which was at that time building its outdoor art collection. As I recall our noted art advisor opined in correspondence he thought was confidential, "Let's bring 'Gay Liberation' and watch Kennedy squirm." I approved the installation, and I still find the piece to be terrific. To date, the sculpture—a white plaster cast depicting two men on a bench and two women, standing—has been vandalized at least three times, and removed from public view for a year, underscoring the vulnerability of the LGBTQ community. The issue deserves thoughtful discussion on a university campus, so I stand behind our decision to accept and prominently exhibit the sculpture.

I had to decline a gift from the graduating senior class of 1986 because of the strings attached to it. As part of its gift, the class created a fund to be held in escrow until the University took the strongest position possible with regard to apartheid in South Africa—total divestment. Yet, there were no specifics as to how Stanford should determine which companies doing business in South Africa were causing harm and which might actually be helping the antiapartheid movement. I spoke to the class on Class Day about why we shouldn't condition gifts on the basis of a single issue, no matter how ubiquitously embraced:

> All of us, surely, share a sense of moral revulsion about apartheid, To many—
> perhaps most—divestment seems an appropriate and necessary signal of that
> moral stance. Others wonder whether divestment will really relieve apartheid,
> or doubt the links between divestment here and divestment there. What I
> would focus on now is not the rightness or wrongness of the conviction that
> led to the attachment of this string. Rather, I hope we might consider the ap-

propriateness of employing our conviction on *any* single issue, however right or however widely shared, as a condition of support and loyalty. . . . I hope we will not form the habit of judging complex, valuable institutions on the basis of their positions on a single matter. Stanford exists for many purposes, all of which are related to the acquisition and dissemination of knowledge—the most precious commodity in humankind's relentless efforts at self-improvement everywhere, including South Africa. The University works toward those purposes in complex ways; its essence is that it is a web of process, with, of course, an appetite. To refuse to feed it because it is wrong in some particular dimension is, I think, to miss the point. We should ask ourselves about the fundamental rightness of its direction and the ultimate value of what it produces—not its capacity to be right every time, here and now, judged by a contemporary standard.[1]

Even without that class gift, the Centennial Campaign was a huge success, exceeding its goal and bringing $1.3 billion dollars to Stanford, catapulting the academic mission to new heights.

DIVESTMENT FROM SOUTH AFRICA

The issue affecting the senior class gift was also of concern to many other constituents. There was little disagreement about apartheid itself but a good deal about how Americans should respond to it. Congress was considering economic sanctions against the South African regime. A number of churches, universities, and other nonprofit organizations divested holdings in U.S. corporations that did business in South Africa—some selectively and some on an across-the-board basis.

At Stanford, there were demonstrations at the 1985 commencement ceremony against the University's policy of selective divestment. In October, two occupations of the Old Union resulted in some forty arrests. One student charged that police had used excessive force in removing him and in processing him later at the county jail. Professor John Kaplan of the Law School was asked to undertake an investigation of the police misconduct charges. He found no evidence of improper conduct but concluded that several procedures required improvement. As the divestment movement gained force, there was a march on the president's residence, and Joan Baez entertained a crowd of about 800 demonstrators outside my office on the Inner Quad. There were at least three major public meetings involving senior administrators, trustees, and large audiences of students; and after one board meeting a group of demonstrators blocked an array of trustees' cars by lying down in the street, creating an unexpected windfall for Hertz.[2]

In the spring, some 200 faculty members petitioned the trustees for full divestment. How best to effect change in apartheid South Africa was something

Students
promoting
divestment from
South Africa.

the Board of Trustees grappled with, and none more intensely than the members of the Special Committee on Investment Responsibility (SCIR). Despite urging by some groups to divest from all companies doing business in South Africa, we employed a case-by-case approach, reaching out to corporate leaders to uncover and understand the nature of their business there and how it affected South African blacks. Other universities—including prominent ones like Columbia—made the decision to divest altogether, but we felt that the case-by-case approach was more prudent, and we were willing to commit the time and resources to pursue it. Among the issues we probed was whether a given company was adhering to the Sullivan principles—the code of conduct developed by the African American clergyman Rev. Leon Sullivan—to apply economic pressure on South Africa. Over time, the principles would gain widespread adoption among U.S.-based corporations.

The Sullivan principles, introduced in 1977, with one addition in 1984, consisted of seven requirements a corporation was to demand of the South African government. In general, they encouraged the equal treatment of employees regardless of race, both within and outside of the workplace, a position that directly conflicted with official South African policies of racial segregation and unequal rights. Based on these tenets, trustees and senior University staff attempted to determine whether a company in which Stanford held shares could be seen as a positive force—supplying technical support or advice, for example, to antiapartheid factions in the South African government. We sought statements about the activities a company might be pursuing to advance the health and welfare of South Africans in general, and nonwhite South Africans in particular. Supplying equipment for the police to use in the practice of apartheid would not have been an action we wanted to support. On hearing from Stanford, a few corporate officers said that they did not want to discuss their policies; if they persisted in offering "no comment," we divested from them. I believe that in the end most of our constituents, including the students, found the case-by-case approach to be reasonable and effective.

The Board of Regents of the University of California took a well-publicized vote in favor of blanket divestiture and was thereby relieved of further student and media pressure. But the divestiture never took place. Regents opposed to the move received a legal opinion that it would result in significant financial losses to the university's endowment, thus exposing board members to legal action. The South African issue raised important questions regarding the origin and purpose of public trusts and the responsibility of trustees. Endless analyses appeared about whether divestiture—or action on any other form of "socially responsible" investment—would penalize the total return of institutional portfolios. Perhaps the inevitable conclusion is that if investment strategy is influenced by any purpose other than maximizing returns, there is likely to be an adverse effect. As a result of the debate, the fiduciary responsibility of trustees became more sharply focused in the public mind. It is better understood now that part of that responsibility is to maintain the real purchasing power of the University's endowments and thus to practice a form of intergenerational equity.[3] As I said in a Founders' Day speech at the time, "We must speak for the students who haven't been born yet, the faculty who haven't been appointed yet, the experiments that haven't been designed yet."[4]

Coincidentally, during this period I had a chance meeting with the South African Bishop Desmond Tutu, a leading figure in the antiapartheid movement. During a brief airport conversation, Bishop Tutu noted that the perceived threat of divestment was actually a more powerful tool of influence than divestment itself. He said that it was important to be considering the issue and talking publicly about it but not quite pulling out, which would thereby forfeit one's seat at the table and the ability to bring change. He suggested that subtle pressure on the U.S. government to influence the South African regime was another level on which the antiapartheid movement could make headway. Neither he nor all those who shared his concerns would have believed that in less than a decade a multiracial democratic government would be established in South Africa.

His devotion to human rights in South Africa notwithstanding, I later opposed Bishop Tutu's nomination to the Harvard Board of Overseers, of which I was then a member. I felt that he would be too focused on the single issue of divestment to respond adequately to the broader range of overseer responsibilities—fiduciary and financial, as well as orientation to the future and institutional values. Tutu was not offered a seat on the board.

An interesting coda to the Special Committee on Investment Responsibility is how it has adapted to serve a useful purpose in contexts other than divestment from South Africa. Always fascinating are the ways in which institutional appendages designed to solve one set of problems can often be useful in addressing others. In this case, thirty years after the apartheid issue, students were lobbying Stanford to reduce its dependence on fossil fuels. Once again, the committee on investment responsibility, since renamed the Advisory Panel on Investment Responsibility and Licensing (APIRL), served as a mechanism by which to recommend at least a partial solution. By demonstrating that natural gas provides a reasonable substitute for coal, the committee persuaded the Board of Trustees that it could be responsive to energy concerns without devastating the entire fossil fuel industry and without jeopardizing the needs of the various Stanford constituencies. To my knowledge, no other major university had decided to limit its use of fossil fuels at that time.

STUDENT ACTIVISM AND PUBLIC SERVICE

When students organize to bring attention to issues like apartheid and sustainability, they are clearly concerned with the welfare of the world around them. By the time I assumed the Stanford presidency in 1980, I had grown quite weary of the general public sentiment that young people were by and large self-centered, primarily career-oriented, and interested only in financial gain. I knew from experience that what our young people at Stanford wanted was to make new ideas, make progress, and make a difference. They were concerned with the needs of others and lacked only a structure by which to engage their altruistic leanings.

The way outsiders were judging the young people in our community led me to two reactions: On the one hand, I felt protective of our students. On the other, I wanted to prove the outsiders wrong. I was struck by the fact that many students on campus were deeply interested in tutoring or serving the public in some way. It seemed to me there was an occasion to try to match community needs with student interest. Until that time, there had not been any systematic way of marrying the need for service with the opportunity to deliver it.

My focus on public service at Stanford was presaged by its Founding Grant. The first section set out the University's object and public service-related purposes: "Its object, to qualify its students for personal success, and direct usefulness in life; And its purposes, to promote the public welfare by exercising an influence on behalf of humanity and civilization, and inculcating love and reverence for the great principles of government." In the years after Leland Stanford's death, Jane Lathrop Stanford prepared several amendments to the Founding Grant. One of them reinforced the public service aspects of the University's purpose: "While the instruction offered must be such as will qualify the students for personal success and direct usefulness in life, they should understand that it is offered in the hope and trust that they will become thereby of greater service to the public."[5]

I was fortunate that a colleague from my time in government, Catherine Milton, arrived on campus in 1982 as the spouse of a newly appointed associate dean of the law school, Tom McBride. Milton had been an assistant secretary of the Treasury responsible for alcohol, tobacco, and firearms when the FDA learned of the danger alcohol posed during pregnancy. I was commissioner at the time, and we wanted to put warning labels on alcoholic beverages, but the Bureau of Alcohol, Tobacco, and Firearms felt such warnings were their purview, not ours. Milton worked with us and did a masterful job of persuading her agency's leadership to implement the warning about drinking during pregnancy that still appears today on alcoholic beverage labels.

Knowing Milton's superb capability and devotion to public service, I reached out to her immediately on her arrival. She clearly saw the potential for addressing both community need and student service and seemed interested in helping to pursue a public service initiative. Among her first steps was to seek input from both the general and student communities. We challenged students to consider dedicating some of their time and talents to serving society and humanity in a way they found personally meaningful. In 1983 I named Milton as special as-

Don speaking to students from the steps of Owen House, the original home for the Public Service Center, May 22, 1992.

sistant to the president to evaluate and advance the state of public service at Stanford. I wanted to ensure that students understood the variety and importance of service opportunities.

In 1984, on Milton's recommendation, Stanford established its Center for Public Service at Owen House, the oldest house on campus, formerly a faculty residence. The Center served as a surface on which to meld community and student service interests. I endorsed it with enthusiasm, and Milton served as its founding director. The "You Can Make a Difference" Conference, a signature program of the public service center, was for years the largest student-run conference at Stanford. Its aim was to inspire students and community members to consider issues beyond their usual experience and explore personal and professional avenues in which they could make a difference. It also invited students

The ground-breaking for what became the Haas Center for Public Service, with Catherine Milton, 1984.

and community members to participate in direct community service. The conference was a pillar of the public service center for more than a decade.

In 1989, with the public service initiative a featured objective in the Centennial Campaign, Mimi and the late Peter Haas committed a $5 million endowment gift to institutionalize public service at Stanford through the creation of the Haas Center for Public Service, bringing new visibility and prestige to the service effort. A $1.2 million gift from the Haas Fund simultaneously established the Mimi and Peter Haas Centennial Professorship in Public Service, with statesman, author, and Haas Center National Advisory Board cofounder John W. Gardner named the first chair holder.

Gardner had served as secretary of the Department of Health, Education and Welfare and had played a founding or sustaining role in one vital civic organization after another. He gradually emerged as the nation's civic conscience, arguing powerfully for citizen engagement with public need and then creating and leading new organizations that could implement that vision. In his books, he explored the relationship between the individual and society. He had a deep grasp of that chronic paradox in American life, one noted by de Tocqueville—our frontier devotion to personal freedom, even license, on one hand, and our strongly felt commitment to social order on the other. Gardner once compressed it into a nine-word summary of the social contract: "Freedom and responsibility, liberty and duty: that's the deal." A frequent theme of his advice was that lives are built on the promises we make to others. He once told a group of Stanford students:

> In the stable periods of history, meaning was supplied in the context of a coherent community and traditionally prescribed patterns of culture. On being born into the society you were heir to a whole warehouse full of meanings. Today you can't count on any such patrimony. You have to build meaning into your life, and you build it through your commitments—whether to your religion, to an ethical order as you conceive it, to your life's work, to loved ones, to your fellow humans. People run around searching for identity, but it isn't handed out free any more—not in this transient, rootless, pluralistic society. Your identity is what you've committed yourself to.[6]

The Haas Center inspires and prepares students to create a more just and sustainable world through service, scholarship, and community partnerships, engaging more than 1,000 students each year in global service across diverse pathways—direct service, engaged scholarship, activism, philanthropy, public policy, and social entrepreneurship. It is a hub for service at Stanford and a national model for how universities prepare students to serve their communities. In addition to showcasing service opportunities, the Haas Center has helped bring public service into the classroom. Courses in public service demonstrate that it is necessary but not sufficient simply to go to work in a soup kitchen. To elevate the experience to the policy level, students are required to bring that experience back to a seminar, where the policies that make soup kitchens a social necessity are examined, exploring, for example, the selection of healthy foods available in soup kitchens and studying food distribution policy.

The Haas Center represents an active statement by Stanford that service is important, involving both personal commitment at the community level and personal engagement with the political process. The Haas family has continued its support, endowing the directorship of the Haas Center in 2004, ensuring an ever-brightening future.

Today, the Haas Center is the hub of Cardinal Service, a university-wide initiative that reaffirms service as a distinctive feature of a Stanford education. Cardinal Service will continue to expand community-engaged learning courses; increase the number of full-time, quarter-long service fellowships; and strengthen efforts to encourage service commitments and careers.

I once suggested to students in a conference at the Graduate School of Business that the other side of the entrepreneurial coin is obligation, that those focused on entrepreneurial success, and who are very likely to achieve it, also have a more direct duty to the society at large—and especially to those less fortunate—that is not discharged merely by the success of their ideas, or even by the tax revenue they generate. Ironically, the more successful those ideas are, the greater the obligation. Stanford students have a charge to live up to the responsibilities their opportunities have created for them.

Catherine Milton went on to become a major national advocate for public service, eventually helping to draft the bill that created AmeriCorps, the national service program championed by President Bill Clinton and organized by Hillary Clinton. When my stepdaughter Cameron attended Stanford in Washington in the spring of 1993, her internship was in the Office of the First Lady, and the project to which she was assigned was the effort to create the Corporation for National and Community Service. Subsequently, my stepson Jamie was an AmeriCorps volunteer. For my part, I worked with colleagues Timothy Healy of Georgetown University and Howard Robert Swearer of Brown University as well as Frank Newman (the president of the Education Commission of the States) to found Campus Compact in 1985, which established the public service move-

He gave an excellent and rather courageous talk, explaining why it's a serious mistake to desert a university because of a single event—that the university exists beyond any particular event, and that to withdraw support because you disagree with something is to damage the institution in the future for students and its contribution to society. It was a very strong and very moving talk and right to the point. I don't know how many university presidents would have taken on the senior class in that form with parents and students there. I admired that a lot.

—Robert Rosenzweig

Many managers want to shoot the messenger; they don't want to hear bad news. But with Don there was a penalty for undelivered bad news. He felt if you don't know about a problem it will only get bigger.

—Bob Freelen

During the early years of Don's presidency I was hired as a young kid to manage Hoover House. Those now seem like the halcyon years at Stanford—perennially number one as an undergraduate institution, with great sports teams, the Queen of England coming for lunch—it was like Camelot. I watched these renowned people come and go who could do anything they wanted with their time and they chose to give it to Stanford. The heavier the schedule, the more it energized Don. The more we did the less tired he became.

Don and Jeanne were such personable, caring, down-to-earth people. After every catered event, they would come into the kitchen and thank everyone. They treated people like family. As the caterers cleaned up, Don would say, "David, come sit down and have a glass of wine and let's talk."

Don and Jeanne insisted that I have my wedding in the living room of Hoover House, and my parents flew out for it. My mother had never been on an airplane. She grew up on a farm, one of ten kids, and no one in her family had ever gone to high school; they went to a one-room country school. My father was a mechanic and a welder. The way Don and Jeanne treated them in their house was a testament to their genuineness and warmth. They made my mother and my Dad feel so welcome. There was an elegant casualness about them.

It was working there, seeing the University from 50,000 feet, that sealed my commitment to Stanford, where I still work in development.

—David Voss

In the president's office, early 1980s.

For that first "You Can Make a Difference" Conference, Don was extremely supportive, contacting deans and taking care of hundreds of little details. At a time when there wasn't much interaction between schools, we got the unprecedented combined support of the Law School, Business School, and Medical School as key sponsors. I was sitting next to Don in the front row of a big auditorium, and John Gardner and Peter Bing and a number of others were giving speeches. I remember Don turning to me and saying, "Wow! I think we have something that's really significant and earth-changing here!" On Monday an article in the *Campus Report* described it as one of those events that was palpable—where you could *feel* the energy, that something new was developing. That conference was the real beginning of the public service movement at Stanford.

—Catherine Milton

Don often opened up his house to dinners for some of the outstanding students and some of the donors, and that's how the Haas family became interested in supporting the public service effort at Stanford. Peter Haas told me that sitting next to some of those incredible students convinced him that this kind of support was the way to really do some good in the world. Those dinners were really important. *—Catherine Milton*

The Rockefeller Foundation offered us a million dollars, a very significant grant in those days, if we would require public service at Stanford. We thought about it and had a two-day meeting, which included about twenty of the top faculty at Stanford, a few student leaders, and a number of other college presidents and experts from around the nation. It was a very intense meeting with lots of discussion, and the decision was that rather than requiring service we would integrate service into the curriculum, exposing students to courses that would encourage them to do public service, which is in fact what the Haas Center has done. They now have well over a hundred such courses. So we turned down the money, and it was Don's leadership that gave us the confidence to go in a different direction. *—Catherine Milton*

Don was such a powerful synthesizer at that organizing meeting for Campus Compact. It was the time of the "Me" generation, and Don understood the importance of having a voice out there to encourage students to do something outside of going to Goldman Sachs and making a lot of money. He led those early meetings and was by far the most articulate person among all those college presidents and in talking to the media.

—Catherine Milton

When Stanford alumnus Peter Ross was a student at Stanford in the late 1980s, he saw President Donald Kennedy give a speech in which he challenged the students to do public service. The next day, Ross signed up to tutor in East Palo Alto. Today, Ross is director of operations for Springboard, a social-entrepreneurial company that places entry-level employees into stable jobs. Springboard President Elliott Brown, also a Stanford alumnus, said he was also inspired by Kennedy. "Kennedy is a hero," he said. "He challenged students to make a difference." *—Gohar Galyan. "Startup Finds Entry-Level Jobs, Mentors." Stanford Daily, April 27, 2001*

ment in U.S. colleges and universities. We invited other college and university presidents to join Campus Compact and support the mission of educating students to be civically engaged. The involvement from presidents was strong, and we strategically created a statewide affiliated network. In 1988, Charles Young (then chancellor of UCLA) and I founded California Campus Compact. Today, there are thirty-four state and regional Campus Compacts and more than 1,100 national college and university presidents who are committed to promoting public service that develops students' citizenship skills, helps campuses forge effective community partnerships, and provides resources and training for faculty seeking to integrate civic and community-based learning into the curriculum. Campus Compact is the leading national higher education organization dedicated solely to campus-based civic engagement.

I find public service extremely important in developing a sense of personal accomplishment. Throughout my career I have made a concerted effort to advocate public service as a priority that enhances individual lives. My own engagement in public service has certainly enriched mine.

At a time when superficiality is endemic to life, we need commitments that run deep. Nothing is more thoroughly satisfying than turning one's own talent productively to the service of others. Addressing graduating classes during my presidency, I continually advised going to work on the world's problems, believing that you can make a difference, that "it is important to keep asking yourself whether you are living up to the responsibility your opportunities have created for you. The reward is not merely the sense of fulfillment; it is nothing less than the infusion of meaning into one's life." Reminding the class of '85 of how aching this world's needs really are, I suggested that "to have gone this far, to have seized the opportunity you now have, without resolving to devote some portion of your lives to addressing those needs would be simply unforgivable."[7]

Change is often easier to manage at the local level and on a reasonable scale. Folksinging activist Pete Seeger once said: "Songs won't save the planet, but, then, neither will books or speeches. Participation is what's going to save the human race. We've all got to be involved. It won't be done by big organizations but by millions of little organizations, often local. You can think globally, but act locally."[8] Though he may have underestimated the crucial role of large organizations, he understood the exhilaration of being a driver of reform, of slipping off the streambank of history and into the flood.

THE BULLY PULPIT:
SPEAKING UP, SPEAKING OUT

Public service is not the only policy issue on which I spoke out during my years as Stanford president. A few of the University trustees hinted to me that it was perhaps not prudent to be as publicly vocal as I was on the range of issues I chose to address, but I decided to ignore them. Whether the issue was K–12 education reform (particularly with regard to teaching evolution), grade inflation, or the undergraduate course serially known as Western Civilization; Western Culture; and Culture, Ideas and Values, I believe I did and said enough to satisfy those who hoped the president would speak out on education policy. I like to think my views were solicited and respected for my insights, but I also realize that as the voice of the University, I spoke not only for the current students, parents, faculty, staff, and community but for the Stanford of the future. Like trustees, presidents have fiduciary and financial responsibilities, to be sure, but also a commitment to posterity.

In that context, I turn to the curriculum issue presented by the evolution of the Western Culture requirement. The move to change the course actually began with a complaint by the Black Student Union, charging that the required course was racist for its absence of books by black authors. Given the rise of ethnic and gender studies since the 1960s, it was not long before women and other recently empowered students of color joined in the outcry against Western Culture as a course with substantial European white male bias.

The course was in fact the outgrowth of the earlier Western Civilization course in European history and culture, discarded during the tumult of the late sixties, only to return a decade later with the title "Western Culture." The syllabus for the required first-year course comprised established classical texts from literature, philosophy, science, and political theory, designed to provide a common, baseline understanding for future intellectual pursuits. The course was admittedly centered on European culture, introducing young people to classics, good writing, and good discussions. It was well designed for its purpose at the time, but as the student body became increasingly diverse, questions arose about the exclusion of non-Western cultures and ignorance of other domains in human society. How were we to understand the cultural values and political traditions of large parts of the world, let alone the diverse ethnic populations that made up our own society, if we let our students hear only from a single tradition of philosophy or literature? It seemed evident that the students' charge of racial bias, though strident, had some merit.

The readings on the Western Culture syllabus were the Hebrew Bible, Genesis; Homer, major selections from *Iliad* or *Odyssey* or both; at least one Greek tragedy; Plato, *Republic*, major portions of Books I–VII; New Testament selections including a gospel; Augustine, *Confessions*, I–IX; Dante, *Inferno*; More, *Utopia*; Machiavelli, *The Prince*; Luther, *Christian Liberty*; Galileo, *The Starry Messenger* and *The Assayer*; Voltaire, *Candide*; Marx and Engels, *The Communist Manifesto*; Darwin, selections; Freud, *Outline of Psychoanalysis* and *Civilization and Its Discontents*. In addition to these required texts, each Western Culture instructor was to choose from a supplemental reading list including such works as the *Aeneid*, selections from Thomas Aquinas, Hobbes's *Leviathan*, Goethe's *Faust* and *The Sorrows of Young Werther*, and a nineteenth-century novel.

With emerging student concern, the course was reviewed by the Faculty Senate— the legislative body of the Academic Council with responsibility for academic and research policy as well as the authority to grant degrees. Two committees made recommendations, and the entire body engaged in a lively and protracted discussion, not only about broadening the syllabus to include more non-Western writers but also about changing the course focus to examine social organization, art, performance, and so on. Those opposed to curricular change charged that tinkering with the required canon was simply political correctness.

It was surprising to me that an academic discussion of which great works ought to be included on an introductory course syllabus was newsworthy, but the pointed interest of William Bennett, Secretary of Education in the Reagan administration, brought national attention to Stanford as we struggled to refine

American Gothic
with Professor
Wanda Corn.

a core curriculum. Members of the Academic Senate hardly knew what to make of the media spectacle that ensued around their discussions. A *Newsweek* headline screamed, "Say Goodnight, Socrates: Stanford University and the Decline of the West." The *San Francisco Chronicle*, hardly known for its education coverage, reported, "Stanford Puts an End to Western Civilization." The Reverend Jesse Jackson came to campus to ignite student protest and, if one is to believe Bennett, led the demonstrators in the now notorious chant, "Hey, hey, ho, ho, Western Culture's got to go." Several reporters on the scene, however, recorded that Jackson did not take part in the chant, and accounts remain conflicting. On the nation's editorial pages, neoconservatives George Will and Charles Krauthammer went toe-to-toe with more liberal columnists like Ellen Goodman and Amy Schwartz, who supported the change. The public was led to perceive the issue as one between polar extremes of educational philosophy—between academic purists and know-nothings, those who favor ultrastructured liberal education and those who believe there should be no structure at all.

As I later wrote in *Academic Duty*,

> Curricular change became an object of intense external concern because of a deep relationship between knowledge and values. Many of the objections to the new course had to do with the fear that Western beliefs and values, and not just a reading list, were being pruned. "Cultural relativism," a phrase used by many of the critics, reflected a fear that if we give too much attention to the non-Western elements that have helped shape contemporary American culture, we will be suggesting that the values represented by them have equal status.[9]

A part of that concern came from a sense that the most successful and humanitarian form of government had evolved out of Graeco-Roman culture, and that the values underlying those roots might be made to appear arbitrary. There was, of course, no such deemphasis implied in the new curriculum.

Bennett himself descended on the campus to meet with students and to debate me on the merits of the existing Western Culture course without multicultural changes. He gave a talk on campus, arranged by the *Stanford Review*—a journal produced by politically conservative students—in which he expressed his disappointment with the people who were, as he saw it, trying to harass the administration into giving up Western Culture and substituting a kind of mongrel non-Western culture. Bennett's point of view was largely informed by Allan Bloom's *The Closing of the American Mind*, which made a powerful conservative case against the introduction of non-Western works. PBS's *MacNeil–Lehrer News Hour* picked up the story, and the controversy culminated with Secretary Bennett and me debating the merits of evolving the curriculum on national television. Bennett characterized the campaign to change the course requirements as one of intimidation and coercion. Few if any minds were changed by that exchange, which many viewers agreed was a draw.

In the end, largely under the leadership of History Professor Carolyn Lou-gee, a new and somewhat enlarged canon of literature was proposed for the basic culture course. Various compromises resulted in further revision, and there have since been many successors to the Western Culture course, including the Introduction to the Humanities (IHUM) programs. The controversy got us talking about things we should have been considering anyway—what comprises the common intellectual property of educated men and women? The discussion was important because it focused on the deep relationship between knowledge and values, and the fear that—more than a list of books—Western beliefs were being challenged. The concern suggested important corollaries that needed addressing—diversity, sensitivity, and the culture of a campus community.

DIVERSITY MATTERS

The question of diversity and why it matters loomed large during my presidency. The rise of ethnic and gender studies in the 1970s led to a focus on minority hiring and student diversity, with the latter much easier to accomplish than the former.

Given the usual student residence time of four years on campus, the half-life of an undergraduate is relatively short. Thus with some reprioritization in terms of financial assistance and need-blind admissions, we were able to include more African American, Hispanic, and Native American students in the freshman classes by the mid- to late-1980s. Although this change presented us with challenges, it offered far more opportunities.

The rise in prominence of instruments like the Myers-Briggs Type Indicator personality inventory, which identify variation in perception, preference, and behavior, has helped rationalize our instinct that diversity is preferable to homogeneity. As these types of instruments demonstrate, diverse teams—whether in the workplace, social sector, or on the college campus—are almost always more effective than those composed of people with similar backgrounds and skill sets. A case in point is Stanford's design challenge, which vexed engineering teams each year to build a better mouse trap, build a paper bicycle, or construct the indestructible egg crate. By accident, we came to recognize that the more diverse teams in these competitions—in terms of race, field of study, and even the Meyers-Briggs profiles—consistently outperformed the homogeneous teams. The management sector has confirmed these observations in practice. When diverse groups work together, productivity and creativity are enhanced.

My colleagues in Stanford's Residential Education program deserve special praise for the environment they helped create outside the classroom, which contributed substantially to what we call a "Stanford education." Dean of Students Jim Lyons was a stunningly effective leader in that role, ably supported by senior associates Norm Robinson, Alice Supton, and Michael Jackson. The "Res

Ed" team persuaded a number of faculty and staff to reside with their families in dormitories as "Resident Fellows" without becoming in loco parentis. Committed to bringing together different cultural norms, Stanford evolved from the ethnic and gender studies of the 1960s to the creation of diverse student living groups in the early 1980s, including "theme houses" based on student interests, cultures, and lifestyles.

In a culturally based theme house at Stanford, such as the African American house Ujamaa or the Hispanic Casa Zapata, only half the residents comprise the ethnic group of focus. That is, by design, only 50 percent of Casa Zapata students are Hispanic. The rest belong to other cultures and are interested in learning more about Hispanic culture. As the "theme house" experiment has evolved, there have been a few unfortunate setbacks in which the nonminority students have grown resentful, even generating controversial behaviors toward the ethnic group.

A case during my presidency took place in Ujamaa, the black theme house. A black student is said to have asserted in a dorm discussion that all American music descended from Africa. "Even Beethoven?" a white resident asked. "Beethoven was black," came the an-swer back. Later, the white student and a friend came on an image of Beethoven on a Stanford Orches-tra poster. Proceeding to modify it, they gave Beethoven an afro hair-style and colored his skin brown, adding exaggerated African lips and nose. Black students were deeply of-fended, and a firestorm of contro-versy ensued.

Was the prank satire? Hate speech? Free speech? Such are the issues that arise in living groups with diverse backgrounds and sensi-tivities, and sometimes with limited perspective and cultural understand-ing. (Perhaps none of it would have occurred if either party to the dis-pute had been aware of the appar-ently obscure fact that Beethoven was not American.) Ultimately, the students who defaced the poster were removed from the residence, and judicial review proceedings were brought against them for vio-

Black Beethoven, Ujamaa dorm, October 1988.

lating Stanford's Fundamental Standard, which requires respectful interaction at all times. Unfortunately, retaliation against the rest of the white students in the dorm was swift, including notices slid under their doors informing them that they were not welcome in the house, and the posting of a dorm photo with the white students' faces scratched out. It was not Stanford's finest hour.

Theme houses are not a bad idea as long as there are rules in place to preclude an agenda on the part of the minority group. It is no doubt of educational value for different kinds of people to live together. As with so many initiatives, the devil is in the details.

The Ujamaa event gave way to an inquiry on race relations at Stanford, producing a 244-page report by a University Committee on Minority Issues, with 117 recommendations for ethnic innovations in courses, admissions, and financial aid and calling for an increase in minority faculty hiring. Through the 1980s, our progress in minority hiring had been slow. Humanities and Sciences Dean Norm Wessells was concerned and spelled out some guidelines to expand the number of minority candidates qualified for faculty consideration, broadening the definitions of the various academic disciplines to cast a wider net, and resolving that if two candidates' credentials were equivalent, the minority candidate would be given preference. The Department of Physics had some people who were passionate about improving minority hiring. To bring more graduate students and young faculty of color to Stanford, they approached bright undergraduates among historically black colleges and universities. Yet the growth in minority faculty remains much slower than the growth in the student body. Stanford continues to work on this important priority.

Ujamaa lounge, after the Beethoven event, October 1988.

In the wake of the Ujamaa incident, I wrote an essay, "Reflections on Racial Understanding," that was printed in the *Stanford Daily*. Although I condemned the insensitivity shown in the incident, I also warned against the dangers of dogmatism: "Time and again we have seen the promotion of racial understanding linked to a more focused—and less broadly understood and accepted—political agenda. That kind of load is probably too heavy for a delicate structure to bear all at once." Multiculturalism should not be characterized by the alienation of communities, polarized debate, or the kind of extreme tactics involved in the menacing takeover of my office and staff in May, 1989, in which fifty-five students were arrested. "We are among the few places in this country," I suggested, "in which it may be possible to test the workability of the multicultural existence that will, ready or not, be the life of Californians and Americans in the twenty-first century."[10]

Multiculturalism must go beyond mere tolerance. In my welcoming talk to the class of 1985, I emphasized that tolerance "implies a kind of live-and-let-live view, one that confuses non-aggression with understanding." I urged "something beyond tolerance: active exploration, risk-taking, a yearning to understand, and a willingness to change. To tolerate diversity is not what we aim for. We aim to celebrate it."[11]

In addition to the theme house innovation, Dean of Students Jim Lyons also came to the Board of Trustees with a solid and thoughtful request to permit graduate students to occupy student housing with their nonmatriculated significant others. The proposal was passing easily until a local newspaper inferred that the policy was designed to permit, if not encourage, gay cohabitation. This led the Trustees who had approved the policy to complain. With the suspicion that Stanford might be condoning, if not encouraging, gay men and lesbian women to have a place of their own, the *San Francisco Chronicle* sent a reporter to campus to do a quick, on-the-spot investigation of who was living in these graduate housing units. As I recall, the bewildered reporter concluded: "We found a couple of gays, but by and large, they were all Jacks and Jills."

TWO MISSIONS

As part of my inaugural address, I observed that "the challenge before us amounts to nothing less than the reformation of undergraduate education."[12] There was a need, I suggested, to rebalance the emphasis given to teaching and research in favor of the former, limiting the emphasis on research quantity as opposed to quality and increasing incentives to good teaching. The university has two missions, the dissemination of knowledge and the creation of new knowledge. The university must create maximum synergy between the teaching and research missions so that it does the most effective job of catalyzing personal and intellectual development and at the same time enhances productivity in the difficult business of discovery. Yet education remains the primary task of

He was a much-sought-after speaker and leader, nationally and internationally, on fundamental issues of university education and research. When the great Mount Sinai Medical Center of New York celebrated its 150th anniversary, he was invited to give the keynote address; it was brilliant. People there talked about it for years afterward.

—David Hamburg

I want especially to thank you for the leadership you have given to education nationally over the past decade. You, far more than any other college president, have spoken out clearly and forcefully and with great wisdom on issues of elementary and secondary education.

—Marshall Smith

Kennedy stuck his neck out very far on the course change and took a lot of criticism. But he stuck to his guns since it was an important direction that Stanford was going in terms of curricular development.

—Albert Camarillo

Kennedy was instrumental in pushing Jewish Studies forward. It was another step in making Stanford more cosmopolitan and more multicultural, something Kennedy supports very much.

—Arnold Eisen

Donald Kennedy will go down as a great president. He clearly raised Stanford several notches in the scale of universities in the world.

—Carolyn Lougee

Don mimics a Rodin sculpture.

On the whole, Kennedy's very vocal leadership on the question of the importance of multiculturalism is a critical, very fundamental contribution to this University.

—Albert Camarillo

Don was a very principled man. He really supported the residential education program, which was so different from that in the East. We were discussing domestic housing at lunch, and I pointed out that since gay couples didn't have the option to get married, they were always out of luck for "married" housing. Don's hand came down hard on the table and he said, "By God! We're doing this because it's the right thing to do." He took some heat from the Board for that. Stanford was the first university to allow it.

—Norm Robinson

President Kennedy is a great national leader, a man of integrity, a man of vision, a man of honesty, and a fearless spokesman on behalf of higher education.

Vartan Gregorian, President Emeritus of Brown University

the university, and society will judge universities in the long run on how well they perform that task.

As I got to know students of various interests and intellectual pursuits, it occurred to me that we risk creating a misunderstanding when we speak of Stanford as a "research university." The term is generally used to differentiate universities committed to knowledge production as well as liberal education from liberal arts colleges that focus exclusively on the latter. The problem arises when the term is interpreted to mean a primary focus on research. Students see it as an invitation that draws their teachers into the library and the laboratory at their expense.

I cited the relentless pressure on faculty members to invest their time in research. In some departments, faculty members could "buy out" teaching time to concentrate on research, or teaching loads were simply reduced to satisfy research objectives. As a result, too many of Stanford's courses were taught by visitors or temporary faculty members. Some of the best teachers of undergraduates were undercompensated and unappreciated. Junior faculty who showed outstanding teaching ability failed at the tenure line too often. There seems to be a myth that research and teaching are mutually exclusive, that a faculty member who excels at one is unlikely to be much good at the other, and that Stanford favors the research faculty. Contrary to this popular belief, I have been privileged to know countless faculty who are excellent at both research and teaching. In fact, those who are gifted in the area of research are often the most enthusiastic conveyers of their newfound knowledge.

The origins of the research university date from two great innovations, the laboratory and the seminar, imported in the late nineteenth century from the German university tradition. Neither serious original research nor training in scholarship had been a significant part of the character of American universities before that. The first university to build a graduate school based on the German model was Harvard. Other universities followed, especially in the new wave of philanthropy that emerged in the late nineteenth century. What ensued was a century-long genteel war between the dominant notion of undergraduate education in the college and the dominant notion of research and graduate education in the university. It's right for that balance to be maintained in creative tension. Presidents should consider it one of their responsibilities to kick and shove it a bit when they think it tilts too far in one direction or another. That is why I initiated a new Humanities Center during my first year as president and in 1991 announced $7 million for programs to improve undergraduate education.

From the beginning, Stanford was a university for research *and* teaching, for theory *and* practice. The Stanfords and first president David Starr Jordan believed deeply in that unity and accordingly made sure not to separate undergraduate from graduate life or fundamental from applied research. Stanford's great period of growth followed the postwar conversion from a military technology to a university-based research system. That technology could easily have been maintained in government laboratories or privatized into the profit sector. But under the guidance of Vannevar Bush (World War II head of the U.S. Office of Scientific Research and Development) and others, it was decided to place the venture in the research universities. Frederick Terman and President J. E. Wallace Sterling had the vision to seize that opportunity as few other academic leaders did, and the result was a great leap forward for Stanford. Of all the fundamental research that takes place in the United States, two-thirds of it is done in universities like Stanford.

But the postwar drive to encourage science and technology created a disparity of emphasis between research and the humanities. Increases in sponsored research brought greater emphasis on kinds of scholarly work usually done without the involvement of undergraduate students. In 1993 a commission was appointed—the first in a quarter century—to study possible changes in undergraduate education at Stanford. By 1995 it had introduced a new set of seminars for sophomores, revised the "breadth" requirement, and instituted a new science core curriculum.

Stanford cares deeply about teaching undergraduates well, and many of the issues we tackled during my time as president emphasized that commitment. There are an increasing number of freshman and sophomore seminars taught by senior faculty; Stanford focuses far more on evaluations of teaching, including

With President Carter in Don's presidential office, 1983.

those from students; and the quality and level of effort devoted to undergraduate teaching has only increased.

TRUST AND TRUSTEES

As president, I enjoyed unusually close relationships with the trustees, particularly Jim Gaither, who served as board chair at the end of my presidency. At the time of my appointment, the board chair was Peter Bing, an alumnus who was perhaps the most closely associated with Stanford of any at that time and possibly for all time.

Bing has, for decades, maintained a relationship that is profoundly vital to Stanford. I so admire all he and his wife Helen have done for the University—whether endowing the professorship in environmental studies to which I returned at the end of my presidency, supporting the centerpiece of the new campus arts corridor by funding the Bing Concert Hall, establishing Bing Nursery School on campus, providing cultural opportunities for students at Stanford in Washington (now the Bing Stanford in Washington Program), or strengthening the Bing Overseas Studies Program with an endowment and naming gift.

Because of my profound affection and respect for Peter Bing, an experience with him after my presidency ended has been difficult to forget. I was teaching in the Human Biology Program, and a topic then being widely discussed in higher education concerned changing standards and grade inflation. I felt that if one is

With Supreme Court Justice Sandra Day O'Connor.

comparing the contemporary university with that of twenty years ago, it's legitimate to discuss changing standards. If it appears there is grade inflation, it may be because current students are achieving more, and we ought not call that grade inflation. I wrote an op-ed piece on this for the *New York Times*. To my surprise, Bing sent me a note admonishing me for speaking publicly on the subject of higher education when I no longer carried the title of Stanford president. Because of my high regard for Peter and our years as collaborators and friends, his suggestion that my public voice could be a detriment to Stanford was unexpected and hurtful.

ANOTHER CAPITAL PROPOSAL

Toward the end of the Ronald Reagan's presidency, Stanford received word of his interest in locating the Reagan Presidential Library and Public Policy Center at Stanford. With a substantial portion of the early Reagan collection already located in the Hoover Institution Archives on campus—somewhat curious because Reagan had not attended Stanford—there was interest in making Stanford a unified home for the presidential papers.

The Hoover Institution is a public policy think tank promoting the principles of individual, economic, and political freedom. The Hoover Institution Archives are dedicated to documenting war, revolution, and peace in the twentieth and twenty-first centuries. The Archives hold Reagan collections dating to the late 1960s and 70s, including radio addresses on dozens of topics relating to U.S. domestic and foreign policy, the Citizens for Reagan records, and the records of Deaver & Hannaford, Inc., a public relations firm based in Los Angeles that worked with Reagan through the 1960s and 70s. Hoover also holds the papers of important advisors to Reagan, including those of William Casey, Director of the CIA; economist Milton Friedman; Edwin Meese, who served as Regan's Attorney General; and George Shultz, Reagan's Secretary of State and perhaps the best-known member of the Stanford faculty.

On a trip to Washington, D.C., Trustees William Kimball and Sandy Tatum and I met with Attorney General Meese, who was representing the president's interests. It was a difficult first meeting, although we made it clear we had much enthusiasm for the library, which would be an enormous intellectual asset for serious historical scholars. Our own Professor of History David Kennedy was involved in the study of what might be available in such a library and had assembled a committee of scholars who might make historical use of the materials.

As to the public policy center, however, we told Meese, we did not feel that a center with a distinct ideological bias was appropriate for collocation on the campus of a major research university. True, the more distinctive the ideology the more interesting the archives of an administration are likely to be to scholars; yet it is important for the University to assure both the fact and the appearance of political neutrality and dedication to academic excellence, both of which are monitored by faculty review, from which the Reagan people were demanding independence. In addition, we had to explain that, contrary to the Reagan team's understanding, the Hoover Board of Overseers has no fiduciary responsibility for the Hoover Institution, as Hoover is the legal property of the Stanford Board of Trustees. With these two sensitive aspects of the discussion out of the way, we agreed to begin to develop plans and proposals for the Ronald Reagan Presidential Library at Stanford. Our zeal for this opportunity was actually quite genuine.

Plans called for locating the library in the Stanford foothills, not far from the Dish, the open space trail beloved by the community. Diagrams were drawn and sketches prepared. At one meeting, Trustee Warren Christopher and I both discussed some of the concerns that student groups had raised about the prominence of some of the features on the library site, but we indicated that the proper committees had done their work and we were prepared to move ahead. There was much concern about how the Reagan people would react to a few minor questions about shape and structure, while David Kennedy reiterated the positive findings his committee had made. Trustee Peter Bing attended that meeting and plainly wanted to move forward. We all did.

To address the design comments, we suggested small modifications that might make the building a bit less conspicuous and more consistent with the natural landscape. Unfortunately, these suggestions seemed to annoy the Reagan people, who interpreted them as unwelcoming. Still, we pressed forward. Although there were some faculty grumblings, David Kennedy's committee managed to achieve a set of agreements the faculty could embrace. We continued to negotiate in good faith and believed it was all going to work. So it came as a surprise and very disappointing to us when the Reagan people abruptly put an end to discussions and pulled out of the negotiations in favor of locating the presidential library in Simi Valley, California.

Sadly, it remained widely believed that Stanford turned down the Reagan Library. We suffered some fallout from alumni and trustees who had wanted the library located at Stanford. Despite some understandable misgivings, the trustees and I made a proposal in good faith and delivered on every commitment we made. Yet there is not a single piece of evidence—no statement, communication, or meeting that could have left the impression that the Reagan Library was unwanted.

It's hard to know what really prompted the sudden change of course. Perhaps fear of controversy persuaded the foundation to change its plans; perhaps some of the acrid public statements made by Hoover director Glen Campbell during the negotiations persuaded the foundation that it had a loose cannon on deck. Some of the commentary in the Faculty Senate with regard to sight lines, architecture, and the advisability of prominent features on a building in the foothills may have been perceived as dismissive of the entire library concept. Apparently, there was

The unique quality of Stanford, attracting a special kind of student, is largely the result of foundations, traditions, and ideals that Don established when he was here. So now you can't be just a great researcher, you have to be a great teacher; it's not enough to be a stellar student or stellar athlete, you have to be both, and ideally give back to the community. It requires that balance; so that shining as an individual without improving the lives of those around you won't cut it. And as long as I've known him, Don has embodied that ideal—a president and a teacher, a scholar who knows and cares about students, an athlete whom athletes love and respect. Don was of the people, getting behind students who were making a difference, and epitomizing that equilibrium between brilliance in what you do and the capacity to teach and encourage it in others. I think the legacy is the endurance of that model in the kind of student that the Office of Admissions seeks today. He created this Kennedy-Platonic ideal that still defines the best students here.

—Jody Maxmin

While he has been president, the university has dealt with an unusual number of volatile issues, and Kennedy is generally regarded to have made astute decisions, defusing crises and remaining popular among students and many faculty members. At the same time, Stanford's reputation as a university has, according to many accounts, risen tremendously in the almost five years that Kennedy has been president.

—Jeff Biddulph, "Stanford University's President Gets High Marks for Leadership."
Boston Globe, *April 30, 1985, p. 2.*

Smiling in the
Quad arcade.

Don was extremely competent, able to handle large complex things in an honorable and decent way. Being at Stanford on the West Coast with a lot of wealthy alumni, the pressure to buy a football team must have been enormous. Clearly he didn't want to do this; he wanted it to be a respectable academic institution. It's difficult to contain those pressures.

—Herbert Levin

For me, Don has always symbolized the bringing together of things, a creator of productive and mutually beneficial mixtures of people—bringing together the right people with complementary talents to create something together that no one could have done alone.

—Russell Fricke

Don was always open-minded about heated questions, waiting patiently for all the factual input. He was sharp, analytic, and fair-minded. And funny!

—Iris Brest

When I first met Don at the beginning of my sophomore year at Stanford in 2012, I left his office with a warm hug and an even warmer heart, knowing that I had found someone who would support me no matter what academic or career decision I made. For the rest of my time at Stanford and beyond, Don was my mentor, a grandfatherly figure who encouraged me in my pursuits yet gently challenged me to consider where my true passions lay. He was the one constant mentor for me throughout my time at Stanford and beyond as I wandered, like a typical college student, from considering a career in medicine to international security and policy, and ultimately to technology and entrepreneurship. With his breadth of knowledge and experience, he was familiar with all my interests, enthusiastically discussing the most recent developments in neuroscience research, and his generosity and kindness meant that he would always take the time to personally connect me with people he knew in the fields and ensure they would mentor me as he had, even personally calling one summer to vet my potential mentors. Don was the one who truly opened my eyes to all that Stanford had to offer, the one who had my back as I navigated all those opportunities, the one who made this campus home for me.

—Josephine Chen

The name Donald Kennedy suggests many things—integrity, tact, humor, intelligence. The man is practically an institution. *—Tanya Paull,* Stanford Weekly, *1989*

Robert Kennedy said of JFK, "He made us feel young again," and that's absolutely central to Don Kennedy. When he was president, we all felt that exuberance, like those who would join his morning run up to the Dish. He made everyone feel young, with a big future out there to look forward to, to contribute to."

—Jody Maxmin

some feeling on the part of the Reagan people that we didn't really want them, which was untrue. We later heard that Nancy Reagan decided that it was going to be too difficult to work with Campbell, who was a challenging and difficult person. Other Reagan team members raised concerns over Stanford faculty complaints about the Hoover Institution and its reputation as a conservative think tank. The reason for the decision is still a puzzle to me. Someday, a careful history from an objective source may solve it.

CHAPTER 7

THE REWARDS
AND RESPONSIBILITIES
OF LEADERSHIP

ON OCTOBER 17, 1989, my flight from New York back home was diverted to Los Angeles. Many will remember it as the date of the suddenly aborted World Series baseball game between the two Bay Area rivals—the San Francisco Giants and the Oakland Athletics. More will remember it as the fateful date of the Loma Prieta earthquake, which devastated the Stanford campus.

On the flight, we learned of the earthquake through an executive passenger who was on the air phone system, speaking with his assistant. "There's been an earthquake!" he hollered. Then, "She's gone under the table!" and "She says there are fires everywhere!" I recognized her mistake almost at once. Looking east from her Marin County office, she saw the flares from the large, Richmond refinery. Later, of course, we learned of the extensive fires in San Francisco's Marina District. The 6.9 magnitude Loma Prieta earthquake disrupted game three of the nationally televised World Series, collapsed a double-deck section of the Cypress Freeway in Oakland, and tumbled an upper section of the San Francisco-Oakland Bay Bridge. Ultimately the quake killed more than sixty people and caused some $7 billion in damages.

At Stanford, although more than 200 structures were damaged, some beyond repair, there were no deaths or serious injuries, only close calls. Pratap Malik had just pulled up next to the Old Chemistry Building to drop off friends when the cataclysmic rumble began—an astronomic shudder that the chemistry graduate student instantly recognized as an earthquake. His instinct to flee the car no doubt saved his life. A huge block of concrete crushed his Ford Granada seconds after he left it. A group of students had just filed out of Memorial Church after a seminar when large pieces of the ceiling began falling. Concrete debris, broken tiles, and the remnants of splintered pews splayed across the dirtied red carpet leading up to the altar. In Green Library, the temblor shifted decorative columns, opened giant cracks in the dome and walls, and spilled an ocean of books—three-quarters of a million in the combined libraries. It seemed a miracle that no lives were lost. We might not have been so fortunate but for extensive seismic strengthening of several old and vulnerable buildings just two years before. Had Roble and the old wing of Green Library not received this treatment, it is almost certain that some students would have died.

More than 1,600 students were displaced that night. Classes were canceled as the registrar scrambled to find new locations for lectures scheduled in uninhabitable buildings. Evacuated from lightly damaged residences, students camped out in tents for a few days until it was safe to return. Others moved, often into more crowded and less desirable venues. A dozen or so residents of Roth, an all-women's row house, moved into Hoover House with me and Robin for a few weeks. Hoover House had thankfully already undergone significant seismic renovation, which was scheduled for many more buildings on campus. As always, the spirit of the student body buoyed the otherwise serious nature of the disaster. Members of the men's swimming team, amused by the expressed fear of one of their own, gathered around his Manzanita Trailer Park residence and shook it with all their might to mimic an aftershock, sending their teammates swarming out the door.

Ten years and $250 million after the Loma Prieta earthquake, Stanford had pieced itself together pretty well. In addition to investing hundreds of millions that had been set aside as a self-insurance fund for repairs, retrofitting, and restoration of buildings that did not meet seismic codes, emergency preparation policies had been fortified. Programs were in place to protect scientific equipment, store food supplies for campus residents, and establish hotlines and improved signage for emergency assembly points. Home to 95 percent of Santa Clara County's unreinforced masonry buildings, Stanford set out to buttress them all.

Some precautions showed a touch of wit. Each fall, around the anniversary of Loma Prieta, Geophysics Professor Gregory Beroza assumed the persona of dashing *Jeopardy!* host Alex Trebek, leading students in a lively game of earthquake *Jeopardy!* The game taught students what to do in the event of an earthquake, with insights into Stanford history in the mix.

Though some may accuse me of characteristically identifying a happy ending, I have to conclude that Loma Prieta was a great windfall for Stanford. It brought us to the attention of the Federal Emergency Management Agency, which helped significantly in our effort to rebuild, including buildings that had already been slated for retrofitting and would have been reinforced at Stanford's sole expense. Several heavily damaged facilities, including the Leland Stanford Junior Museum, Green Library, and Memorial Church, provided huge fund-raising opportunities, which succeeded with help from faculty and administrative leaders who rallied the donors. In other instances, iconic buildings were restored with strong support from donors who wanted to rescue them and receive credit for doing so. Ironically, Loma Prieta turned out to be one of the best things that could have befallen Stanford. As of this writing, the last reminder of Loma Prieta—Old Chemistry, condemned for years behind chain link fencing, has been demolished and replaced by the Science Teaching and Learning Center.

THE STANFORD SPIRIT

The buoyant, compassionate, and creative spirit of Stanford students was much in view in the weeks and months after the earthquake. People worried about one another more than about themselves, and the level of complaint was astonishingly low. Spontaneous acts, such as artwork on the wooden buttresses installed to support the Quad arches, brightened the scene. Looking back on my years as president, my interactions with students were the enduring highlight. Academic initiatives, campaign goals, and curricular development all lead back to creating an environment where talented students and faculty can flourish.

For most of my years as president after Robin and I were married, we served together as freshman advisors, which brought us closer than most to an intimate group of newly arrived students. Generally, I took the "techies," the students interested in pursuing math, science, and engineering, and Robin counseled the "fuzzies," those interested in the arts, social sciences, and humanities. We came together around meals and social events, including a memorable trip to a bowling alley! We still have close friendships with a handful of those former advisees, some of whom we consider part of our extended family.

An apt word for the general spirit of students at Stanford is communitarian. They take pleasure in being together, having common goals, and resolving those goals collectively. Their societies are generally cooperative and seldom competitive. One hears stories from elsewhere, for example, about clever concealments of library books. Nothing of that sort seems to happen at Stanford. Moreover,

Robin and Don preparing to shake hands with graduates and their families.

rather than an envy of others' successes, there is a culture of support and appreciation. Those cheering on the sidelines often include students who are achieving outstanding but different accomplishments of their own but who are delighted to applaud their roommate or friend who is succeeding at something equally worthy of acclaim.

Humility, too, is a word that comes to mind in distinguishing the Stanford spirit. Nearly every freshman arriving on campus each fall wonders silently, "Did they make a mistake?" "Do I really belong here?" Imagine checking into your dorm to find you are now living under the same roof as tennis great John McEnroe, child actor Fred Savage, teen actress Reese Witherspoon, or first daughter Chelsea Clinton. The list goes on. The ethos at Stanford is to treat such "celebrity" students like any other. To merit the attention of the student newspaper or a faculty member, they must do something notable in the Stanford context. Their rights to privacy are respected; they are not celebrated simply for being famous.

Among my academic heroes are the deans of admissions with whom I was privileged to work, who capably identified who belonged—and all the students I encountered did. The admissions team responsible for each incoming class waited as eagerly as the rest of us to see what these talented, witty, and modest young people would accomplish at Stanford and beyond. I was often struck by the late Dean Fred Hargadon's ability to discern from a slew of college applications which of those seventeen-year-olds are likely to make the most of what he called "the keys to privilege." His successor, Dean Jean Fetter, made equally marvelous assessments. Both of their records were impeccable.

There is a sense of humor that is characteristically Stanford as well. Though controversial on occasion, the shenanigans of the Leland Stanford Junior* University Marching Band, like the annual Wacky Walk into Stanford Stadium for Commencement, exhibit humor and audacity designed to entertain and enlighten. There is an intellectual wit that accompanies the antics, while costumes reflect current events and social puns. A critical piece of insider expertise is knowing *exactly* when to jump when the Band plays "It's All Right Now" after every touchdown or field goal. A glossary of campus locations reveals the silly shorthand reserved for those in-the-know: Mem Aud (Memorial Auditorium), CoHo (Coffee House), Mem Chu (Memorial Church), and Mem Claw (the fountain statue in front of the bookstore).

Although I had discerned much of the at-once laid back and intense student environment as a faculty member, becoming president brought still greater opportunities to recognize all that is truly unique about Stanford. An example of

---

*After students at the University of California, Stanford's arch rival on the gridiron, attempted to goad our fans with the sarcastic cry, "What's a *Junior* university?" the band's announcer was prompted thereafter to insert a pause between "Junior" and "University" ("Junior" being a reference to the name of Leland and Jane Stanford's son, Leland Junior, who perished in Florence from typhoid fever when he was only fifteen and in whose name our university was founded by his grieving parents.)

the casual, yet achievement-oriented spirit arose when I was asked to pose for a photo with the 1985 NCAA Championship Men's Swim Team. All the swimmers lined up in their Speedos, while I stood in the center in my presidential suit and tie. Team captain Pablo Morales seemed perfectly comfortable cajoling me despite his state of relative undress.

"Okay, Prez," he said, "What do you say if we repeat and win the championship again next year, it's us [swimmers] in the suits and you in the Speedo?"

Morales would eventually hold a record eleven NCAA championship titles, but at the time, he was a somewhat prematurely cocky swimmer sidling up to his university president. I naturally (and perhaps foolishly) accepted the challenge. Twelve months later, as fate (and talent and discipline) would have it, the Stanford Men's Swimming Team won the NCAA Championship again. In fact, the swimmers added the next two years, 1986 and 1987, to the string of excellence led by Coach Skip Kenney. True to my word, in the second year of their remarkable three-peat, I posed in a Speedo with a team of swimmers fully clad in jackets and ties. The team also took NCAA highest honors in 1992, the last year I was president.

When I first arrived at Stanford in 1960, I was a fan of student athletics, attending games with my family and faculty friends. The football team record that year was 0–10. Years later, as president, I regularly went to the locker room at halftime to hear what the coaches were saying to motivate the teams. It seemed uncanny

NCAA championship men's swimming, year 2 challenge, 1990.

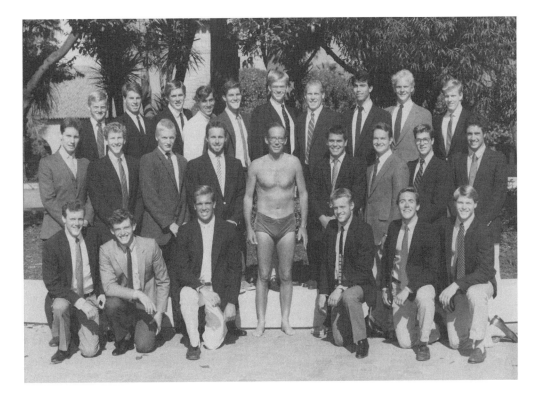

that the Cardinal was able to perform credibly over teams ranked far higher. Our capacity was once described by a dismissive sports writer as "reliably competitive."

Of all the plays in all the games I attended, nothing comes close to the last play in the Big Game of 1982—a last-second kickoff return so spectacular it has come to be known simply as "The Play." No matter the record of the California Golden Bears and the Stanford Cardinal in any given season, the Big Game is a high-stakes rivalry with a trophy all its own, an axe mounted on oak that is padlocked to the winning team's yell-leading squad to ensure against theft by the other side. Enthusiasm runs high. A victory is cause for enormous celebration.

Stanford had taken a 20–19 lead on a field goal. With four seconds left in the game, members of the Stanford Band began making their rag-tag way into the end-zone to launch the victory party. What could happen in just four seconds? But on the ensuing kickoff return, Cal made five lateral passes, and, undeterred by the scattered Stanford band members, scored the winning touchdown to earn a disputed 25–20 victory. There remains disagreement among Stanford loyalists over the legality of two of the laterals.

Four days after the game, student editors at the *Stanford Daily* penned and published a phony issue of the *Daily Californian* with the lead story proclaiming that the NCAA had declared Cal's last play to be dead. The bogus account handed victory to Stanford, sending Cal students into pandemonium until they realized the newspaper, distributed widely on the Berkeley campus, was a hoax.

Graduate student Cory Booker at Hoover House, 1992.

Regarding the band's controversial role in The Play, Stanford Athletic Director Andy Geiger commented that although the band did not cause The Play, it

was typical that they would have been in the wrong place at the wrong time. To this day, the incumbent Stanford band manager annually passes his baton to the newly elected manager when the Big Game clock indicates that four seconds remain.

As a fan of student achievement in every realm, it was a privilege I invoked as president to get to know some of the football players who wore the Cardinal jersey. One athlete who has gone on to greatness in the political and social justice arenas is Cory Booker, a champion of public service and a dear family friend. Initially recruited as a wide receiver, Cory was transformed into a tight end when coach Jack Elway took one look at him, handed him the keys to the weight room along with his jersey, and told him to get himself in shape to play a new position. Cory's service on the Council of (senior class) Presidents foreshadowed his meteoric political career—as a member of the Newark, New Jer-

"The Play,"
November 20,
1982.

Don and
Cory Booker
celebrating
Stanford's 1990
Big Game victory.

sey, City Council; Mayor of Newark; and U.S. Senator representing New Jersey. As an undergraduate, he volunteered at the Bridge Peer Counseling Center and organized Stanford students to help at-risk youth in East Palo Alto, presaging his devotion to mentorship and community service.

Cory finished his undergraduate degree in 1991, coinciding with the University's centennial. He elected to remain a fifth year, pursuing a master's degree, but had nowhere on campus to live. When I learned he was at risk of being homeless, I invited him to move in with us at Hoover House (the campus home of Stanford presidents), which cemented an already close friendship.

Cory made the All–Pacific Ten Academic team and was awarded a Rhodes Scholarship to study at Oxford University, where he earned an honors degree in U.S. history in 1994. He went on to earn his Juris Doctor in 1997 from Yale Law School, where he operated free legal clinics for low-income residents of New Haven, Connecticut. Baptist by religion, he was a founding member of the Chai Society (now the Eliezer Society) for the scholarly study of Jewish texts, and a Big Brother with Big Brothers Big Sisters of America, an organization he touts regularly. My family and I are exceptionally fond of him and enormously proud of his commitment to public service.

Running the Dish.

During my Stanford presidency, I adopted a practice of making myself available to anyone interested in having my ear, an open invitation to those who wished to join me on early mornings to "run the Dish," the dish-shaped radio telescope in the Stanford foothills behind the campus. A loop trail of approximately four miles snakes up the hill, past the satellite dish itself, along the ridge paralleling Alpine Road, and back down again. Among native grasses and live oaks, with the aroma of eucalyptus in the morning mist, it's a wonderful workout and a great way to start the day. Local community members treasure the undeveloped land as a natural resource, and many use it as a private park.

On the Tuesdays and Fridays I was in town, I would be joined on the Hoover House lawn at 6:30 AM, where students assembled and stretched. At times I would find nervous young fraternity men who clearly were out to complete a pledge task. The women's crew sometimes showed up and ran with me. More intense was PattiSue Plumer, who was holding international records at 5,000 meters. Another regular companion was Rob Levitsky, a local affordable housing guru who owns about a dozen rooming houses in Palo Alto, each named for a Grateful Dead song, in which Stanford students reside. Designed to replicate the popular, funky, co-op housing on campus, in which students live communally, preparing and eating meals together and carrying out household tasks by rotation, Levitsky's houses offer students below-market rent in somewhat historic homes with names like Terrapin Station, Box of Rain, and Truckin'. Levitsky is a real, albeit unheralded, friend of the University (though sometimes disputing its policies!) who continues to provide affordable housing opportunities for many Stanford students.

"Dash to the Dish with Don at Dawn" T-shirt, June 1992.

Years later, as my Stanford presidency drew to an end, my wife Robin planned a wonderful surprise to mark the end of the morning Dish runs. As I emerged onto the lawn for the last morning jog, hundreds of students, faculty, staff, and community members greeted me wearing red-and-white T-shirts reading, "Dash to the Dish at Dawn with Don." To my great surprise and delight, they joined in my final loop from Hoover House, across Junipero Serra Boulevard behind the main campus, up the trail into the foothills, across the ridge, and back, where we celebrated with balloons, fresh orange juice, and a "concert" by the Stanford Band. The fact that the band members were up and dressed at that hour of the morning was perhaps the biggest surprise of all!

FRIENDSHIPS AND ANGLING

As I noted earlier, my father taught me to fish when I was a young boy. Decades later, we came together again to fish—not just the two of us but with a small group of men who were among my closest friends. It included my friend Bill Kaufmann from Syracuse days, Norm Wessells (Dean of Humanities and Sciences), Colin Pittendrigh (cofounder of the Program in Human Biology), Al Hastorf (one of three provosts during my presidency), Pitch Johnson (a Silicon Valley venture capital pioneer who taught, at Stanford, the first venture capital course in a graduate school of business), David Kennedy (professor of history and a Pulitzer Prize winner), and, for a number of years, my father.

In coining the phrase "the duck syndrome"—that Stanford students are placid on the surface but paddling like hell underneath—Don was aware early on of what has become a much more significant part of student mental heath and well-being. It was another manifestation of his caring about students, about the many challenges they have to confront that he didn't.

—Patricia Karlin-Neumann

In a meeting of the faculty senate, after Don had recently banned all skateboards from the arcades and elsewhere, a few faculty members objected seriously to this action against civil liberties. Don sat there and listened to the objections and said, "I hear what you're saying and there are, in the course of running a University, many extraordinarily difficult decisions that are terribly vexing, especially when personal liberties are involved, and I can tell you that this was not one of them. This was in fact the easiest decision I've ever made."

—John Schwartz

Kennedy will always be remembered as the "Students' President"—a great teacher and student advisor, for sure, but much more. He welcomed students to join him on his morning runs; he walked and talked and laughed with them; he attended their rallies and performances; he even posed with the swim team—he in swimming apparel (what little there was of it) and the team in business suits—after they met the challenge of winning a second NCAA title. He brought scholars and singers, athletes and student leaders, graduate students and postdocs into his home and his daily life.

—Jim Gaither

I remember as a freshman going out to Sunken Diamond, and behind home plate is Don Kennedy, passionately engaged in the game, providing the constructive input to the umpire, who was clearly nearsighted. And I said, "That's my president, I like that guy!" He was not a passive observer. Passive is not his strong suit. Engaged is his strong suit.

—Kai Anderson

Don had an intense interest in sports. You didn't jog in those days, you ran against a clock, and his two-mile times were impressive. During his teaching years, there was Frisbee at noon in the Quad. Don played the game with gusto, of course. I recall him making spectacular catches while leaping into one of the manicured hedges that decorate the Quad. He was accomplished at the single and double-skip Frisbee delivery, but one time his throw was a little errant and his Frisbee hit a stylish young woman walking through the Quad. Her response, as I recall, was to address the future president of Stanford University as "you shithead."

—Ron Hoy

Don had an unbelievable passion for people he cared about—very broadly, since he cared about everyone. And for all things intellectual. But so enthusiastic, and so interested in anything you could tell him.

—Deborah Zarin

Kennedy's tenure will be most remembered for a few unqualified commitments: a love of students, an interest in their individual accomplishments as well as their aggregate success, and not just a willingness, but a desire to communicate with them on a personal level. And thanks to Kennedy's twelve years of service, these commitments are now an integral part of the presidential job description.

—Ari Richter, "Unqualified Comments." Stanford Daily, June 3, 1992.

We called ourselves the "Flood Society" in honor of Old Eben Flood, from the poem "Mr. Flood's Party" by Edwin Arlington Robinson, about nostalgia, loss and grieving:

> And Eben, having leisure, said aloud,
> For no man else in Tilbury Town to hear:
> "Well, Mr. Flood, we have the harvest moon
> Again, and we may not have many more;
> The bird is on the wing, the poet says,
> And you and I have said it here before.
> Drink to the bird." He raised up to the light
> The jug that he had gone so far to fill,
> And answered huskily: "Well, Mr. Flood,
> Since you propose it, I believe I will."[1]

A favorite spot was the northern California Bollibakka Fly Fishing Club, established in 1904 as a private fishing club on the McCloud River. The club surrounds more than 3,000 acres and more than seven miles of some of the best wild trout fishing in the American West. It is said by some that the McCloud River rainbows (*Salmo Shasta*) may be the most famous strain of trout on planet Earth. Pitch Johnson recalls that there was some discussion between the purist dry-fly fishermen and the guys who used nymphs and caught most of those beautiful McCloud River Rainbows. A day of fishing would be followed by an excellent dinner at the up-river lodge, complete with tablecloths and the best silver. In the spirit of Old Eben Flood, we raised a glass or two to both the birds and the fish!

Don and his father, Bill Kennedy, at the Stanford Athletic Awards Banquet, mid-1980s.

It was time away from the campus, savoring nature knee deep in a river abundant with trout, sharing evenings of food, wine, and companionship with dear friends. After each adventure, I returned to Stanford reinvigorated, ready for whatever awaited me.

RESPONSIBILITIES—
TO STANFORD AND TO MYSELF

The mission of the University is to train leadership for the successor generation and to enrich the store of basic knowledge so as to power a cycle of improvement through innovation and extensions of culture. Carrying out this task was a privilege for me, one I accepted with a kind of astonished gratitude. Among other things, it gave me a perch from which to view the most extraordinary young people in our country as they passed by.

In response to those who asked what my parting wisdom might be with regard to the role of university president, I suggested that they should pay attention to students and ask them the hard questions to find out whether programs are really accomplishing anything. And get out of the office. If you sit in your office and wait around for what comes to you, it will be mostly sorrows. You need to get out and really find out what's going on. Make commitments that force you to participate at the working level in the institution, like doing some teaching, giving the occasional lecture, or interviews with the campus newspaper. Get out to student residences and take first-year advisees every other year to discover where they are finding the road bumpy. Meet with the faculty often, in both formal and informal circumstances. And get out on the road and talk to alumni to find out what is bothering them. The president should be a strong national spokesperson on issues in which education has a legitimate voice and for the institutions values.

In that list of presidential responsibilities, I neglected to add that the one thing a president does not do is get divorced while in office. Nonetheless, early in the fall of 1986, I discussed with Jeanne my hope that we could end our marriage in a mutually respectful way. Another conversation took place in Jacksonville, Florida, where Stanford was playing Clemson in the Gator Bowl. I said that I loved our children, now in their twenties, and that they had become wonderful young women thanks in large part to Jeanne's attention as a mother, but that we had too few common interests to hold the marriage together any longer. We were not focused on the same priorities, and with my new obligations to the University's centennial campaign I asked her to consider a separation.

To accommodate Jeanne, which I wanted to do in every way I could, I actually moved out of Hoover House for a few months before our impending divorce was publicly announced. Jeanne had calendared several events that were important to her, including the wedding of two staff members we had agreed to host at the house; I did not want to be an impediment to her ability to follow through on these commitments or to plan her return to the Palo Alto home we had rented out for several years. I took a small apartment at Oak Creek Apartments, a complex adjacent to the campus, at which more than one separating spouse has logged time.

It was a difficult period. The announcement of our divorce prompted questions about why, and eventually, which of us might have provoked the decision. Nobody knew exactly what to do or say about it. And there were major consequences, almost immediately. One was the resignation of Henry "Hank" Riggs, who had stepped up as Stanford's Vice President for Development following Joel Smith's departure. Riggs may have felt that a divorce by the president in the midst of the most ambitious fund-raising campaign in U.S. higher education was unacceptably adverse. Shortly after he learned of it, he left Stanford.

Obviously, the decision to divorce was not one I made lightly. I knew it would have consequences affecting attitudes among the faculty as well as observers of Stanford and that it had to be conducted in a thoughtful and respectful way. Although Jeanne and I had a friendly relationship based on mutual regard and love for our daughters, I had become impatient and I think a little difficult to live with over the first part of my presidency. Despite that history and Jeanne's usual willingness to support what I wanted to do, her input became ever less apropos to my increasingly complex professional life. I was willing to weather the negative consequences, confident in my ability to survive them and that my presidency would thrive.

But the other shoe was yet to drop—some years earlier, I had fallen deeply in love with Robin Hamill, then Stanford's Director of Real Estate Programs and Lands Management. My love for Robin was not, however, the reason for my divorce. What eventually precipitated my decision to divorce was my increasing sense of the limitations of my marriage to Jeanne and our divergent interests.

ROBIN'S RETURN TO STANFORD

A Stanford undergraduate ('68) and law student ('78), Robin was a respected colleague, an active university citizen willing to serve on committees and take on responsibility. She was deeply compassionate—a side I discovered during my visits to Joel Smith. Robin visited him as well, and occasionally one of us was walking in as the other walked out of his campus home.

In 1980, Robin Hamill was a single mother of two, living in Los Angeles pursuing a career in entertainment law at a law firm that required long, grueling hours, disrupting family life. The disruptions became so frequent that Robin's eight-year-old daughter threatened to take her younger brother and live with their father if Robin could not get home at night in time for dinner. Distraught, Robin vowed to make a change. She contacted some of her law school faculty friends and others to whom she had been close at Stanford, and they encouraged her to find work there.

The most well-known Kennedy trait was his personal touch. His jogs to the Dish, his constant attendance at athletic events, his visits to student dorms, and his regular performances with his wife, Robin, in Gaieties all indicated to the Stanford community that Kennedy was an open president.   — *Juthymas Harntha,*
"Kennedy's Style: An Asset, Liability." Stanford Daily, May 29, 1992, pp. 1, 6–7.

Memory teems with recollections of Don—from his gallant effort to teach me biology as a Stanford undergraduate to fly-fishing with him on the McCloud River and to the countless occasions when our surnames led to a confusion of identities. Of all those occasions, the one that yielded the most lasting amusement took shape in Tearney's, the once-upon-a-time men's clothing store in the Stanford Shopping Center. When I presented my card to make payment, the clerk noticed my last name and asked, "Oh, are you Don Kennedy's son?" Of course I went home and immediately shared the moment with Don. Ever after we greeted each other as "son," and "dad." I chuckle about that even as I write this—and, to be honest, swell with a bit of pride, too, just to be associated with someone for whom I have long had so much affection and regard.   —*David M. Kennedy*

He saw what was wonderful about the world and about being a human being. Others might have been oppressed by the same job, or simply felt that they could and should do it; but for Don it was more like "This is great! I love having my own fire department."
—*Howard Fields*

I did a brochure for a conference at which Don would be giving a luncheon address. I did pictures and write-ups of the other participants but forgot to include Don—just "the president will speak." It was the first one I'd worked on. The phone rang and it was Don on the other end. He couldn't have been nicer. He said "I just saw this brochure and I just thought I'd mention that having the president come to a city is a big deal, and it probably would be good to have a picture or a write-up of me." I was mortified; but he did it in such a kind way, with such grace—always the teacher. He wasn't critical; he was just helping me to do a better job next time. It was something I needed to learn, and I've never forgotten it.   —*Carolyn Manning*

Don was an alumni director's dream president, noted for his energy and enthusiasm, a knowledge base and curiosity seldom found in a single package, a superb speaking ability, strong academic values and instincts, and a genuine love of people and scholarship.
—*Bill Stone*

He had so much charisma, a friendly informality and approachability—and always flexible, willing to speak at a moment's notice.   —*Carolyn Manning*

He was extremely well liked and highly respected, always warm and generous, with a great curiosity and a wonderful sense of humor.   —*Larry Horton*

He's a great writer and wrote his own speeches. Almost every year his talk at the graduation ceremony was better than the commencement speaker's.   —*Bob Freelen*

At one of his early commencement addresses, before he said a word, he had a loud, long,
standing ovation from the students. I had never seen a student body respond to a university president that way.   —*Tim Goldsmith*

I first met Don when I was a first-year professor. Imagine what it was like to have the
president of the University know your name and what you would be teaching. I was
blown away. But I came to understand that it was vintage Don. He was a terrific president and leader because he always cared first and foremost about students, faculty, and
staff—he understood that a university is only great because of its people. Don was an
important influence on me—and on the way that I tried to lead. I learned a lot from him.
                                                                        —*Condoleezza Rice*

Inside Hoover
House, early
1990s

Among the many interviews she endured during a two-day whirlwind assessment of her ability to manage faculty/staff housing programs was one with then-Provost Donald Kennedy. The job was to solve the problem of faculty recruitment and retention, which was a significant issue due largely to the high cost of Bay Area housing. Robin was convincing in her knowledge, her strategic approach, and her enthusiasm. She got the appointment and returned to campus in the fall of 1980, living in graduate student housing as she had during law school.

Over the next seven years, Robin excelled and the job expanded. She became director of nearly all nonacademic campus real estate and a member of the senior staff of the vice president of business and finance, who reported directly to me. Robin attended many meetings—and a few retreats—at which I was present. Our friendship and mutual esteem grew out of those meetings as well as our passion for Stanford. As a university citizen, Robin stepped up, agreeing to serve as staff on the committee seeking to hire a new provost. When the Super Bowl came to Stanford in 1985, Robin agreed to serve as "host" for some of the visiting dignitaries, including Senator Ted Kennedy and his delegation. For many years, we were excellent colleagues—and colleagues only.

The turning point in our relationship came in the wake of personal trauma for Robin. One night, with her two young children asleep upstairs, a man who was a well-known campus figure whom Robin had every reason to trust, paid her an unexpected evening visit at her campus home, ostensibly to discuss a presentation she had made earlier that day. Without hesitation, she invited him in and, in a turn of events so extremely unexpected that she was caught completely off guard, the man forced himself on her against her will.

Fearing for her security and that of her young children and the possibility of a repeat assault, Robin turned to a friend, then working for the Stanford Police Department, who had provided child care in exchange for a room when she first arrived on campus in 1980. She swore the officer to secrecy, fearing for her safety and her job if she reported the assault. He repeatedly urged her to report the incident to Stanford Police Chief Marvin Herrington, whom she had long known as a colleague on the business and finance senior staff. She remained reluctant but, without her knowledge or consent, her friend decided on his own to report the matter to Herrington.

When Chief Herrington called Robin, he explained that he could not keep the matter to himself, that he needed to know the identity of the perpetrator to protect other women on campus. It took several weeks and many such conversations but, in the end, Robin gave him permission to tell me what had transpired and to convey her fear about the potential loss of her job.

Apart from my outrage and overwhelming concern for the victim, Robin was my friend. After several weeks, when I thought she could manage it, I met with her in my office to offer consolation and support. Robin recalls my being far more compassionate than she would ever have expected. She reminds me that

I told her, "I don't care if you were walking down the middle of the Quad with no clothes on, a rape would not be your fault." In sharing the trauma and dealing quietly but decisively with her assailant, I came to see her in a different light, precipitating an unexpected leap in our emotional intimacy.

Over the months that followed, I did my best to discourage Robin from having any expectations about a future with me, telling her, on one occasion, that I was a "bad bet." She understood that I would likely never end my marriage, at least not during my presidency for which, at that time, there was no end in sight. I never felt any pressure from Robin to change my marital situation. When the time came that I did so, it was entirely at my own initiative and independent of my relationship with Robin.

In the end, I was not doing well at hiding my love for Robin, which raised speculation and a cascade of issues related to indiscretion. The announcement of my divorce from Jeanne came in February 1987, following a Stanford Travel Study trip to Antarctica in which Jeanne and I had to interact with a great many other people. Jeanne behaved beautifully through the whole ordeal even though she wasn't happy with me, and neither were our children, by then both grown women. It was soon after the carefully crafted public announcement of my divorce that my relationship with Robin became public knowledge.

We were married on the Friday after Thanksgiving in 1987, although I'm sure the timing, so soon after my divorce became final, caused a lifted eyebrow here and there. Cantor David Unterman of Congregation Beth Am officiated; Rabbi Richard Block offered a blessing. Robin's Judaism has provided an enduring spiritual foundation that I respect, although I never chose to convert.

Many years earlier, I had addressed a meeting of some fifteen senior staffers at Stanford selected to learn more about university operations, of which Robin was one. I recall Robin's asking a lot of questions I couldn't answer, but I remember one that she asked me pointedly—"Do you think you would have gotten to where you are if you hadn't been subsidized by your wife, who took care of everything at home and let you devote yourself to your career?" She was very concerned with giving credit where credit was due, and I did not hesitate to answer that no, without the "subsidy" of Jeanne's traditional role as wife and mother I could not have achieved what I had. Robin was hardly a bra burning feminist, but professional injustice was—and continues to be—intolerable to her.

Of course, I was in love with Robin long before the announcement of my divorce. We share so many mutual interests and activities—a deep interest in politics, policy, and the way politics make policy. We love the many Stanford traditions and the zeal the students exude. Among those traditions is one called Full Moon on the Quad, in which freshman girls are transformed into Stanford women by the kiss of a senior. When it was finally legitimate for us to do so, Robin and I joined the students on the Quad under the light of the moon, and just before I leaned in to kiss her, I recall asking Robin, "Does it count if it's a Harvard guy?"

A quiet moment in the Hoover House front hall before sixty guests arrive for dinner during the Centennial campaign, early 1990s.

When you have a promising and important love in your life to whom you are not married, it raises your attention to future possibilities. It is a frame-of-mind changer. My relationship with Robin was important to my state of mind and my wish to make sense out of a difficult transition in my life. I remember discussing my inner turmoil with John Gardner, a hero of public service whom I deeply admired and considered a close friend. His advice moved me profoundly, and I took it to heart: "You do not want to die with the music still in you."

THE PRICES PAID FOR PERSONAL CHOICES

Few personal choices come without price tags, and my decision to marry Robin certainly cost us in ways we anticipated and in ways we did not. At the time our engagement was announced, Robin was running nearly all of Stanford's nonacademic real estate. Among her duties were faculty housing programs, representing Stanford at local council meetings, and identifying a location for the soon-to-be launched Stanford in Washington program.

It wasn't long after our announcement that Provost Jim Rosse invited Robin to meet with him. He raised concerns about the public aspects of her position, now that she was to be married to the University president. He suggested it might be unseemly for the president's wife to be blasted publicly—at meetings and in the local press—by the opposition to any given real estate project. In short, he indicated (in prettier words) that the personal decision to marry me would cost her the high-profile and challenging job she loved.

Not one to be dismissed lightly, Robin insisted she would not resign her position unless she could continue to work for Stanford, albeit in a different capacity. The compromise reached was that Robin would join the Office of the General Counsel, as an attorney for half her time and as business manager for the other half. In the event, she was treated quite poorly, given a very small, windowless office and excluded for a year from the office's weekly staff meeting—the only attorney on the staff to be excluded. Robin walked away from a very senior administrative position—one of very few women at her level—and was, in essence, sent to Coventry. I never asked, so I don't know, whether this long fall was intended to be punitive. In recent years, Robin has expressed her disappointment in herself for not having refused to step down. To this day I am grateful that she does not resent me for the acute professional setback she endured to spend her life with me.

Despite early apprehension and ambiguity, the Board of Trustees finally came around to our new reality. A silver lining of the Centennial Campaign was the opportunity it presented to introduce Robin directly to the various Stanford key stakeholders. They got to experience firsthand her intelligence, her enthusiasm for the University, and her interest in the fund-raising activities so essential to our eventual success. It was a great opportunity to demonstrate to trustees, alumni, and donors that Robin and I were campaigning together, with equal energy, and participating together as well as anyone could have asked. Warren Christopher (Secretary of State during the Carter Administration), then Chairman of the Board of Trustees, thought it important that the board put its official stamp of approval on my new marriage. To that end, the trustees hosted a large party at Hoover House about a month after our wedding, to which were invited all current and former trustees, major donors, and many faculty. This was quite separate from the wedding reception we threw for ourselves at the Garden Court Hotel in Palo Alto.

Who could have foretold that just a few years later the two receptions would be erroneously conflated in the press covering the indirect cost controversy, and that we would be accused of staging an elaborate wedding reception for ourselves at university expense? Still, it occurs to me that a lot of personal capital was expended to attain the personal life that I wanted, and perhaps that capital might

Russian President Gorbachev and Don on the Memorial Auditorium stage, May 1990.

have come in handy a few years later during the indirect cost scandal. It is a question whose answer we will never know.

A WELCOME INTERLUDE

A glorious respite from the marital and indirect cost controversies was the May 1990 campus visit of Soviet President Mikhail Gorbachev as part of his U.S. tour. Hoping for a glimpse of the world-renowned couple, community members, faculty, students, and staff lined Palm Drive, the post card perfect promenade to Stanford's front door and the route the Gorbachevs would take up the oval drive to the Main Quadrangle. Robin and I were at the curb to greet them, host them on a walking tour of the campus, and escort them to Memorial Auditorium where President Gorbachev was to give a nationally televised live address.

Despite all the Secret Service protection afforded a foreign head of state as well as his own Soviet security detail, Gorbachev turned out to be quite a crowd plunger! He could scarcely contain himself from extending a hand for a high-five and diving into the crowds to embrace their fervent hospitality, donning a Stanford baseball cap handed him from someone in the throng. His wife, Raisa, could not have been lovelier; she and Robin enjoyed an amiable walking tour.

When, at last, our entourage landed backstage in the Green Room at Memorial Auditorium, we took a moment to relax and regroup before taking the stage. The Gorbachevs and the Kennedys were joined by Jim Gaither, Chairman of the Board of Trustees; and the Hon. George P. Shultz, recently returned to the Stanford faculty after serving as secretary of state under President Reagan.

With much help from Secretary Shultz regarding protocol and expectations, I had, over many weeks and multiple drafts, crafted an introduction—not of Gorbachev to Stanford, for he needed no introduction—but of Stanford to Gorbachev. I had reviewed my brief remarks with Shultz, who had offered helpful pointers to prevent any foot-in-mouth occurrence. With Gorbachev's first visit to the United States and to Stanford being televised to millions of people worldwide, you can imagine my shock and dismay when I stepped up to the podium, pulled my speech from my pocket, and looked down to find only the pronunciation guide for the names in the Soviet delegation! No speech! I recovered, working from memory (fortunately, I always wrote my own speeches), and even got a few compliments from those who had heard me rehearse the scripted version, saying they thought the version delivered from memory made for a superior speech!

Gorbachev was in every respect a delightful visitor. It was a joy to host him and his visit put Stanford in the national spotlight in a very positive way.

CHAPTER 8

OF PATENTS, PROFITS,
AND THEIR ENSUING EFFECTS

IN HIS POST-WORLD WAR II LETTER in support of federal science, Vannevar Bush envisioned the future in a sweeping metaphor. Science, he wrote, was to be an "endless frontier" in which government-supported basic research created a "science commons"[1] that could be made broadly available for commercialization. As head of the U.S. Office of Scientific Research and Development, through which almost all wartime military research and development was carried out, Bush argued for government support of basic research in universities and laid out the case for putting that investment in the very places where the next generation of scientists were to be trained.

For me, the choice of metaphor suggested the Western frontier explored by Meriwether Lewis and William Clark. Like the basic sciences, the Lewis and Clark expedition was not directed toward a specific goal but was rather a loosely guided foray to find, describe, and ultimately understand what was new and unknown, an exploration without a limiting boundary. The frontier image implied not only unknown but unowned space—a commons inviting free access without the hindrance of proprietary claims. Citing the limited funding available at the time for universities and research institutes, Bush argued that if U.S. research institutions are to meet the rapidly increasing demands of industry and government for new scientific knowledge, their basic research should be strengthened by the use of public funds. For a time, that vision worked perfectly. Tax money supported good science practiced in universities and a few independent laboratories. By 1980, however, Congress was questioning why the commercial and economic benefits publicly supported research was meant to yield hadn't materialized.

At that time, federal research contracts and grants were requiring researchers to assign to the government the patent rights to inventions they developed with federal funds. The rationale was that intellectual property rights on things developed through government-sponsored research should belong to all the people. Yet, if something belongs to all the people, it belongs to nobody; thus there is no incentive to *develop* the idea that belongs to everybody.

Hoping to jump-start the flagging economy of the late 1970s and noting that the federal government had gained very little from the number of patents produced by government sponsored research, Senators Birch Bayh of Indiana and Bob Dole of Kansas introduced the Patent and Trademark Law Amendments Act, which changed the assignment of patent rights, giving a university, small business, or nonprofit organization—or the inventors themselves, if the institutions agreed—the ownership of inventions developed with federal funds. Although taxpayers had financed much of the research supported by government grants awarded, for example, by the National Institutes of Health, this was an extraordinary gift by the government. Under the Bayh–Dole amendments of 1980, the government would relinquish intellectual property rights on tax-supported research to the researchers who could patent their discoveries—or their institutions could do so on their behalf—and develop them commercially.

In an editorial published in *Science*, I continued the "endless frontier" motif, noting that Bayh–Dole did for intellectual property what the Homestead Act of 1862 had done for real property. In both cases the transfer from public to private hands was implemented by purposeful government intervention, accomplished through statute. Just as the Homestead Act had transformed the frontier from public land into a checkerboard of holdings owned by private settlers, allocating 160-acre tracts virtually free to those who would promise to live on and improve them, Bayh–Dole moved research into private hands, while extending such incentives as a reduced tax on capital gains and more generous allowances for deductions.

But, like the Homestead Act, which did not envision vast differences in land use, available water, conflicting claims, and range wars, the endless frontier of Bayh–Dole replicates the problems of private enclosure—patent disputes, hostile encounters between public and private ventures, and faculty distress over corporate deals with their universities. The benefits—growth of industry jobs and hundreds of companies contributing research at no cost to the taxpayer— were balanced by new problems for faculty and university administrators: conflicts of interest, licensing policy, royalty distribution, and the propriety of commercial relations.

BAYH-DOLE COMES TO CAMPUS

The Bayh–Dole amendments opened new opportunities for our faculty: a professor could patent through Stanford a new technology for gene splicing, start a company funded by others, and then build an independent off-campus laboratory to work on commercial applications. Administering such arrangements, however, presented challenges for the University. If we hoped for the science commons that Vannevar Bush offered, the Bayh–Dole amendments now allowed new possibilities for limited enclosure. But with the opportunity that intellectual property rights presented came new disputes over who stood to profit.

Assignment of patent rights to the university or the professorial inventor presented a terrific opportunity but also a challenge within the university political structure. If a patented invention were to generate licensing fees and royalties, who would reap the profits? The inventor personally? His or her department or school? The general university budget? We had an immediate question at hand in the case of Professor Stanley Cohen who, along with his colleague Herbert Boyer of the University of California, San Francisco, had developed recombinant DNA technology. Stanford and UC shared the patent equally on the basis of a National Institutes of Health waiver made shortly before the passage of Bayh–Dole.

Early in my presidency, I met with Cohen to discuss how Stanford should distribute its half of the patent proceeds. It was a short meeting, less than thirty minutes, over a cold sandwich shared in my office. Cohen proposed that a third of the distributions from patent rights should be awarded to the inventor and his laboratory, another third to his department, and the last third to the school—in his case, the School of Medicine. That sounded fair to me, and it is how we handled the matter of the distribution of patent rights proceeds throughout my presidency. Later, looking at what other places were doing with licensing revenues, we saw that they were using about the same formula, so I think we may have been instrumental in setting a pattern for dealing with royalty or licensing revenue.

WHO OWNS? WHO GAINS?

During my presidency, Professor Irving Weissman and his postdoctoral collaborator Michael McCune had made an extraordinary series of discoveries about the formation of the blood elements and the immune system in mammals. They found that they could transplant embryonic tissues containing stem cells from humans and thus reconstitute an entire immune system of genetically different origin in an immunologically suppressed strain of mice. The prospect that the human immune system could be created in a mouse raised the potential for commercial development, which we all agreed might better be pursued through an off-campus venture than in their university laboratory. The work required for commercialization was not novel; the basic methodology for isolating hematopoietic stem cells had already been developed. The scale was much larger than could be accomplished in Weissman's crowded campus laboratory, which also accommodated projects he was pursuing as a principal investigator for the Howard Hughes Medical Institute. Accordingly, Weissman decided to organize a company to pursue commercialization of the stem cell technology.

Weissman consulted with Stanford colleagues and lawyers, and with me in particular, about the specific arrangements. He was careful to distinguish which work would go over to the new company, to be known as Systemix, and which would stay in his university lab. He accepted no formal position with the new company, and Stanford made no financial investment in the new venture. No scientific work moved back and forth across the divide we constructed in the original agreement. I couldn't have imagined a more carefully conceived understanding, essentially creating a firewall between the two labs.

So bright did Systemix's prospects seem that the large pharmaceutical firm Sandoz purchased a major interest. The stock swap was negotiated on very favorable terms to the Systemix shareholders and, as a result, the founders, including Weissman, made a great deal of money, which was quickly noted by the *Wall Street Journal.* When that article appeared, the Howard Hughes Medical Institute leadership expressed deep concern over Weissman's financial gain. In an extended series of negotiations with Weissman and Stanford, they took the position that the level of equity held by Weissman was inappropriate. They demanded that he take divestiture despite the nonexistence of any equity limitations in the agreements they had made with Stanford or with Weissman. A sharp argument ensued, with complaints from the Howard Hughes Medical Institute reaching such a strident level that we eventually determined the relationship had to be severed. Weissman continued in his faculty position, unfortunately without the research support of the Howard Hughes Medical Institute.

The reaction on campus was also swift and not all positive. Most scientific colleagues who knew Weissman were happy for him, but the reaction of some contained equal parts of resentment and envy. As the case illustrates, even the best-intentioned policies sometimes generate a result that people have difficulty accepting. The vision of a professor getting rich—really rich—just gets under people's skin. Teaching and scholarship are supposed to be activities that bring their own psychic rewards and don't require financial ones. I don't think this is a fair attitude, but all my experience tells me that it represents political reality and that universities and their faculties need to recognize it and live with it.

SHARING THE INTELLECTUAL "WEALTH"

One might ask why the commercialization of scientific research falls in a "gray area" when it comes to earnings for work initiated in the university setting. Faculty members in all sorts of disciplines have the opportunity to profit from work undertaken as part of their university responsibilities, but the rewards in both reputation and remuneration are limited.

Faculty members who do exciting, important research with obvious product applications have attracted the attention of various people in Silicon Valley who are either eager partners wanting to participate in the development themselves or venture capitalists who want to invest. The faculty inventor might therefore be invited to join the board of a new company that is building a commercial portfolio based on her basic research, or to become the chief scientific officer, or to serve as advisor to the new company. A chief scientist might be tempted to persuade a talented graduate student with whom she has been working on a related problem to abandon her academic pursuit to work at the new offshore company, where she could earn a salary and receive stock options or other benefits unavailable to a graduate student.

The Committee on Graduate Studies took up this conflict and determined correctly that it is not in the best interests of our students to veer from their research projects, which they hope will eventually lead to employment and their own path to success. Although we reached agreement in principle, this conflict left Stanford in a bit of a free-for-all as to what rules apply to faculty—with whom Stanford has diverse relationships, ranging from landlord (many Stanford faculty own long-term leases for the land their campus homes occupy) to employer, to procurer of research funds, to seeker of philanthropic contributions. The relationship between an off-campus and a university laboratory, each engaging the same scientist, also raises issues. Would it be all right, for example, for a company to make a gift to Stanford to support the work of its scientific advisor's research on campus? Or for a university fund-raiser to seek a gift from the private lab based on "indebtedness" to the original research that spawned its opportunity? What about the potentially lucrative opportunity for the university to invest in the new offshore company the faculty member has helped to launch?

My friend Derek Bok, a Stanford graduate and then president of Harvard, found himself in the pages of *The New York Times* as he weighed the opportunity to invest Harvard endowment funds in an outside faculty enterprise. Compelling to Bok was the inequity that would inevitably result by investing in one professor's company and not another's. He ultimately decided—prudently, I believe—that the university ought not invest in faculty ventures. The newspaper account challenged all of us operating in the new Bayh–Dole environment to consider issues ranging from conflict of interest to conflict of commitment.

THE CONFERENCE AT PAJARO DUNES

At this point, it seemed that it might be constructive to bring together a group of university administrators along with a number of their governing board members and some thoughtful members of the business community. I came to this in part from a sense that Derek Bok and I needed to find some way of sharing with others what we were learning. Extra encouragement for such a meeting came from a conversation I had with Dr. Arnold Beckman, with whom I had been visiting in search of support for a new Stanford center. As a young faculty member at Caltech, Beckman had been a marvelous developer of new technologies like the pH meter. He then chose to work independently on his projects rather than continue on a university faculty. Our discussion led me to ask whether he would join a meeting to discuss the issues being raised by the Bayh–Dole amendments and the new roles being undertaken by universities and their faculties.

A Stanford alumnus offered access to an appropriate seaside venue at Pajaro Dunes on the Northern California coast. In addition to Beckman, we invited the presidents of the University of California, Caltech, and MIT. To insure the inclusion of business leaders in the conversation, we invited the six presidents to bring along trustees or especially knowledgeable alumni. We felt that the subject matter was complex and challenging, so we risked keeping the meeting private and did not invite journalists. For that, we received the expected criticism but hoped that the discussions would at least yield guidelines for managing the difficulties that were likely to arise in the new era of patents, licensing, and off-campus laboratories.

We were delighted by the diversity of the participants as well as the degree of technical knowledge needed to deal with a sharply changed institutional environment. One of the first general guidelines reached by the group focused on the issue of conflicting commitments: Professors' relationships with commercial firms should not interfere with their primary responsibilities of teaching and research. The participants called special attention to the problem in biotechnology, where the needs of off-campus commercially focused laboratories might burden professors with managerial duties and ownership responsibilities that would compete with their university obligations.

The Pajaro Dunes meeting also tackled troublesome problems that had arisen in recent historical settings. At that time, serious questions had been raised, in particular by the aforementioned *New York Times* story in which Harvard's president had been invited to coinvest in a company founded by one of its faculty members. President Bok had declined that opportunity, and in the Pajaro discussion we focused on that issue. The guideline discouraged that kind of coinvestment largely on the grounds that it placed the university in the position of potentially benefiting from one faculty member's work and not from research done by a colleague. Given the choice to invest selectively, how then could the university allocate salary, space, or other resources in a way that would be seen as evenhanded?

The Pajaro Dunes group began discussions about ways in which the universities might, or should, regulate other aspects of the relationship with the faculty member who owns an off-campus laboratory and has an active research program in the university. We touched on a number of topics without attempting to set formal guidelines. For example, should the university accept or discourage gifts from the offshore company designed to support the on-campus research program? Should the professor encourage graduate students in the on-campus laboratory to interrupt their thesis work and move over to the company? At Stanford we introduced policies designed to discourage both of these practices.

Not discussed at Pajaro Dunes were a few other issues regarding potential conflicts of interest with off-campus companies. Suppose one or more members of the Board of Trustees have undertaken financial or management roles in a company's formation? Should academic leaders in the university undertake roles in the governance or management of the new company? In this new environment, such problems continue to pose challenges to universities.

In regard to conflicts of interest, in which the faculty member's position as an independent researcher is at odds with statements he might make to advance the commercial value of the company he helped spawn, we examined where the faculty member's primary commitment lies and determined it is to the university employer. Eventually, we developed a policy at Stanford that limited faculty to no more than one day a week devoted to outside consulting, or thirteen days per academic quarter. Otherwise, primary obligations are to the university, focused on the teaching and research missions. According to Stanford's policy, either the provost or president had to approve outside faculty involvements from both conflict-of-interest and conflict-of-commitment perspectives.

BALANCING PRIORITIES

Professor Carl Djerassi, celebrated as the father of the birth control pill, took a different approach from Weissman in managing his faculty and commercial interests. Djerassi, who had a long personal history of research discoveries that turned into commercial successes, actually reduced his Stanford professorship to half time so that he could devote the other half to his commercial interests. He maintained a rigorous separation between the work done at Stanford and the work done in his commercial ventures.

Another case arose at Harvard. Professor Walter Gilbert, a winner of the Nobel Prize, helped to found a company called Biogen, maintaining laboratories in both the new company and at Harvard. The problem arose when he announced technological advances benefiting the company in a press conference identifying him both as a principal at Biogen and a Harvard University professor. In which

Pajaro Dunes Conference: Don, Derek Bok, and David Saxon.

role was he speaking? After the announcement, Biogen stock advanced significantly, putting Harvard in the unwitting position of potentially being viewed as helping to hype a stock. The blurry lines were severed when Gilbert ultimately left his faculty position to work full-time at Biogen. The case is instructive as universities continue to grapple with the careful relationships between inventors, entrepreneurs, and investors, on the one hand, and faculty members, graduate students, and trustees on the other.

CHAPTER 9

MONEY MATTERS

The Indirect Costs of Doing University Business

GOOGLE MY NAME, and your search results will be populated with articles and items pertaining to an arcane accounting practice that gained national headlines in the early 1990s—the recovery of the indirect costs of government-sponsored scientific work by the nation's research universities. The subject was a controversy in which government and media allegations of wrongdoing were amplified to indict Stanford as a first-order villain that bilked the taxpayer out of millions of dollars for such extraneous expenses as maintenance of a luxury yacht, expensive home furnishings, and lavish parties. As is so often the case, appearances belie the truth. But it took enormous heartache, time, and expense for Stanford's leaders to eventually obtain exoneration. Yet, although the allegations had been front-page news, the exoneration was buried in the back pages. In the end, I would leave a job I loved.

Indirect costs are exactly as one would expect from the name—expenses that are related to scientific research projects but not directly attributable to them, such as utilities, depreciation of buildings, and administration of departments and the university. The government representatives assigned to Stanford had previously always understood that there are certain indirect costs associated with research that cannot be charged to a particular project, and that universities are entitled to reimbursement for these as well as the costs of direct research. For example, some of the journals and books in university libraries are essential references for scientists, and others clearly are not. The tortuous process of counting how many scientific journals are checked out by scientists, in contrast with how many Regency novels are borrowed by others, is ideally the basis for calculating the percentage of library expenses attributable to the indirect cost of research. In practice, however, by analyzing the traffic and looking carefully at the pattern of book and journal purchases, it is possible to arrive at a reasonable estimate of how much activity is research related. If the estimate were 30 percent, that percentage would then be treated as a cost "pool" for convenience in auditing. The government would then assume that 30 percent of all library costs were attributable to research and reimburse the university for applicable library expenses based on that rate.

Indirect costs are calculated by creating the pools associated with each function, determining the fractions of each pool attributable to research and instruction, and then negotiating an overall percentage rate for the institution. Because an increasing number of expense categories directly related to research were excluded from indirect cost recovery during the ten-year period for which the overall negotiated rate was contracted, the rate appeared to increase although in fact remaining fairly constant in terms of actual cost recovery. This apparent increase contributed to some of the misunderstandings animating the controversy.

Most universities used a default rate for calculating indirect costs as set forth by a federal Office of Management and Budget paper, known as A-21. But some, particularly research-intensive universities, were not sufficiently reimbursed under A-21 and were allowed to sign supplementary agreements called memoranda of understanding (MOUs). The MOUs were negotiated with the Office of Naval Research (ONR), the federal agency administering government research contracts with Stanford. The MOUs were supposed to be audited annually by another federal office, the Defense Contract Audit Agency (DCAA). But for reasons never explained—overwork, incompetence, or carelessness—the Stanford audits had not been done for ten years, beginning in 1981, despite frequent requests by Stanford to finish them. Add to that the fact that the ONR used a different method than other federal agencies in recording MOUs, dividing, for example, two basic agreements for equipment and buildings into subparts, making it appear that there were thirty-two MOUs instead of two. This made it appear that Stanford's coverage was excessive when in fact it was only more highly catalogued.

The issue was the validity of the MOUs, which Stanford had negotiated with the government in good faith following a complex set of rules. In the end Stanford was cleared of any wrongdoing, but the incomplete audits, the ONR's inflated number of MOUs, and inevitable small errors prompted a disturbed whistle-blower and a rancorous congressional committee to do Stanford considerable harm. Given the pooling of costs and the fact that Stanford had conducted research under nearly 18,000 federally sponsored contracts and grants involving many millions of transactions during the unaudited years, a handful of accidental or misplaced items was to be expected for any large university.

We had hoped to focus on the research values involved, on the complexity of the regulations governing indirect cost recovery, and on Stanford's record of compliance with them. But the Subcommittee on Oversight and Investigations of the House Energy and Commerce Committee zeroed in on the "sensitive" items. These also involved purchases for Hoover House, a national historic landmark that is the president's residence and was at that time the site of all official university entertaining hosted by the president.

The problem lay in the concept of pool accounting. Hoover House is a university facility used for academic meetings, donor engagement, and other official purposes that required a certain level of quality in presentation. Because expenses of the president's office and the official residence are legitimate parts of the "general administration cost pool," these items, included in accounts along with secretarial salaries, maintenance, and the like, were grossly misrepresented. The government's auditors failed to recognize that vendors often lump purchases. The alleged "$1,600 shower curtain," for example, was one minor item in a $1,600 bill for upholstery and drapery work for the entire House, while the "early-nineteenth-century fruitwood commode" was a cherry chest of drawers that the committee chairman misconstrued as a $1,200 toilet. Then there was the yacht—*Victoria*—that had been donated to the Athletic Department and inadvertently depreciated in an indirect cost account. There were also simple errors by the auditors, such as misplacing decimal points to Stanford's disadvantage.

The implication, however—aggressively pursued by the committee and the media they fed—was that I was living the high life at taxpayer expense, despite the fact that we hosted seventy to eighty official events a year at Hoover House, welcoming some 15,000 guests annually. There was no division between public and private space at the house; it is the policy of Stanford's Board of Trustees to furnish the house in a comfortable standard for private spaces, and an elegant standard for entertaining. About a quarter of these expenses were charged to the general administrative pool, from which a percentage was reimbursed as an indirect cost of research routinely approved by government auditors in the past.

When testifying before the congressional hearing in Washington, D.C., in the spring of 1991, I offered such explanations, but the enmity Stanford faced in that hearing room was palpable. There was little room for detailing the complex elements of indirect cost recovery, all of which had been prenegotiated and approved by government partners. Up against determined congressional legislators, one doesn't really have a chance to say "that's an unfair accusation"—even when the chairman is deliberately misrepresenting reality.

Although it was obvious we had not been allowed to put a good face on Stanford's obligations to the government in that hearing, we were strong in defending the memoranda of understanding as well as our professionals responsible for Stanford's performance under the agreements. Still, I left the hearing room feeling dejected. The proceedings had been outrageously unfair, demanding that I explain random items out of tens of thousands of entries that inadvertently wound up in one indirect cost pool or another. I was concerned over the appearance created and worried about the consequences, specifically that there might be a permanent suppression of the indirect cost rate, as well as continued, ongoing challenges to the processes by which we negotiated our memoranda of understanding with the federal government. At a time of tight university budgets, such consequences could present even more challenges than we already faced in containing the costs of our teaching and research mission.

THE SCANDAL UNFOLDS

The road to the hearing room began in the spring of 1990, when Dean of Research Robert Byer paid me a visit out of concern over the new government auditor's posture and his questions regarding indirect costs. In June, I met with Paul Biddle, the new resident representative of the Office of Naval Research, the federal agency that was and is the principal correspondent to Stanford. He expressed dissatisfaction with the level of cooperation he was receiving from his contacts in the Controller's Office, but his demeanor was not unfriendly. I offered to assign him new contacts and invited him to bring any lingering concerns directly to me. At that meeting, Biddle showed none of the righteous hostility that characterized his later discussions with the press and, presumably, with congressional staff members.

Later that summer, when we learned that reporter Jeff Gottlieb from the *San Jose Mercury News* had filed a Freedom of Information Act request with the Office of Naval Research to obtain correspondence concerning indirect costs at Stanford, we made a similar request to learn what he would learn. We discovered that Biddle was in communication with the *Mercury News* and the staff of the congressional subcommittee. Biddle accused his ONR predecessor of having formed a cozy relationship with the University and suggested that Stanford's liability for ten years of unaudited indirect cost recovery could amount to $200 or even $400 million. In an adoring profile in *Reader's Digest* ("How He Caught the Campus Chiselers"[1]), he emerged as a white knight intent on saving taxpayers from a grasping university and complacent bureaucrats.

In August we received a letter from subcommittee chairman John Dingell (D-Michigan) informing Stanford that he had asked the General Accounting Office to undertake an investigation of indirect cost accounting practices at several universities, starting with Stanford.

No doubt mistakes were made among the countless entries handled by the Stanford Controller's Office. But to say that these errors were intentional, malicious, or designed to dupe the taxpayer were unfounded. The University's interest and obligation is to maintain the public trust.

When the hearing was over, I felt battle weary, harassed, disappointed, and fearful for the consequences that might come to Stanford. It was an absolute trough—not only in my career, but in my life—so personal were the accusations. Although, as the Commissioner of the FDA, I had testified at more than fifty congressional hearings, including some hostile ones, none bore any resemblance to what took place that day.

Dingell, whose antagonism toward Stanford was foreshadowed by the parade of investigators he had sent to Stanford in advance of these proceedings, took apparent pleasure in dredging up alleged improprieties and denigrating Stanford's professionals. Our Stanford team had been advised that Dingell might be placated by a humble public apology for our "wrongdoing." But we were convinced we had done our best, with some inevitable instances of human error, to uphold the agreements we had negotiated with the government. Hiring professional help to guide us through the media and government maze of questioning, we took the high road, focusing our testimony on the importance and public benefit of the research enterprise and our adherence to government rules.

I was accompanied at the hearings by Jim Gaither, then Chairman of Stanford's Board of Trustees, one of the most loyal friends I've had in my life. His presence was a tremendous comfort to me, emotionally and spiritually. A student later approached me to ask why in the world I had brought my lawyer to the congressional hearing, which he thought me look culpable. "That was no lawyer," I responded. "That was my boss!" Jim's support in my bleakest hour meant everything to me.

HOW IN THE WORLD DID IT COME TO THIS?

Imagine that you are a principal investigator in the basic sciences, competing for government grant money not only with faculty colleagues within your own institution but with colleagues across the nation's research universities. Imagine, too, that your university—for reasons quite beyond your control—has an indirect cost recovery rate near the top of the curve. That is, were you to win government sponsorship of your research project, the government would pay the university an additional 73 percent of modified direct costs of research. Compare that with a rate of say, 55 percent at a public university on the other side of the country, and you understand why some Stanford faculty members were unhappy with the rate we had negotiated. They supposed that the higher rate provided a disincentive for the government to sponsor their research projects. Disgruntled faculty did not keep these concerns to themselves. Biddle, moreover, initiated luncheon meetings with a few of the discontented science faculty members "to see if we can do something about the indirect cost rate at Stanford."[2]

Three conditions, I believe, conspired to bring the issue to the attention of government investigators:

- Whistle-blower Paul Biddle, who represented the government in its dealings with Stanford, and who had allegedly been an unsuccessful applicant for a staff position at Stanford.
- A powerful congressional subcommittee misinterpreting accounting records.
- Media, both inside and outside the University, whose salacious accounts of an otherwise arcane topic resulted in an inquiry that would damage the University and its administrators for years to come.

This triangular trade among ambitious congressional investigators, a whistle-blower with a personal agenda, and selectively fed media produced an unexpectedly powerful impact on public opinion, comprising the impetus for an extraordinarily damaging and costly battle between Stanford and the government, one that dominated the next two years of the University's life. By the summer of 1990, the usual two government auditors at Stanford grew to thirty-five, outnumbering the Stanford staff in place by two to one!

Since the beginning of my presidency in 1980, Stanford had been receiving a fairly constant one-third of its total research support in the form of indirect costs, similar to that at many other research-intensive universities. But an increasing number of exclusions gave the impression that the rate was rising. Moreover, some universities—including Harvard, to which Stanford has often been compared—separate out the costs of research in their medical centers. Stanford does not, and with an active medical research arm, this, too, contributed to the perception that our indirect cost rate was, relative to our peer institutions, relatively high. By the late 1980s, Stanford's rate, similar to those at many other research-intensive universities, had climbed to 73 percent.[3]

At the March 1991 hearing, Congressman Dingell praised representative Paul Biddle, criticized the Navy for sloppiness, and urged the Office of Naval Research to cancel Stanford's MOUs, which it did. This left Stanford with a provisional indirect cost recovery rate of 55.5 percent and a retroactive bill in excess of $25 million per year for ten years. Add to this the expenditures required to respond to the burden of government audit requests, install new accounting systems, and meet an evolving standard that more and more resembled that for defense contractors in the for-profit sector. This was a harsh new reality. Fortunately, it was a time-limited one.

Quite apart from the focus and attention required to deal with the indirect cost matter and to ensure that Stanford's research enterprise would not be crippled by the newly imposed provisional rate, the University was celebrating its centennial with the most ambitious fundraising campaign in higher education to date—a $1.1 billion goal.

Even the May 1990 visit of Soviet President Mikhail Gorbachev—a fabulous endorsement of all the University had accomplished in its first hundred years—was not completely joyful, plagued as I was with worry over the accounting controversy. Because I was pretty clearly identified as someone responsible for the indirect cost problem, it was evident that it would be very difficult for me to be part of the solution. So, after careful consideration, and against Robin's impassioned advice and counsel, I told the Board of Trustees in June of 1991 that I would resign the Stanford presidency at the end of the following academic year. I would spend that year working hard to make sure we corrected every problem that we felt had been correctly identified by the Dingell committee.

EXONERATION

In the aftermath of the Dingell hearing, because of the cancellation of our MOUs and the provisional indirect cost recovery rate of 55.5 percent, Stanford appealed the decision to the Armed Services Board of Contract Appeals. We hoped to recover the previous rate and to negate cancellation of our MOUs for 1991 and 1992. Three and a half years after the Dingell hearing, Stanford and the U.S. government agreed to a settlement of all disputed matters related to the billing and payment of the indirect costs of federally sponsored research for the years 1981 through 1992. In settling, the Office of Naval Research acknowledged that the Navy "does not have a claim that Stanford engaged in fraud, misrepresentation, or other wrongdoing with respect to the Memoranda of Understanding, costs, submissions, claims or other matters covered by the settlement agreement."[4] The settlement provided that Stanford owed *only* $1.2 million as payment to cover *all* "over-recovery" during the ten largely unaudited years—about 0.1 percent of Stanford's annual research business with the government and a far cry from the $25 million per year that Congressman Dingell wanted to levy! All University personnel were fully exonerated. To fight the charges, however, the University had paid heavily. By the end of the crisis, the cost for lawyers, accountants, and related services totaled about $37 million.

Two features of Stanford's case were decisive in the settlement. One was the plainly political circumstances that caused the cancellation of the contracts—in particular, Chairman Dingell's direct instruction to the Navy during the hearing. The second was the demonstration that personnel of the Defense Contract Audit Agency, contrary to their testimony during the hearing, not only participated in the signing of many of the memoranda but had conducted audits on the basis of these agreements in a way that plainly acknowledged their validity. Thus when Stanford countersued, the government saw the obvious need to settle.

Paul Biddle later filed a legal action of his own against Stanford with the Department of Justice. Under the *qui tam* provision of the False Claims Act, citizens may file such actions and the plaintiff may receive up to 30 percent of a treble-damage award, a huge windfall if Biddle's estimate had been correct. But, based on conflict of interest, the Justice Department declined to prosecute Biddle's suit. Should a government employee be permitted to use his or her official position to obtain information or take actions that might produce such an extraordinary personal reward? The Justice Department had in fact asked for legislation to outlaw the filing of such lawsuits by government employees. Biddle left Stanford, ran unsuccessfully in a congressional primary, and pursued a suit against the University until his appeals were finally thrown out of court. His predecessor at Stanford, who had been fired as a result of Biddle's accusations, was reinstated. Sensational accusations, however, are the stuff of headlines, whereas exonerations dot back pages.

AFTERMATH

Full analysis of the indirect cost matter shows that the damage to Stanford's reputation was transient and the price paid, mine aside, was quite small. Despite all

We all learned a lot about the operation of congressional committees that want to hold hearings that will get them on the six o'clock news. They feed bits and pieces to the press, where they're used to distort the facts. It was at the beginning of electronic archives, and we discovered that once anything got into computer storage it was almost impossible to get it corrected. So story after story would repeat an error because it would come up in the data base and just get plugged into the story. The athletic department had a program of soliciting gifts, and one of them was a large plush yacht with a hot tub. Don didn't even know about the boat but was accused of partying on it. It got buried in everyone's computer and the whole thing became a scandal as opposed to an auditing issue.

—Bob Freelen

Don was forthright, clear, and appropriately uncompromising in his explanation of Stanford's position in the indirect cost issue. Every research university in the United States owes him a debt of gratitude for that. He could have been obsequious or arrogant, but he was not. He was direct. He stood up for the universities and made clear what seems pretty obvious, that in any system with hundreds of thousands of transactions, there are inevitably going to be a few unintentional errors.

—Paul Brest

The Dingell crowd were bad people. They were the underbelly of the House of Representatives, they were bullies, they were cynical. They weren't interested in substance. They didn't give a damn what Stanford had done or hadn't done. Once they got hold of the issue, and they saw that it had a lot of public resonance, they were going to drive it for all it was worth. I think they got a lot of personal satisfaction out of it. They were really some of the most unpleasant people in town.

—Jerrold K. Footlick, "How High the Cost: Indirect Costs at Stanford University,"
in Truth and Cconsequences: How Colleges and Universities Meet Public Crises
(Phoenix, AZ: Oryx Press, 1997)

After Don and I went to the editorial board of the *L.A. Times* on the indirect cost matter and Don had explained things to them, we had some time afterward, so we went across from the *Times* building and just walked around the park. That was the first and only time during this that Don talked about what was deeply troubling to him about it—that he had spent his life working hard to attain a good reputation and the thing that distressed him the most was seeing his integrity questioned. It was very moving and completely uncharacteristic of Don to open up like that. Perhaps it was because we'd been in the foxhole together at other times. But he wasn't complaining or looking for sympathy, he was just reflecting on what was deeply troubling him.

—Larry Horton

Suddenly in the hearing Dingle roared at Don: "Why is it that you charged the Japanese government one cost and you charged the taxpayer another cost? How do you defend that?" Don said it didn't make any sense and he needed more facts about it. It turned out to be a grant to the School of Education for a few hundred dollars for a seminar, and we had waived the indirect cost—little things like that. But they knew—they *knew* what they were doing. They don't tell you it was a hundred dollars for a seminar. They make it appear as though we were cooking the books and stuffing everything in there for the taxpayer.

—Larry Horton

Throughout the problem we had at Stanford, Don could have taken alternative actions that might have been very damaging to the University. If he had suddenly said, "We've got to stop this; let's fire everybody over at the accounting office and admit that we've done wrong in some way," when we really hadn't, it might have stopped Mr. Dingle from holding hearings, but at what cost—at what human cost? Don was not someone to throw other people under the bus to protect himself. He went out and absorbed the arrows for the rest of us.

—Larry Horton

I'll never forget those conversations we had a few days before his resignation. I was so impressed by Don's complete self-awareness, and his perfect analysis of the situation on the campus. I have encountered others in such situations, but rarely with such clear perceptions—he was not sorry for himself or worried about his reputation. He was analytical, finding what would be the right thing to do. Others would lose control, and not be that cool or thoughtful.

—Henry Muller, managing editor of Time

A shameful mark of the long years when Democrats controlled the House of Representatives was the abusive record of John D. Dingell of Michigan, chairman of the Energy and Commerce Committee. In the arrogance of his power, he terrorized individuals and institutions that he wanted to humble.

—Anthony Lewis, New York Times

Through the whole indirect cost controversy, Don insisted on taking responsibility himself. Most people at the top of the pyramid say, "Well, it happened on my watch, and I'm responsible," but they don't usually mean it. What they mean is, "What the heck was I supposed to do? I run a big organization; I don't know what the hell's going on there, but I'm responsible so I'll take the responsibility." People were undermining Don, but he said, "I don't believe in throwing people overboard." I think he might have protected himself a little more.

—Bob Rosenzweig

the accusations reported by the *San Jose Mercury News* and on ABC TV's *20-20* and those that came out in the Dingell hearing, Stanford completed a very successful Centennial Campaign, exceeding its $1.1 billion goal.

In the end, I had to admit that my divorce and remarriage while in office likely left some residue, which probably interacted with the intensity of negative attention given to the indirect cost matter. Even the eventual clearing of the University and its officers, including me, and a favorable financial settlement with the sponsoring government agency did not immediately remove the taint nor fully undo the financial damage caused by the dispute. Nonetheless, I am grateful that it did not permanently damage the University.

HOW CAN WE LOOK SO RICH AND FEEL SO POOR?

How private universities can look so rich and powerful and yet confront consistent pressures on the annual budget is an issue that no doubt contributed to the allegation that Stanford was somehow cheating the public. Part of the answer lies in the growth of the endowment—managed funds that must remain invested and untouched, with only a single-digit payout supporting the annual budget. Thus, a million-dollar endowment gift, celebrated by the development office and noted in the newspapers, adds just $50,000 annually to help pay the bills. And even some of that must be reinvested because Stanford's trustees are required by law to protect the purchasing power of the endowment against inflation, conserving it in the interest of future generations of faculty and students. Add to that the fact that donors often give money to support highly specific purposes, which may or may not help the budget. Nor can Stanford draw much profit from its 8,200 acres of highly valuable land, the sale of which was wisely prohibited by its founders.

In a visit with a group of Los Angeles alumni, their worry over the application of admissions standards for their own offspring quickly shifted to the financial consequences of acceptance, as they expressed concern about the growing rate of annual tuition increases. Indeed, some of them had been made aware of Stanford's success in fund raising over recent years and wondered why we needed that money at all. (When Stanford opened in 1891, matriculation was tuition free!)

It is important to understand the difference between the *cost* of education and the *price* of education. The cost of education is a number reflecting the university's budget divided by the number of students enrolled. The price, however, is that fraction of cost that is charged to students and their families. Because we want a diverse and capable student body, we set a tuition value that is significantly less than the real cost. So while we count on tuition income from students and their families, we add a significant subsidy from general funds that may appear to the student as financial aid or may be invisible to those footing the education bill, covered by annual fund raising, investment income, and endowment

I once asked him what the limits of the presidency were, and he said, "I always felt that when you entered office you were given a limited number of silver bullets, and when you ran into a lot of trouble, you pulled out one of your silver bullets and you got out of trouble. But eventually you run out of these silver bullets, and then it's time to go."

—Bob Rosenzweig

One of the most courageous acts of Don Kennedy's presidency was his decision to accept full responsibility for the integrity of Stanford University and its financial staff against the charges of widespread fraud in its indirect cost accounting—malicious and patently false charges, inflamed by the media and John Dingell. While he had virtually nothing to do with the application of arcane rules of indirect cost accounting, Don Kennedy stood up for the University and its financial staff—no pointing at others, no attempt to walk away from the political attacks. Don's tenure was not always easy. His character showed most brightly when the clouds were darkest. When Stanford was challenged on legal and ethical grounds, he insisted that the buck stop with him, however wrong or exaggerated the charges. He would not let anyone point fingers at anyone else, nor did he do so.

—Jim Gaither

Don, you called me Boss, when I was honored to serve. You elevated me when I was elevated to be in your presence. Your greatness has grown as you have suffered for us all. These have been tough times, eased for all of us and lifted from Stanford's back by your willingness to accept the burdens of the last eighteen months. You have placed Stanford before yourself with remarkable spirit and good will. We had no right to expect so much, but on reflection we should have known that no less would be given. *—Jim Gaither*

Don could have done virtually every one of the top jobs at the university as well or better than the incumbent.

—Norm Robinson

Our son's twenty-fifth Stanford reunion reminded me of that Sunday morning in 1991, sitting in the Stanford Stadium and listening to Don's graduation speech—the most brilliant address I have ever heard from a university president, transforming a painful experience into an inspiring message for the students. I will never forget it.

—Derek Bok, President Emeritus, Harvard University

payouts. And because those subsidies are dependent on external economic factors, tuition becomes the one source over which the University has significant and immediate control. Thus it rises at what seems a disproportionate rate to cover ever-increasing costs.

Those costs include professors, administrative staff, and modern high-technology facilities along with the highly skilled professionals who can run them. In our economy these human costs, comprising two-thirds to three-quarters of our overall budget, tend to inflate so as to give Stanford an annual budget increase that runs two or three points ahead of the consumer price index. Stanford is a research university. It attracts brilliant faculty scholars, with whom our students are privileged to work in the laboratory or classroom. Not only must salaries improve to remain competitive, but intellectual inquiry is subject to the economics of knowledge. The German physicist Max Planck pointed out that each discovery raises another question that will inevitably be more difficult and more expensive to solve, requiring new methods and ever-more sophisticated equipment.

It is important both for those inside the academy and its outside critics to understand some of these economic realities. The paradox is that to finance even modest levels of improvement in faculty salaries, research programs, and student financial aid, Stanford had made painful cuts in expense budgets during thirteen of the sixteen years before the mid-1970s. But universities have the unique misfortune always to be labeled by their total assets. Thus, we wrestled with the ongoing dilemma of looking inordinately rich while feeling poor, which no doubt contributed to our becoming a target of Chairman Dingell and his congressional subcommittee.

CHAPTER 10

POST PRESIDENCY

Picking up the Pieces

ONCE I ANNOUNCED MY DECISION to resign from the Stanford presidency, I knew, of course, that a search would ensue for my successor. Although a few supporters urged me to hang on, I believe they disregarded the depth of my discouragement about the damage the indirect cost investigation and my association with it might have done to Stanford. Whether out of respect for my feelings or a sense that the matter was none of my affair, I heard nothing of the presidential search process, despite the fact that some of my closest colleagues were no doubt involved in advisory capacities, if not direct participants. That silence was pierced by a telephone call early one morning when Robin and I were still asleep. A voice on the other end of the phone informed me that "as I perhaps knew," the selection process had resulted in the appointment of Gerhard Casper, the provost of the University of Chicago, as Stanford's ninth president.

For the remainder of the 1992 academic year I continued to work hard on the university budget and was lucky to recruit Ted Mitchell, an experienced former Stanford trustee and a tireless ally in managing that challenging year. Mitchell was a good friend who had served as professor of education at Dartmouth and understood how to navigate the landscape among the president, provost, faculty, and Board of Trustees. The recent Centennial Campaign had been a major success, and some of its objectives raised departmental hopes for specific projects. Mitchell was an adept partner as we found ourselves dealing with a number of the postcampaign expectations by departments that proposed new programs and initiatives.

Looking ahead to the changing of the guard, I realized the need to make plans for postpresidential life. In June, bidding farewell to a number of students I had known and valued at a sad but meaningful Stanford commencement, I realized that, like them, I was preparing for an unknown and uncharted future. I began my commencement address, as I always had:

And now, members of the class of 1992 . . . it is time to turn our attention once again to the ancient question: "Is There Life after Stanford?" I know what

you're thinking. "His last year, our last year, get ready for some heavy stuff."
Forget it. I'm not leaving Stanford; you are. We need the beds![1]

On the more serious note of our entering a new and perhaps perilous phase, I
shared with them this poem, "Faith," by Patrick Overton:

> When you walk to the edge of all the light you have and take that first step
> into the darkness of the unknown, you must believe that one of two things
> will happen:
>
> > There will be something solid for you to stand upon, or, you will be
> > taught how to fly.[2]

After commencement, the pace of Robin's life and mine changed dramatically. Some colleagues in the Institute for International Studies—the economist
Wally Falcon and the law school's Tom Heller—generously invited me to join
them in thinking about problems linking the environment and national policy.
That experience was fulfilling enough, and I certainly wasn't looking around for
other things to do. I believe strongly that university presidents emeritus ought to
resume regular duties on the faculty, thus signaling a bond with the teaching and
research mission of the institution. The Human Biology program was still active,
and I was glad to be available to teach in it for the next
several years. We did an interesting modification of the
core curriculum at that time: A number of our students
were especially interested in health, including public
health; others were focused on environmental and conservation issues. By emphasizing these challenges in a
special section of the Human Biology core, we hoped to
attract some students who perhaps had not been drawn
to the standard program. It was a return to my roots,
teaching a new generation.

Staff farewell to
Don, Sunken
Diamond,
summer 1992.

NEW DIRECTIONS

The new administration of Gerhard Casper brought
many changes to Stanford. The one that most affected
me and Robin was the appointment of a new general
counsel, Michael Roster, a Stanford alumnus and partner in the Los Angeles office of the prestigious Mor-
rison and Foerster law firm. Within a few months of
Roster's arrival, he made clear to the in-house lawyers
that his charge included a substantial reduction in professional staff in the Office of the General Counsel and
their substitution with outside law firms.

The day that Robin and her General Counsel colleagues were asked to present their portfolios to an assembly of representatives from major Bay Area law firms was embarrassing to both University attorneys and partners from the outside firms. In an expression of solidarity with one another, all the staff attorneys wore black. Days before, they had learned that their role during the long session was to explain their individual areas of expertise including matters in which they engaged on a regular basis. The goal was to facilitate the subsequent bidding by the outside lawyers to acquire Stanford's legal work.

A virtual decimation of the incumbent legal staff ensued over the following six months. Robin was the first to go, the second time she had been compelled by a University vice president to leave a professional role she cherished. In both instances, I could not help but think I was to blame, although Robin always assured me that I was not.

NEW OPPORTUNITIES

I left the Stanford presidency at the end of August 1992 under a bit of a cloud. Yet it wasn't long before the clouds parted, and I found myself transitioning to a new kind of teaching opportunity, returning to my roots in biology. I was offered the chance to teach at Stanford in Washington during the winter quarter of my first postpresidential year. It was a quarter devoted to students interested in policy issues related to environment and health, subjects with which I was familiar, as they had been emphasized in the Human Biology core.

The Stanford campus in the nation's capital was itself an early collaboration between me and Robin. In her real estate role and as a member of the committee setting the criteria for this new venture, she had the task of identifying suitable premises for the new campus. Over the course of nine months, Robin made six trips to Washington, viewing grand homes, estates, and a large site known as the Senate Stables—a place with historic significance for Stanford, Senator Stanford having boarded his horses there during his years in the Senate. The Senate Stables was not in a great neighborhood, and the facility would have required extensive work. Still, Robin flew home dreaming of its promising possibilities.

On arriving home from her penultimate trip, she received an urgent call from the real estate agent who insisted she return immediately. The Connecticut Avenue property housing David Lee's Chinese Restaurant and hotel rooms above had just come on the market. After touring the property, she determined that it met all the criteria required by the committee. Fearful of losing the opportunity, she prepared a letter of intent while she was still in Washington, negotiating the best price she could. Before returning home, she found herself on the telephone with a representative of Anne T. (MLA '07) and Robert M. Bass (MBA '74), the generous donors who had committed to fund the purchase of property to house the program. She learned in that call that the Basses had hoped Stanford in

Washington would find a home in Georgetown. Robin deployed all her powers of persuasion to convince the Bass representative that locating this program near a metro stop was essential.

The effort was successful, and the property became Stanford's home in the capital, opening its doors in 1988. Housing what is now known as the Bing Stanford in Washington Program, the property has provided classrooms and residence for generations of Stanford students and faculty spending an academic quarter there. It has also been a venue for panel discussions, alumni gatherings, student recruitment events, and lectures by local luminaries, including members of Congress, Supreme Court justices, and other government dignitaries as well as distinguished Stanford alumni. In 2005, thanks to a gift from Victoria ('61), and Roger Sant, Stanford was able to purchase the adjacent building. Renovated in 2007, it accommodated bicoastal classes and conferences, and additional guest space for faculty and students. Exhibits in the first floor art gallery satisfied a retail requirement imposed by the District as a condition of approving the new construction and operation.

The location, just across the street from the Woodley Park metro station on the Red Line, has been lauded by both students and faculty. My student Marc Fioravanti stayed in shape for rugby by regularly running up the 204 foot "down" escalator—the steepest in the entire Metro system!

As faculty in charge that quarter, I was required to live in Washington with a group of students I was delighted to mentor. This meant that I had to leave Robin behind in our campus home, as she was at that time still working full time in the Office of the General Counsel. She visited as frequently as her schedule allowed, and in January of 1993 we were lucky to attend Bill Clinton's inauguration.

By that time, I had settled in with my twenty-three students. I was teaching a seminar encompassing health and environmental policy challenges. My feeling was that biologists who have a serious interest in evolution, behavior, and biological systems ought to devote a significant amount of time worrying about what is happening to biological diversity and environmental quality. So we talked about the FDA, the EPA, the Toxic Substances Control Act, Endangered Species Act, and the Federal Insecticide, Rodenticide and Fungicide Act, under which pesticides were regulated. We also turned to the more global or transboundary issues, considering the kinds of international arrangements necessary to deal with the whole question of tropical forests, ozone depletion, and global warming.

Each of the students had organized internships with government agencies, individual legislators, or the occasional nongovernmental organization or policy institute. We ate together, explored for fun together, and lived a lively cultural life. I got to know those students well and have loved keeping track of them. Their academic performances were imaginative and creative. It is hard to know which was more remarkable: their intellectual caliber, the intensity of their commitment, or the ability they had to support one another and accomplish things together. It had a transforming effect on my views about experiential education and the value of merging academic work with practice.

During that quarter, we arranged for the students to meet with Vice President Al Gore in the Lincoln Room at the White House to discuss climate change, an area of Gore's interest at the intersection of science and public policy that is broadly recognized. We also enjoyed an interesting session with Gro Harlem Bruntland, former prime minister of Norway. The Stanford in Washington experience was a timely break from the campus environment and provided me with a cherished experience, becoming extremely close to an outstanding group of Stanford students with the hope and determination to make a difference in the world.

LAYING A FOUNDATION

There is a widely held assumption that one leaving a major job will soon be pursued by new opportunities. On my return to Stanford in the spring of 1993, I was not exactly flooded with offers, but one especially welcome invitation came my way when Susan Packard Orr and her husband Lynn Orr, former dean of Stanford's School of Earth Sciences, talked to me about possible membership on the board of directors of the David and Lucille Packard Foundation, which Susan chairs. The Packard family has taken seriously its obligation to society. In addition to a strong program in local grants, the foundation has a major program supporting children, families, and communities, while a more global program focuses on population, reproduction, and family health. In addition to these strong family members, some bright leaders in environmental policy served on the board, including Ward Woods of the Woods Center for the Environment at Stanford and Bill Reilly, noted for his past leadership at the federal Environmental Protection Agency and elsewhere. The board took on interesting and occasionally tough topics, and for me it was an exciting educational experience.

I'm often asked why family foundations invite nonfamily members to serve on their boards. In some cases, the policy of appointing "outsiders" to the board arises as a result of the family's experience. David and Lucille Packard and three of their children had carefully worked out a set of social needs that had concerned all of them—changes in education, the status of children, conservation, the preservation of first-rate science, and the dynamics of world population, committing their family resources to these objectives. It was the Packard family's habit to seek outside advice from individual and institutional experts, seeing consultation of this kind as essential in educating program staff and reviewing priorities. Thus the family sought a few area experts for the foundation board. One of the very first Packard Foundation commitments was to identify and support the research of young scientists, providing funding and experience to help these protégées become candidates for the most competitive kinds of federal fellowship support. The foundation continues to track and meet with that original cadre of scientists. The Packards' leveraging of their research careers has laid down a legendary track record in prizes and membership in the National Academy of Sciences.

NEW OPPORTUNITIES, NEW CHALLENGES

My Washington teaching experience indirectly generated two different opportunities, each based on friendships. Jim Gaither had helped recruit me to the FDA in the late 1970s and had been a source of emotional support as chairman of Stanford's Board of Trustees during the indirect cost hearing. In 2003, Gaither became chairman of the board of the Carnegie Endowment for International Peace. At his initiative and invitation, I joined that diverse and interesting group of men and women. Several board members were academic refugees as I was, and others came from strong business organizations.

The other initiative that meant a great deal to me stemmed from my early work at the FDA, where my first general counsel was Richard Merrill. We developed a relationship of mutual trust and even had some fun together. After Merrill returned to the University of Virginia, where he soon became dean of the law school, some interesting things were brewing at the National Academy of Sciences. Under staff leadership from Anne-Marie Mazza, members of the academy were considering how best to integrate policy considerations in the areas of science, technology, and law. There was enough enthusiasm from various academy members—many of whom had noticed the frequency with which scientists made important connections with the legal profession—to launch a commission on Science, Technology and Law, to which Merrill and I were nominated as cochairs. The ten-year collaboration that ensued was a bright spot in my professional experience and led me to consider some of the most vexing challenges at the intersection of these three policy arenas.

PRESIDING PRESIDENT EMERITUS

With many other opportunities and interests to command my focus, I soon was making new inroads and establishing new priorities. Serving as president of Stanford University was my most rewarding career experience, but it was not my only fulfilling professional role. With each new opportunity I was invited to consider and explore, I found myself picking up the pieces, rebuilding a life with different priorities, and moving forward. Despite our vastly different styles and approaches, I did my best to give a wide berth to Gerhard Casper to define his own presidency without the undue burden of a lingering emeritus.

The only occasion on which Casper asked my advice was on the appointment of Professor Condoleezza Rice as provost—a position that I held briefly at Stanford and at which Casper himself had excelled at Chicago. Casper invited me to his office and expressed minor concern over Rice's relative youth, as well as the possible faculty response to her already-established political orientation. He asked if I thought the faculty would be distressed by her appointment.

My assessment was straightforward and unequivocal: Rice's record as a faculty member was exemplary. Her knowledge of Russia and Russian military affairs was renowned. Although some faculty might disagree with her political views, she was and is intellectually strong and tough minded. I advised Casper that, in my opinion, Rice would manage the job capably and effectively and would be a respected holder of the office of provost. Casper did, in fact, appoint Rice to that office.

As she has written extensively, Rice does not favor the practice of affirmative action. She believes that precisely equal qualifications are nearly impossible. And she believes that the successful candidate deserves the assurance that the position was won on the candidate's merits and not as restitution from some historic slight.

I am grateful for the many postpresidential opportunities that came my way after serving as president of Stanford. They allowed me to move forward and sustain the privilege to serve. In fact, there was only one other professional engagement that came close to the love I had for the job of president of Stanford—serving as editor-in-chief of the journal *Science*, the subject of the next chapter.

THE STANFORD AURA

I have often tried to explain to others the extraordinary feeling that binds the Stanford family together, and as often I have failed. Perhaps, as we say when a funny story falls flat, "You had to be there." There is a sense of belonging that overtakes one at Stanford, a feeling of open friendliness and youthful informality—people say hello and call you Prez; older alums console football players headed for the lockers after a tough loss; fifty students in a residence stage a surprise party to cheer up a friend, or the band shows up to play free for someone's birthday. I reflect on wonderful times with PhD students, all of them undergraduates from other places and nearly all now faculty members elsewhere who still speak of the Stanford magic.

Stanford is, of course, not one but many things: a selective, residential undergraduate college with extraordinary students, a much-admired set of professional schools, and a distinguished research faculty that contributes much to our national life and innovative capacity. But above all there is a cooperative spirit that unites people of widely different backgrounds, ethnic heritages, and beliefs and invites them to share in the life of the mind. I recall the anguished discussions that took over my biology class the day of John Kennedy's assassination; the sometimes inspiring, sometimes deeply troubling challenges of the late 1960s; or the Human Biology program of the 1970s, where a new tradition of enthusiasm for interdisciplinary work and policy studies was formed.

The abiding backdrop is the Stanford landscape—the desert smell of dry grass and eucalyptus on a hot October Saturday; the green hills behind Lake Lag on an afternoon when breezy sunshine follows a March rain; or what novelist and

Don Kennedy built a legal office at Stanford from scratch, one without peer in any other university. It was a fabulous office, protecting Stanford against those various risks that a university faces.

—*Paul Brest*

Don could be very direct. There was an article by the new head of the legal office, who had dismantled much of the office, bragging that until he arrived it had been a kind of retirement home for spouses of important people and what a fabulous job he had done in reducing the legal costs at Stanford. Don took exception and went to meet with the man, who said, "I never went to the press seeking publicity, they just came to me and I answered their questions." Don looked at him and said, "You know, I didn't just fall off the turnip truck on the way here."

—*Iris Brest*

One of the early things Don and I worked on was how to get a campus program in Washington, D.C. We had many meetings and discussions, trying to get a faculty committee to do the actual planning. In the end, we were able to create a terrific program which is still thriving. In the early days Don was the one person who really understood the power of Washington—that you can make that difference, that you can have that government job and impact the world in a significant way. He understood how important it was for a student to have that chance and that exposure to Washington, D.C. Without his personal support and guidance we would never have had that campus.

—*Catherine Milton*

When I took Don's class at Stanford in Washington my senior year, he was coming off of what must have been a challenging departure as president, but I swear you would never have known. He was just indefatigably positive, optimistic, and energetic, a truly inspirational person. Most of us tend to waste a certain amount of time and talent, but you felt like that was something he just didn't do. He was the embodiment of work-hard-play-hard in a fantastic fashion. Every day was a day lived fully.

—*Kai Anderson*

When Don was president emeritus, teaching at the Stanford in Washington program, a number of us scrapped our senior year plans so we could take his class. That winter quarter with him in Washington was transformative for me, and my guess is that if you asked that whole roster, they would point to it as a very important, if not definitive three months of their lives. Don had a remarkable way of making us believe in our individual and collective capacities, in what we could do in the world. It's very hard as an undergraduate to understand what the world of opportunities looks like, and I had no idea how I would end up—especially when I sometimes felt I was at Stanford accidentally, chosen, perhaps, for demographic reasons as a poor kid from redneck Oregon, woefully unprepared for the place. But Don was stubbornly optimistic about what I could do in a way that was almost a self-fulfilling prophesy. He would not allow you to think you couldn't succeed. My courage to forego a PhD in sedimentary geology and enter public service, working on energy policy and biodiversity, creating wilderness bills, conservation areas, and national monuments, was inspired by Don Kennedy.

—*Kai Anderson*

Don proved to be one of the most stimulating and delightful presidents the University has had. He engaged faculty, students, and board members with enthusiasm, excellent ideas, dignity, and respect. His ability to relate to people of various ages, professions, and backgrounds made him very effective in solving the complicated issues facing a great university.   *—David Hamburg*

Don would routinely come over to the alumni center for lunch, and I would be down picking up my salad to take up to my office and he'd say, "Nah, come join me," and we'd sit and he'd just tell stories. The impression I was left with in all of those chance encounters was that with this man—whose resumé is stunning by any measure, whether it be his academic chevrons, his time leading the FDA, as Stanford's eighth president, or as editor of *Science* magazine—there was no pretense, no suggestion of even emeritus status. In the café he was just another guy.

Introducing Don to a student walking by, I would say, "I'd like to introduce you to Don Kennedy; Don was the president of Stanford from 1980 to 1992," and Don would get upset with me, embarrassed that that should be a part of the conversation. It wasn't how he defined himself. I was just struck by the level of humility and graciousness and lack of even a scintilla of arrogance or ego. I think he would rather I said, "This is Don Kennedy the current editor of *Science* magazine." It reminded me of the Jeffersonian concept of governance, where if the farmer has certain talents he's asked to go and lead and when he's done leading he goes back and farms. That's the way Don approached it. He's of the people.   *—Howard Wolf*

Three presidents at the 1992 commencement (Lyman, Kennedy, and Casper).

One of the most significant but little recognized long-term triumphs of Don's presidency was establishment of the Jasper Ridge Biological Preserve at the western edge of the Stanford lands. Through the 1940s, 1950s, and 1960s those undeveloped lands and the Searsville Lake evolved into a near public set of facilities for thousands of swimmers and picnickers on summer weekends. After complaints, police visitations, and literal trashing of the lake shore, it became clear to Don that Stanford needed to take or lose control of the 1,200 acres. I recall touring the Ridge lands with trustees Sandra Day O'Connor and William McCoy and seeing their shock at the detritus and garbage left by the public after a busy weekend. Don worked hard with them, other trustees, and several generous donors to achieve the difficult vote that excluded the public from the Stanford lands, establishing the Preserve.

—Norm Wessells

Don Kennedy took the lead in transforming Stanford from a good to a great university. As we look at the faculty, the transformation that Don and his provosts, Al Hastorf, Gerry Lieberman, and Jim Rosse, brought about was extraordinary. He was a magnet for great scholars (both established and promising) and brought incredible enthusiasm for promising ideas and opportunities—a willingness to innovate and bring about major change in Stanford's teaching and research.

—Jim Gaither

Don lecturing alumni about the natural world at Jasper Ridge.

Donald Kennedy is a thoughtful man, given to pondering the role of the university in the historical continuum, the role of the individual in the university, the place the university has as a bastion of free and challenging thought.

He is an eloquent man, unafraid to shrug off the presumed formality of his office to talk about the beauty of a spring rain or the joys of fatherhood.

He is a giving man—of his time, of his thoughts, of his feelings.

It is fitting that his departure led him not to some well-financed institution with its own political agenda, but back to the classroom.

It is fitting that the finest tributes to him were ones of his own fashioning—the grace and dignity of his departure, the nobility of his philosophy, the idealism of his future plans.

—Mark Simon,
Peninsula Times Tribune, *1992*

Stanford alumnus Allen Drury called the long, lingering, hypnotic spring of Santa Clara Valley. The core of the campus—its spiritual heart—is the red-tile-roofed, adobe-colored Quad. I like it in the evening—the rhythm of the arches, gold in the sunset, or in the tule fog on a winter morning. Approaching the campus, the near ridges of the foothills are visible to the west. Just beyond them, thickly wooded elevations that belong to the Jasper Ridge Biological Preserve are set against the distant mountains, rising in that blue mist.

Stanford's extraordinary good fortune in having its own biological preserve on land contiguous with its campus flows from a special piece of original wisdom: Senator Stanford's decision forbidding the trustees to sell any of the University's endowment lands. What began as a modest conservation effort and an attempt to protect continuing research has become a full-scale research facility and a community resource of inestimable importance. It gives vigorous life to field studies at Stanford, the terrestrial equivalent of the University's Hopkins Marine Station in Pacific Grove. It has encouraged a generation of research commitments by a remarkably distinguished assembly of population biologists. And now it is used by school children and groups of all ages, drawn to the greening hills and golden fields on an early spring day.

When the pressures of institutional life grew heavy toward the end of April, I would find myself driving through the gate, parking near the bridge at the upper end of the lake, and setting off on a walk. The path leads through riverine woodland, with trees newly in leaf. I pause and listen to hear if the black-headed grosbeaks have returned on schedule. As the path turns around the end of the lake and rises into the chaparral, I look to the water for wood ducks and ring-necks, and on the ascent scan the manzanita to see if by chance this time the wrentits are violating their usual rule: that it is proper to be heard but not seen. I listen for the first orange-crowned warbler in the oaks and try to remember which path leads down to the Ohlone Indian acorn mill. My trip ends with crossing the dam and wondering how many weeks will pass before the flow in San Francisquito Creek will decline to summer levels. The circuit never fails to produce a sense of peace and joy—a serenity that seems in a way to echo the aura of quiet civility and vibrant idealism that endure behind the bustle of the University.

CHAPTER 11

SCIENCE

The Final Frontier

OVER THE COURSE OF MY CAREER as a practicing scientist, I regularly read the journal *Science*, published weekly by the nonprofit American Association for the Advancement of Science (AAAS). Many of the world's great researchers have hoped that the distillation of their new findings would culminate with publication in *Science*, broadly regarded as one of the two prestige publications for scientific research along with *Nature*, issued by Macmillan Publishers.

In 2000, the AAAS Board of Directors was considering new editorial leadership for *Science* and one of its members, Dr. Alice Huang, suggested I might consider undertaking the role of editor-in-chief. When discussions had moved along far enough, I heard from AAAS Board Member, the late Stephen J. Gould, a distinguished paleontologist, evolutionary biologist, and historian of science who spent the bulk of his career at Harvard. "Well, Don, I guess we owe you this one!" he said, plainly referring to the indirect cost controversy at Stanford. Despite Gould's reminder of that painful episode, I was honored to be offered the *Science* post.

So it was that I found myself commuting cross-country to Washington, D.C., where *Science* is headquartered. I maintained a condominium there while Robin continued her law practice in California. Although it was a great advantage to be there, the distance was a challenge. I often forgot which shirts I had left in Washington and which I had kept at home.

Although my predecessors as editor-in-chief generally limited their regular visits to Washington, D.C., to one week a month, taking the red-eye on Sunday nights and returning on the latest flight out of Dulles on Friday nights, I spent far more time at *Science* headquarters and on occasional visits to other destinations on *Science's* behalf, including its offices in Cambridge, England. Over the eight years as editor-in-chief, I was away on average twelve to thirteen days a month. I didn't realize until much later what a hardship this worked on Robin, who rarely complained, knowing how vital it was to me to return to a prestigious position in the scientific and academic universe.

Being editor-in-chief afforded me the opportunity to work directly with a much broader range of scientists than I had in any of my roles at Stanford. The journal represented the scientific community, and its editors worked hard to manage the tasks of submission, evaluation, review, and economy of language. They worked especially hard to ensure that the writing in each paper would be understandable to intelligent people outside its particular discipline. One couldn't expect that every paper on, say, neurophysiology, would be easily understood by a geologist or paleontologist, but the editorial staff strove for comprehension and readability. That task was difficult. We sometimes failed, but most authors and reviewers understood that the editors were themselves committed scientists who had given up their own research careers to assume editorial responsibility for a discipline at *Science*. Being accomplished in their own right gave the editors authority to deal effectively with scientists submitting their work.

It was rewarding to experience firsthand the intense passion, often accompanied by displays of competition within a field and occasionally by envy. During those eight years, I had a platform, the 700 words of the editorial page, on which to explore issues of scientific practice and policy and news of science breakthroughs. I soon began to view *Science* through a different lens than I had as a consumer of the journal.

I gradually learned from an extraordinary group of co-workers at *Science* about pitfalls—confidentiality, questions of data falsification, and disputes between colleagues—that had led to wise policies and practices. I was fortunate enough to inherit both my administrative assistant, Sylvia Kihara, who seemed to know everyone and everything, and executive editor Monica Bradford, who was an indispensable source on the history of why things were as they were—along with informed and thoughtful guidance for a newcomer. Bradford's amazing management skills kept me going to her office time after time to resolve problems I couldn't figure out.

SEPARATE BUT EQUAL

Almost all prestige journals employ a process of peer review, and rarely do questions of ethical standards arise. Confidentiality is the norm; the scientific community shares the expectation that the editor will take primary responsibility for considering submissions, calling on the advice of experts in the particular discipline to review their peers' contributions.

A frequent aspect of my job involved dealing with appeals from prospective authors claiming unfair refereeing by our editors or unreasonable adverse judgments by peers. A protective policy was developed to mitigate the possibility that past grudges may have led to unfair reviews: For example, authors were permitted to submit the names of reviewers they did *not* want us to call on—antagonistic competitors in the same field, unhappy students who had left the researcher's lab, or former romantic interests, for example. *Science* almost always honored these "blackball" requests. Interestingly, their frequency was somewhat field-dependent. They were far more common in highly competitive fields like biochemistry and genetics and relatively rare in fields like archaeology, geology, or ecology. My intuitive assessment of this phenomenon is the difference in opportunity for friendly collaboration from one discipline to another: reductionist biologists in laboratories don't have the opportunity to share coffee in the field.

In addition to publishing new research findings, *Science* also comprises a team of journalists whose reports occupy roughly the first ten pages of each issue. As the new editor-in-chief, I quickly discovered the challenges involved in publishing both new findings and news reports on the nation's scientific enterprise: conflicts of interest, confidentiality issues, and ensuring the highest ethical standards.

The physical manifestation of this partition between editorial and news departments was placement of the editorial staff on the tenth floor and the news staff to offices on the eleventh floor of 1200 New York Avenue, Washington, D.C., where *Science's* offices are located. Most of *Science's* editors were based in Washington, but a few were resident in the international headquarters in Cambridge, UK. A research paper could go to an editor in either place, depending on the editor's specialty and the content of the submission. The editor then recruited peer reviewers to assess the validity of claims made in the paper, and a determination was made regarding publication or rejection.

On the eleventh floor, journalists tracked news about science—new findings or issues that brought science into some political or policy context. The potential for conflict between the research and news sides gave rise to several policy guidelines. One was strict confidentiality regarding the peer review process and its participants. Suppose, for example, that the editors and the experts they have consulted have accepted a paper that may upset a generally accepted principle. A news reporter, seeking interviews about the published result, may report several contrary views about the paper's claims and even some doubt that the paper should have been published. The editor who approved the publication would surely be unhappy about this, but the journalist surveying the field did well in seeking a range of views. However, if the news reporter elicits from the editor the name of a negative, minority-view reviewer and seeks out that person for comment, it could jeopardize the relationship between reviewer and editor. The reporter would place the reviewer in the uncomfortable position of being publicly at odds not only with a competitive colleague who won publication but also with the *Science* establishment that agreed to publish the paper. We followed a policy of confidentiality regarding communications between news editors and peer reviewers.

Despite pragmatic reasons for confidentiality, in the past few years a few new journals have launched with an "open peer review" model, in which the evaluation is transparent, including the reviewers' identities. I see two advantages in such a system. Peer reviewers perform a vital and uncompensated contribution to the scientific enterprise. A thoughtful public argument about the value of a new contribution may be useful in coaching others about how it's done well—or badly! There is also a positive benefit for the reviewer: he or she may have contributed a superb piece of scholarship in improving a peer's submission. Why shouldn't that effort become part of a professional portfolio that brings rewards to both the reviewer and his institution? It could even make the meetings of tenure committees more interesting.

In my eight years at *Science*, there was never a serious quibble between the news and editorial staffs. And regardless of the firewall, we all celebrated together when a big story on a new scientific discovery came out in the *New York Times* or an equivalent publication citing an original piece of research first published in *Science*. The generally high level of respect among staff members usually extended throughout the peer review process, but the troubling example of one peer reviewer who went rogue remains with me. He felt that a particular paper should not have been published, though other reviewers had agreed with the editor that it should.

The disappointed peer reviewer took his quibble to the *Los Angeles Times*, where a story critical of the *Science* publication appeared. *Science's* policy on confidentiality precluded the possibility of commenting on his assessment. We could not even acknowledge that he had been a peer reviewer! Nor could we offer the contrary opinions of the majority of reviewers or the editor, as all were protected by confidentiality. The reviewer was not invited to evaluate any future *Science* submissions.

GETTING IT WRONG?

A controversy that persists today involved publication in June, 2005, of the documented sighting of the ivory-billed woodpecker, previously suspected to have been extinct. As a birdwatcher myself, I found the discovery so exciting and the analysis so compelling that I had the cover of the June 3, 2005, issue feature an illustration of the rare bird, spotted in the Big Woods region of eastern Arkansas—to the delight of some and the dismay of others!

Visual encounters during 2004 and 2005 and analysis of a video clip from April, 2004, seemed to confirm the existence of at least one male ivory-bill. The bird's acoustic signatures had also been heard and recorded. Although extensive efforts to find additional birds remained unsuccessful, the researchers, led by John Fitzpatrick of Cornell Ornithology Laboratories, were persuasive in pointing out that the potential habitat for a thinly distributed source population was vast—nearly 850 square miles—so it was not unusual that other birds had not yet been spotted.

The report that the purportedly extinct ivory-billed woodpecker had been discovered deep in the swamps of Arkansas made front-page news across the country and even around the world. This rarest of rare birds is so spectacular that, according to folk legend, those who see it spontaneously cry out, "Lord God!" giving rise to the nickname "the Lord God bird." The news reports were read not only by the 60 million birders in North America but also by millions of others swept up by interest in the rediscovery. For many Americans, the sighting came as an unexpected piece of rare, good news; to the inner circle of bird enthusiasts it was a remarkable story of hope and survival.

The editorial staff celebrated the sighting and the publication coup for *Science* with a great party given by passionate environmentalists Roger and Vicki Sant. They named one of their philanthropic organizations, devoted to the arts, education, and the environment, the Ivorybill Foundation. But nine months after the ivory-billed woodpecker appeared on the cover of *Science*, another team, led by renowned ornithologist David Sibley, a distinguished validator of bird species identification, reanalyzed the video presented to confirm the sighting. "None of the features described as diagnostic of the ivory-billed woodpecker eliminate a normal pileated woodpecker," the Sibley team wrote. "Although we support efforts to find and protect ivory-billed woodpeckers, the video evidence does not demonstrate that the species persists in the United States."[1]

Debate has ensued in the academic press ever since. It's hard to tell who won that battle. Although I was disappointed that *Science* published a paper that was likely in error, a silver lining came in the form of a victory for the environmental movement. The Big Woods in eastern Arkansas, where the bird was alleged to have been espied, is now a government-protected habitat. In the end, there are still people who believe that the sighting was legitimate, and there are people who still believe *Science* got it wrong. Although we were lobbied to retract the paper, we opted to let the debate continue. Science doesn't have to be absolutely neat, clean, and decisive in every case, and one doesn't give up on a finding merely because it is controversial.

Rarity is important, but I also like unfamiliar birds. Because most of my bird watching was done as a young man in the East, I enjoy trips to Las Vegas to visit our granddaughter, where I encounter the blackbird called the great-tailed grackle, absolutely characteristic of that area, although in the woods of my childhood it would be a rare bird. I started watching birds as a child in semirural Connecticut and have found in my later years that it is a wonderful escape from everyday tensions. Americans have experienced an explosion of interest in birds as a way of getting to know nature. More than 6 million enthusiasts now buy "birding stuff," and half a million pay dues to the National Audubon Society. The trend is fortunate because it supplies a veritable army of capable observers as data gatherers to support research in conservation biology.

A few years ago I wrote two books with the artist Darryl Wheye, *Humans, Nature, and Birds: Science Art from Cave Walls to Computer Screens* and *Birds of Stanford: 30 Species Seen on the Main Campus*. We used birds as a model to illustrate some connections among art, science, and nature. Our approach used art, both contemporary and historic, along with thoughtful and compelling captions to situate the images in ecological and behavioral reality. Our hope was that we might help refute the conventional sense that there is a clear divide between science and

Don's love of science, policy, good writing, and people, combined with his extraordinary communication skills, made him a perfect choice for editor-in-chief of *Science*. He was a natural in the position. Our editorial page was a must-read during Don's tenure. He did not shy away from controversy, and his gift with the written word raised the impact of our editorial page at a time when scientists and scientific research needed an effective advocate. Equally important was Don's skill as a decisive leader. He guided us through some pivotal moments in the journal's history, including the publication of the human genome paper, the establishment of processes to handle papers reporting dual-use research, and the unraveling of the stem cell papers and subsequent retractions. He was diplomatic, fair, and completely open in handling these high-profile events. Don did not make excuses when the journal made mistakes. Rather, he insisted that we learn from the past and make changes to improve future performance. The staff loved being on his team, and his enthusiasm for producing the magazine was infectious. As a result, the staff performed better, enjoyed work more, and flourished under his supervision. The journal and the staff owe Don a debt of gratitude for his leadership and his friendship. His tenure as editor-in-chief has had a lasting impact on AAAS, *Science*, and everyone who had the honor of working with him!

—*Monica Bradford*

It was always a pleasure to work with Don. He valued the news component of the magazine and sat in on many of our meetings—sometimes suggesting ideas, sometimes simply observing, but always interested and engaged (and sometimes amused) by the mind-set and process of iterative decision making. He enjoyed being part of the magazine and loved the bully pulpit of the editorial page. His enthusiasm and sheer gusto made the Kennedy administration a great pleasure for those of us who were here. Don holds a special place in our hearts.

—*Robert Coontz*

I most appreciated Don's gentlemanly enthusiasm and generosity in taking the time to meet with and mentor his junior colleagues.

—*Kelly LaMarco*

One year, the Newcomb-Cleveland prize was one of Ian's physics papers, and Don came to my office and asked me about it, giving me a short oral summary of a paper on quantum mechanics. He took a lot of time to digest a paper so far from his expertise (which was very broad), and indeed, his summary was correct. He felt he really needed to know what was getting the Prize. It was one of many testaments to his dedication and his interest in everything scientific.

—*Phil Szuromi*

Don's wide vision of the world we live in, related to his deep knowledge of environmental matters, soon brought him onto the international scene in a most constructive way. His research on the structure and function of simple nervous systems led to his election to the National Academy of Sciences at an exceptionally young age. As a member, he stimulated interest there in science education, convincing the leadership that it was not only a wonderful place for research but for education as well.

—*David Hamburg*

Don was very open, approachable, and incisive, always saying interesting things. I recall a moment walking through the old executive office building next to the White house. "Do you see those little fossils embedded in the marble floor?" he said. "That one's a Paleo-zoic nautiloid. You know you could teach a whole course on this floor." He knew about the granite and about what had happened with the fossils, and it was just fascinating.

—Larry Horton

Don loved writing op-eds and had a good sense about what readers would be interested in. He had a magical way of engaging people, with just the right style for each piece. He was generous with the editorial page as well, offering the platform to voices he didn't always agree with, but felt it was the right thing to do. Don taught me the power of diplomacy.

—Lisa Chong

Some of my strongest memories of Don come from our many group discussions. Whether he agreed with your viewpoint or not, and whether his final view and goals matched your own, it was clear from his summaries that he listened to what everyone had to say and acknowledged the perspectives each had to offer. I learned leadership from Don.

—Marc Lavine

I was so nervous when I was given his first piece to edit. I think he knew that I might be. He came into my office and said, "Don't hold back, let me have it!" So I did. And he de-manded that with every piece after that.

—Lisa Chong

Don challenged us to take risks, and stood by us after we took them.

—Valda Vinson

Unbeknownst to Don, he was actually an honorary and beloved staff member of the business and publishing office. Under his splendid editorial direction, the magazine flour-ished, and he was a wonderful asset with our advertising clients, librarians, and members. While Don understood the wall between business and editorial, he also respected the role that business played in the magazine's success and engaged in many thoughtful con-versations with us on a wide range of publishing issues including international expansion, access rights, licensing, advertising placement, and subscription pricing. His intelligence and integrity were always evident, and we saw him as the embodiment of the qualities to which the business, publishing office, and magazine as a whole should aspire.

—Beth Rosner

art. This kind of art traces back to the paintings found on cave walls and contains a valuable storehouse of information. We argued that it ought to be given the name "Science Art," art that is both aesthetically engaging and scientifically informative, making the discoveries of science—as well as the need for protecting and restoring habitats—accessible to a much wider audience. I'm reminded of the art of Chesley Bonestell in the mid-twentieth century, cited as a significant personal influence in their youth by so many of those who launched the space program. The right image can often bridge educational, cultural, and economic divides, slipping past language and political barriers.

When I go out on my campus walks I don't really expect to see rare birds, though the occasional surprise is always welcome. Instead, I go in anticipation of the peace and comfort that settles over me when I'm in fairly natural surroundings in the company of other living things. The birds are nature's big bonus.[2]

THE CASE OF SCIENTIFIC FRAUD

Often the editor-in-chief was required to settle disputes between authors who should have been collaborating. These could generally be resolved by widening the discussion to a slightly larger pool of thoughtful colleagues within a discipline. At times, we called on the assistance of deeply respected senior scientists when a question arose about balance in subject matter. In my time, this panel was chaired by my somewhat gruff but altogether loyal friend John Brauman, who was chairman of Stanford's department of chemistry. It comprised half a dozen members, most of whom belonged to the National Academy of Sciences. In addition to participating in the annual meeting of the AAAS, we would call on them when crises arose. Their guidance was most needed when research ethics and questions about cheating were on the table. Some make the broad claim that scientific fraud is everywhere. My view is that it happens rarely and that detecting it is possible if the journal's procedures are in order.

During my tenure three cases arose involving ethical lapses. When disputed authorship or fraud was concerned, we usually referred the problem back to the institution of origin for resolution. When a particular author was accused of academic fraud in producing a paper under consideration, we typically returned as much information as we could to the scholar's institution and asked for a decision by the dean, provost, or their standing committees. One such case concerned an experiment involving the development of stem cells by a group at Seoul National University (SNU) in South Korea.

In February 2004, Dr. Hwang Woo-suk and his team at SNU announced that they had successfully created an embryonic stem cell with the somatic cell nuclear transfer method—the first reported success in human somatic cell cloning. Energized by the claim, a U.S. delegation traveled to South Korea and returned impressed with the experimenters and their work. On the basis of this corroboration, *Science* accepted a key paper. In the March 12, 2004, issue of *Science*,

Hwang explained that his discovery would enable every patient to receive custom treatment for an enormous range of diseases and conditions—with no immune reactions.

A year later Hwang announced an even greater achievement, creating eleven human embryonic stem cells using 185 eggs. This work, published in the June 17, 2005, issue of *Science*, was instantly hailed as a breakthrough in biotechnology. But close scrutiny revealed that several of the photos of purportedly different stem cells were in fact photos of the same cell. Researchers raised questions about striking similarities between the DNA profiles of the cloned cells. Hwang and another coauthor asked *Science* to withdraw the paper when it emerged that much of his stem cell research had been faked.

Science sent the published papers and the editors' and reviewers' comments to an internal panel set up at SNU to investigate the allegation. On December 23, 2005, the panel announced its initial finding that Hwang had intentionally fabricated stem cell research results, calling Hwang's misconduct "a grave act damaging the foundation of science."[3] Publication of the paper was withdrawn. It was my unpleasant task to explain why *Science* retracted a paper it had found acceptable in its first iteration. SNU took responsibility for the fraud investigation, and we had no reason to doubt that they did an excellent job.

Another case involved a long series of multiauthored papers from one of the most distinguished scientific institutions in America, Bell Laboratories, describing major breakthroughs in physics, including the development of a transistor where the main switching component was a single molecule. As recounted by Dan Agin in his book *Junk Science*, soon after J. Hendrik Schön published his work on single-molecule semiconductors, others in the physics community noticed anomalies in his data. Lydia Sohn, then of Princeton University, noticed that two experiments carried out at very different temperatures produced identical data. When editors pointed this out to Schön, he claimed to have accidentally submitted the same graph twice. Paul McEuen of Cornell University then found the same data in a paper describing a third experiment. More research uncovered a number of examples of duplicate data in Schön's work, triggering a formal investigation by Bell Labs, chaired by my Stanford colleague, Professor Malcolm Beasley.

The investigation concluded that the data in the disputed research, published between 1998 and 2001 in various prestige journals including *Nature* and *Science*, had been improperly manipulated, if not fabricated outright. Schön had conducted the bulk of the experiments while on leave in independent labs in his native Germany, not at Bell Labs where colleagues could participate, replicate, and confirm his work. The investigation found that he kept no laboratory notebooks, his raw-data files had been erased from his computer, and some of his graphs, presented as plots of experimental data, were produced using mathematical functions. Further doubts arose because it seemed impossible to do the quantity of work that Schön submitted. In 2001, he averaged one scientific paper every eight days. For most scientists, a few papers a year is considered very productive.

Bell Labs immediately fired Schön who, until then, had looked to be well on his way to a Nobel Prize. On October 31, 2002, with the agreement of his coauthors, *Science* withdrew eight papers written by Schön. These anecdotes show that the peer review system underlying scientific publication is not designed to snuff out fraud, which raises the question of where fraud detection rightly belongs. The scientific community continues to grapple with this problem. Thankfully, the phenomenon is not widespread.

A third encounter with academic fraud struck closer to home, occurring at Stanford much earlier in my career. Frank Morell, a candidate for head of the neurology division at Stanford Medical Center, turned out to have falsified all kinds of records, but one in particular struck a nerve. Morell claimed he had recorded a response from a patient's single "command" nerve cell, but when I looked at the slide, I recognized the responses as having come from a neuron from my own laboratory. When confronted, Morell offered a variety of excuses akin to "the dog ate my homework." It was a most embarrassing situation for all involved.

In retrospect, I am disappointed we did not reveal Morell and his fraud for what it was. He eventually left Stanford. Dean Robert Alway decided that Morell should be released without blemish, which allowed him to continue the ruse a bit longer, although in time everyone in the academic medical community learned the truth.

THE HUMAN GENOME PROJECT

Science has always had a strong competitor in the journal *Nature*. Breakthrough scientific findings are usually published in one or the other and make news in the major media. We used to worry about the relative standing of *Science*, partly because we knew that some papers submitted to us had previously been reviewed and rejected at *Nature*. In fact, we learned that the reverse was also true, that *Nature* would occasionally publish papers we had declined. I soon realized that there was a simple explanation: any paper carefully reviewed by one of the journals is likely to be accepted by the other because the very process of review has raised the quality of the contribution.

Both journals figure in the very first challenge I undertook in my new role at *Science*. A major project to discover the nucleotide sequences that characterize the human genome was under way, with competing organizations pursuing different sequences of the project. The so-called public project was led by Francis Collins and sponsored by the National Institutes of Health and various collaborating institutes around the world. The competing, privately funded project was pursued by a powerful team led by Dr. Craig Venter and colleagues at the high-technology company Celera.

In 2000, just as I arrived at *Science*, principals from both research teams were meeting with government officials and were saying highly uncomplimentary things about the other. The rivalry between the teams was occasionally intense enough to induce profanity—one instance involving a story in the *New Yorker*![4] A meeting I attended at a downtown Washington hotel had been arranged at which leaders from both research groups were scheduled to meet, and I had hoped to persuade them to publish their findings together in a single issue of *Science*. But the level of hostility between the two groups was so high, the personal animosity so deep, and the genuine difference in philosophies so great that over the ensuing months my hopes were dashed. Although mediation was an interesting personal experience, there was simply too much bitterness—some taken out on the *Science* staff—to make progress toward a joint publication. In any case, such a joint paper would have stretched our capacity to its limit. The resulting journal would have rivaled the Neiman Marcus Christmas catalog in heft. On reflection, I don't know how we would have managed the postage.

In fact, that meeting was merely the introduction to a series of difficult interactions, many of them initiated by representatives of the publicly funded program, whose attitude suggested some entitlement on the basis that "after all, we stand in the public interest." Venter and the Celera group plainly wanted to take advantage of what the other group was producing in the public domain, which in turn produced anger. Venter's results were not available to the public project scientists, but theirs were available to him. In the meeting's aftermath, several advocates of the public program telephoned me and my colleague Barbara Jasny to insist that Celera should be required to make its data public, a matter clearly not in our hands. After much negotiation with both groups, it became clear to me that we would not be persuasive in compelling a single publication comprising the work of both groups and that *Science* would have the privilege of publishing only one human genome sequence—Celera's.

That was a clear ending for an unpleasant passage. It struck me as ironic that the public program, with its idealist, open-access philosophy, wound up publishing its sequence in the commercial journal, *Nature*—whereas *Science*, the professional society's nonprofit journal, published the privately funded Celera sequence. I developed respect and even friendship with Venter, whom I found personally engaging. And the good news is that when the two sequences were published in competing journals—virtually simultaneously—they matched up well, thus providing confidence in the mutually confirmed results.

THE POWER OF THE PEN

Among the privileges I most enjoyed at *Science* was oversight of the weekly editorial page. In my nearly eight years at the helm, I had the opportunity to express my views on more than a hundred occasions, writing opinion pieces on such areas of science and policy as dual use, government secrecy, bioengineering, stem cell research, and climate change that I continue to find most compelling and in need of attention. On occasion I would inject a bit of humor, allowing me to flex my creative muscle.

Readers old enough to remember Don Marquis's syndicated *New York Sun* columns may recall that at night, a cockroach named Archy took over his typewriter to write short pieces about Mehitabel, an alley cat with a celebrated past. Because Archy typed by jumping on the typewriter keys, he had difficulty with uppercase letters and punctuation, yielding a rather free-form text. The July 27, 2007, issue of *Science* ran a piece asserting that domestic cats derive from at least five species found across the Fertile Crescent region of the Near East, probably coincident with the development of agricultural villages; the descendants of these domesticated cats were transported throughout the world with human assistance. Cats being among the more aloof creatures—at least as compared to domesticated canines—I thought it would be amusing to manufacture a cat's response asserting her independence and adapted the Archy and Mehitabel construct in my editorial of August 3, 2007:

> boss, I sent archy to the keyboard to say how upset I am about the terrible treatment of cats in the papers its because of a report in science telling all about how we cats got started pretty interesting but some of the papers are saying that's how we got domesticated. Domesticated hell! Domesticated is for dogs not us boss. Action needs to be taken against this slander . . . why do they think we occasionally bring a bloody present into the house and lay it on the bed or the best rug its because we want to remind everyone that we are volunteers not repressed conscripts like the damn rovers and Fidos.[5]

A perpetual issue of my more serious commentary involved the concept of dual use—that is, science that can be deployed for good or for evil, depending on the end purpose. For example, in the wrong hands, the new discovery of an infectious agent could be developed into a bioweapon. On the other hand, a committee of public health experts would likely cheer such a finding, given all that we might learn from the discovery about infections and how to control them. Publication in a journal like *Science* cannot control for the end use of each new discovery— whether the specifics of a new strain of infection make their way into the laboratory of an epidemiologist focused on vaccine design or the cell of a terrorist intent on biological warfare. My view is that the public may be more concerned about dual use than the issue merits. The leadership of the AAAS, *Science*, and *Nature* ultimately issued a joint policy, generally advocating with respect to dual use that the question of whether or not to publish is up to the journal and its editors.

SCIENCE VERSUS SECRECY

The tension between scientific discovery and secrecy is particularly murky when the government applies rules intended for military matters to the basic scientific enterprise. In the case of classified research, scientists are clearly prevented from publishing the findings. Perhaps worse than the micromanagement of the editorial process, the government imposed policing responsibilities on research universities like Stanford, either instructing them not to host foreign visitors or requiring them to monitor the movements of foreign visitors around places like Silicon Valley, where industry laboratories abound. Foreign nationals were sometimes barred from participating in scientific symposia; others were not permitted to work on projects in academic laboratories; still other visitors had to be tailed by their faculty hosts if they visited other labs in the area. Academic institutions and their faculties objected strongly to what they perceived as a misapplication of the arms control statutes. As early as 1982 I wrote an editorial for *Science*, asserting,

> If a Soviet scientist is viewed with such alarm that universities must be asked to police his visit, then the Department of State can apply visa controls. And if a technology has such military value that exposure in an open environment presents clear risks to national security, the government can classify the technology, thereby permitting the universities to decide in advance whether they can accept the restrictions that come along with the work. But to apply a burdensome set of regulations to a venture that has gained such great strength through its openness will cost the nation more than it can be worth.[6]

Attempts to resolve these matters were undertaken by a group called the Department of Defense—Universities Forum, which I co-chaired with Dick DeLauer, Undersecretary of Defense for Research and Engineering and a former Stanford baseball player. The Department of Defense was inclined to be cooperative, but DeLauer had to contend with an internal struggle involving the Assistant Secretary for Policy, Richard Perle. Eventually, a National Academy of Sciences committee chaired by Dale Corson, the physicist who had been president of Cornell University, recommended eliminating the use of such regulations as proxies for classification.

A deafening federal silence was followed by the recommendations of the Forum and Corson committee. But eventually President Ronald Reagan issued an executive order establishing National Security Defense Directive (NSDD) 189. It said, in part,

> It is the policy of this Administration that, to the maximum extent possible, the products of fundamental research remain unrestricted. It is also the policy of this Administration that, where the national security requires control, the mechanism for control of information generated during federally funded fundamental research in science, technology and engineering at colleges, universities, and laboratories is classification. . . . No restriction may be placed upon the conduct or reporting of federally funded fundamental research that has not received national security classification, except as provided in applicable U.S. statutes.[7]

NSDD 189 is still in effect, confirmed in 2002 by then-National Security Agency Director Condoleezza Rice in a letter to former Secretary of Defense Harold Brown. Known as the Reagan Rule, it ensured among other things that the federal government would not use classification as a way of preventing access to scientific research.

To me, the tension between science and secrecy seemed a paranoid fear of espionage, and I used the editorial page of *Science* to comment:

> There is an old and by now familiar edginess between two important threads in American culture. We depend increasingly on science and technology, activities heavily based upon the free flow of information. At the same time, our national security interests often require efforts to conceal information—and so, increasingly, do the interests of commercial research sponsors. Not surprisingly, the science values sometimes collide with the security values.[8]

Six years later, not much had changed. I wrote,

> There has long been an uncomfortable relationship between the scientific community in the United States and the regulations of its government regarding exports. In the early 1980s, that conflict flared up in protests against restrictions on the publication of basic research findings and on the admission of foreign nationals to seminars or symposia in the United States. The issue is of increasing international concern, not only because it hampers useful transnational collaboration, but because restrictions have been applied to exports that might improve other nations' economic competitiveness with the United States, as well as to those with potential military applications.[9]

Universities and their faculties have to recognize that they confront two different sponsors, government and industry, with different but often equally insistent demands for secrecy. Those demands require consistent responses, recalling a wise observation first made by Admiral Bobby Inman: Society will judge harshly those who are willing to keep for profit the same kinds of secrets they are reluctant to keep for patriotism.

In a concept known as "deemed export," the federal government has attempted to restrict the flow of research findings to and from unapproved countries, most often for security concerns. So if, for example, a paper came in from a group doing ecology in the Cuban forests, my natural instinct was to edit it. But it turns out that offering editing services to an unlicensed Cuban entity constituted a "deemed export." My choice to edit such a paper literally became a federal case!

Scientific culture is by nature oriented toward disclosure. Because the research venture grows by accumulation of information, it depends on the open availability of previous work through publication. Yet it was not uncommon to encounter bizarre uses and applications of regulations designed to prevent the flow of information to sources that might be "inappropriate." I was tempted to publish a paper allegedly from an unlicensed source—which was permissible—full of the most egregious errors of construction and spelling, with an editor's note explaining that the Office of Foreign Assets (OFAC) allowed me to publish but not to edit the submission! Fortunately, OFAC came to its senses before I did anything so foolish.

Other problems arise when science faces political opposition. Take the case I editorialized on in June of 2002:

> In a case recently brought to *Science*'s attention, an Israeli researcher asked an author of papers in two peer-reviewed journals to supply cells from a clone used in expression analyses. The author declined, citing her institution's protests against the recent Israeli military actions. It was a particularly ironic refusal because the research being conducted by the group in Israel involve[d] a collaboration with Palestinian scientists . . . aimed quite directly at benefiting Palestinians.[10]

My view is that personal political convictions do not trump authors' obligations to share experimental material. The author's refusal was a clear violation of the policies in place at most journals and commonly understood in the scientific community. When authors submit a manuscript, they make a commitment to supply cells, special reagents, or other materials necessary for verification. They are not free to violate that commitment once their paper has been published. At *Science*, we set out the expectations this way: "Any reasonable request for materials and methods necessary to verify the conclusions of the experiments reported must be honored."

"Perhaps," my editorial concluded, "there are plausible excuses for failure to comply with the sharing requirement like 'We ran out' or 'The dog ate my culture,' but 'We don't like your government' just won't do."

SCIENCE AND REGULATORY POLICY

I have long been interested in how science is used to inform regulatory policy. From time to time, the federal government has wrestled over the composition of committees put together to resolve the relationship between a statute and its regulatory derivative. Both the executive branch agencies and congressional committees have struggled earnestly to keep political influence out of the scientific committees, to adopt and empower peer review judgments, and to establish rules to limit conflicts of interest.

A major effort of this kind was instituted by the Bipartisan Policy Center in Washington, D.C., which resulted in production of a final report on August 5, 2009, entitled "Improving the Use of Science in Regulatory Policy." The report was the product of a committee co-chaired by me and the Honorable Sherwood Boehlert, former chairman of the House of Representatives Science committee.

I remember his sense of humor, which helped get us through some difficult situations with the genome project. He has been the quintessential renaissance scientist—amazing for his ability to move from plant taxonomy to energy science to genomics. I admired his editorial writing ability and his willingness to take on authority. I still remember when he suddenly had to fill in a hole in the calendar and said, "It's a good thing a lot of people in government have annoyed me lately."

—*Barbara Jasny*

As editor-in-chief of *Science,* Don routinely impressed me with his skill as a science communicator, particularly his elegant and masterful command of an extraordinary vocabulary, which he leveraged in countless media interviews and insightful editorials. He was also unfailingly diplomatic and magnanimous in all of his dealings with me.

—*Ginger Pinholster*

What I loved most about talking with Don was his endless curiosity about the human condition, his deep understanding of policy matters, and his exquisite sense of context—understanding what particular bit of information would shed the most light on the subject and get to the heart of the issue. Most "experts" would have been happy to possess just one of those qualities. Don had all three and wore each one of them modestly. I greatly miss talking with him.

—*Jeff Mervis*

If there's one legacy that Don left with me, it is that policy simply has to be informed by good science. Scientists need to get better at operating in the world of policy, and policy makers need to get better at incorporating science. I think Don was really one of the first champions of that concept. He played a key role in my understanding of this and in my future career.

—*Thomas Butler*

Don made *Science* and AAAS a very pleasant place to work. What I remember most from his tenure as editor-in-chief was his curiosity and his passion for the causes he particularly believed in. It was inspiring.

—*Nancy Gough*

I remember thinking when Don hired me here at *Science* that he had a contagious enthusiasm for such a broad sweep of science, combined with such a kind and personable manner. He made a deep impression on me that motivates me still.   —*Jake Yeston*

Don would be the first to congratulate any student for advancing science by disproving any of his previous work. He has impeccable manners and no trace of paranoia. He has an omnivorous and insatiable curiosity about the world around him. He delights in learning, and he inspires others to learn and to excel. He knows how to nurture a thought as well as how to spot a weak idea, and he has an ever-present good humor, which he uses to good effect.

—*Larry Horton*

It was fortunate that David Goldstone, an old friend from *Science* and *Nature*, served as project director. The report pointed out that in recent decades the use of science in the regulatory process has been a "flashpoint"—with frequent objections to the politics or scientific credentials of those involved. The plain intention of the report was to support the morale of the scientists and public faith in the process. Much attention is given to how scientific advisory committees should be appointed, and how concerns about conflicts of interest or bias in prospective members should be managed.

The appointment process for science advisory panels should be as transparent as possible, with potential conflicts of interest or possible biases identified for proposed appointees. In general, the National Academy of Sciences has rules of disclosure for appointment to proposed advisory committees that should be adopted by the science advisory boards. In each case, a clear conflict of interest would be a financial interest that might impair the individual's objectivity. The report added that it would be improper to appoint anyone with a conflict of interest to chair a committee. Agencies should not frequently invite the same scientists for service on advisory committees. Data on selected members of advisory committees should be kept, including disclosure forms, records of objection, and responses from the agency. In the words of the panel: "To build public trust through transparency, much more information on federal advisory committee members needs to be available than is now the case."[11]

Here again, the panel took the National Academy of Sciences as an appropriate guide in dealing with bias as an entity quite different from real conflicts. Its position was a reflection on how Academy committees were sometimes constructed so that members with contrary views—enough to qualify them as "outsiders" with respect to a particular scientific issue—were present with more conventional members. Often such pairings produced the kind of debate that is more productive than routine agreement on the merits. My own view is that our project succeeded in clarifying a difficult set of issues.

The report was a response to the George W. Bush administration's practice of subjecting Scientific Advisory Committee appointees to tests of political loyalty. Committees were shut down and reconstituted with new members closely associated with administration positions. Past administrations had certainly made politically friendly science appointments, but what was unusual about the Bush administration was how deep the practice cut—in particular, the way it invaded areas once immune to this kind of manipulation. George W. Bush had signaled his disinterest in serious science and scientific opinion from the outset. Security was being imposed not to protect the public from the possibility that science might fall into hostile hands but to shield them from information that might otherwise cast doubt on government policies. Obstructing stem cell research and efforts to mitigate climate change, the Bush administration coerced scientists or twisted facts to encourage policy outcomes it favored. The results of congressional testimony by the Union of Concerned Scientists in relation to these practices were frequently summarized in *Science*.

Delivering a Clark Kerr Lecture in Berkeley in 2007, I observed that "presidential claims to exclusive power over knowledge may sometimes be justifiable in our national interest," but that we should not be misled. "We are not an empire and our president is neither an emperor nor the commander-in-chief of anyone who doesn't happen to be in the armed services."[12] An example of the Bush administration's reluctance to acknowledge climate change occurred after Julie Gerberding, head of the U.S. Centers for Disease Control and Prevention, presented congressional testimony on the potential impacts of climate change on public health. Her testimony was reviewed at the White House and soon made to disappear. Virtually all of what she said about climate change—six pages of it—was blacked out of the document filed with the Senate Environment and Public Works Committee.

Congressional decision making on science issues has not been much better. "If you look at the voting," noted Daniel Greenberg, for many years editor of the *Science and Government Report*, "it's mostly along party lines. I don't think many congressmen could answer ten basic questions about science."[13] One recalls Senator Proxmire's sarcastic bestowal of the "Golden Fleece Award" on the Search for Extraterrestrial Intelligence (SETI), though success in that project would be the most significant discovery in human history.

President George W. Bush's 2001 executive order banning use of federal funds to support stem cell research, along with his veto of the 2007 Senate bill that would have authorized such research, highlight the fact that certain kinds of science are now proscribed on what amount to religious grounds. There has been a convergence in American society between religious conviction and partisan loyalty. When this convergence leads to managing the nation's research agenda, its foreign assistance programs, or high school curriculum, that marks a very important change in our national life. I penned a number of *Science* editorials on this issue, suggesting, for example, that candidates should be asked hard questions about science policy, including how those positions mirror belief.

SCIENCE ILLITERACY

The problem reflects in part the escalating contention between science and religion. The increase in the number of Americans committed to evangelical forms of Christianity has created a new fissure in the public regard for science. In many Christian schools, the science curricula assign texts that do not teach about evolution and use scriptural arguments to set the age of Earth at 6,000 to 10,000 years. Creationist alternatives to teaching evolution have been debated in no fewer than forty states, while surveys suggest that one in eight biology teachers believes in creationism, statistics that place us first among developed nations in the denial of evolution.

Surveys suggest that 95 percent of Americans are scientifically illiterate. Something like half of American adults do not know that Earth goes around the Sun and takes a year to do it. Sixty-three percent are unaware that the last dinosaur preceded the first human. Three-quarters of Americans believe in angels. It is painfully obvious that we have difficulty bringing the most rudimentary scientific rules to bear even on the business of discriminating sense from nonsense. Numbers of our fellow citizens can readily be persuaded that they can be made more powerful by pyramids, cured of cancer by eating apricot pits, or lost forever in something called the Bermuda Triangle.

In any given year, our democracy has to decide on a host of issues that have important scientific and technological content: what to do about climate change, how to organize human or robotic exploration of space, how to develop a sustainable national energy policy, or how to treat the health potential offered by embryonic stem cells. To be an educated citizen increasingly requires a familiarity with the basic concepts and the vocabulary of science. The challenge of education is to instill in our youth enough curiosity and basic understanding to qualify them as useful citizens of the modern world. A nation without some system of scientific belief—one in which astrology is taken as seriously as astronomy and in which mysticism is accorded the same respect as rational analysis—is not likely to give sustained support to serious scientific inquiry.

The 2001 Hart-Rudman Commission Report concluded that domestic terrorism was the number one threat to national security but that widespread scientific illiteracy was number two. When a nation invades another with little clarity about the science and technology underlying the war's proximate cause, when a population is seized by fears that science has shown to be unreasonable, or when children may not learn basic building blocks of knowledge because scientific understanding and moral judgments are conflated—then a widespread understanding of science seems a compelling need.

Scientific illiteracy has many roots—underfunded schools, oversized classes, uninspired textbooks, poorly trained and underpaid teachers, peer pressure, failure to group students by ability, and most important, a culture that promotes short-term gratification while expecting little of its youth.

We might start by limiting the overdoses of vocabulary and comprehensive information that now overstuff too many textbooks. We need to transcend the memorization of facts, figures, and formulas. Rather than presenting the packaged load that is characteristic of virtually all introductory courses we need to teach what science is about: the larger concepts, the history, the *method*, and the *wonder*—the mysterious and awe-inspiring phenomena that will sustain interest in science long after the minutiae are forgotten. If science teaching were to begin with the great mysteries—things strange beyond comprehension, immensities beyond imagination—and work backward to the familiar, more students might become inspired. The result might be adults less susceptible to pseudoscience and superstition and more in tune with the transcendent yearning to both comprehend the cosmos and see more deeply into the self.

American science deserves the respect of the American people—because it has earned it. If our society cannot bring itself to understand science—if instead it prefers fantasy and myth to data and evidence and is the willing victim of charlatans—it will soon find that science is being done somewhere else, and that others are reaping its benefits.

Science education—the public understanding of science—is requisite to the survival of civilization, if not of our species. Ignorance is the prime medium for every war, act of terror, and myopic "ism." "It is only through science that we have been able to pierce the infantile, dysfunctional need to be the center of the universe," said *Cosmos* producer Ann Druyan. "That we even *do* science is a hopeful sign for our mental health. In some far future, when all our conceits are revealed to be but a product of our history and inborn imperatives, science will still be ratcheting ahead, finding bits of reality. No single bit is sacred. But the quest is."[14]

If science is a belief, it is simply a faith in the inherent potential of humanity. As the only reliable road to whatever reality is accessible to us, scientific knowledge is the result of open inquiry and debate, accepted only when a range of compelling evidence is corroborated and replicated by a community of inquirers. Science is structured like a web; its facts are bound tightly in place by many supportive threads. When they enable us to make accurate predictions and build powerful devices, we know we have tapped into some form of reality. "It is not the 'true' story," said science writer Chet Raymo, "but it is certainly the truest."[15]

CLIMATE DENIAL

In a *Science* editorial, published July 26, 2002, entitled "POTUS and the Fish," I commented on a *New York Times* front-page photo of President George W. Bush landing a striped bass, intended for his daughter, Jenna, off the coast of Kennebunkport, Maine. I called this bass "a fish with a message":

> In my summertime reverie, I imagined that the 43rd president might have turned to No. 41, who was driving the boat, and said, "Gee, Dad, did you catch 'em like this when you were Jenna's age?" Although tempted to employ the usual fisherman's license to lie, former President Bush would have had to answer, "No, son, I don't remember that we did."

And with good reason! Back in the day, when George H. W. Bush fished these same waters, such stripers were scarce north of Cape Cod, which is why, I added, "It always surprises me when thoughtful outdoorsmen like the president don't buy into the reality of global warming right away without requiring persuasion from bevies of advisers."

"The next time he meets with a group of old friends who are still in denial about climate change," I concluded, "he should tell them a fish story. The message from Jenna's striper could just as well have come in a bottle from the scientific community: Climate change is real, and it's time to do something."[16]

Science editorial "Potus and the Fish," July 26,

EDITORIAL

POTUS and the Fish

Summer is the time for fun—and as I write, looking at today's *New York Times* (8 July), there is the president of the United States having some. In a four-color photograph above the fold, he is helping his daughter Jenna boat an impressively large fish. It is not named in the caption but is readily identifiable as Morone saxatilis, called striped bass by us New Englanders, though doubtless known to the White House chef by its Chesapeake name, rockfish. Everyone in the picture is having a wonderful time. But the president, without his knowledge, has just captured a fish with a message.

In my summertime reverie, I imagined that the 43rd president might have turned to no. 41, who was driving the boat, and said "Gee, Dad—did you catch 'em like this when you were Jenna's age?" Although tempted to employ the usual fisherman's license to lie, former President Bush would have had to answer: "No, son. I don't remember that we did." In fact, when I was Jenna's age and studying fish biology at Woods Hole, it was almost a mantra that stripers (and bluefish, another sport-fishing favorite) were relatively scarce north of Cape Cod.

The recent northward redistribution surely delights the Bushes and other Gulf of Maine fishermen. More important, these changes in biogeography have many parallels, as the striper's message to the president is repeated elsewhere. On the West Coast, in the intertidal at Hopkins Marine Station near Monterey, California, old transects made in John Steinbeck's day have been reexamined, demonstrating a massive replacement of northern invertebrates by ones with a more southern distribution. On land, around the Bush estate in Kennebunkport, Maine, American cardinals, birds unknown in New England in my youth, now not only breed but even come to feeders in the dead of winter!

These observations typify a growing host of phenetic studies that have documented biological responses to global warming during the past century. The list is rich indeed: significant advances in the dates for first breeding in a number of bird species; changes in the dates at which British plants first flower; upward shifts in the distribution of Alpine flowering plants, at rates up to 4 meters of elevation per decade; and northward adjustments in the distribution of several species of North American butterflies. Such changes document the reality of global warming, though we are not necessary for that purpose, as we now have so much physical data (ranging from average global temperature to rates at which glaciers are receding or river ice breaks up) to show that it's happening. But examining the biological impacts is useful for at least two reasons.

The first is that it tells us something about what continuing change may portend. What is clear is that natural communities will not be displaced intact as the temperature rises. Each ecosystem depends on a kind of coevolved synchrony, in which flowers and pollinators, predators and prey, herbivores and their food plants not only depend on one another but also on one another's timing. If the flower isn't blooming, the butterfly can't pollinate it: result, no nectar for the insect, no seeds for the plant. Most of the studies show that different species respond at different rates, dismembering communities that once worked well together. It is something we should expect in estimating the impacts of climate change.

The second is that the biological effects tell us things directly that we can otherwise learn of only from someone else's numbers. Anyone my age (I'm 71) can document such changes as a result of personal experience. That's why it always surprises me when thoughtful outdoorsmen like the president don't buy into the reality of global warming right away, without requiring persuasion from bevies of advisers.

My impression is that President Bush is coming awake to this particular problem, and he probably doesn't need much help from me. Nevertheless, here is a suggestion. The next time he meets with a group of old friends from the oil bidness who are still in denial about climate change, he should tell them a fish story. The message from Jenna's striper could just as well have come in a bottle from the scientific community: Climate change is real, and it's time to do something.

Donald Kennedy

Bush and bass.

Climate change threatens the loss of biodiversity and the human services that depend on natural ecosystems, and the depletion of such resource stocks as clean air, fresh water, and ocean fisheries. These relentless engines of change have three things in common. They are nonlinear, dynamic events that promise surprises. They are complex, with many interactions among them. And they are caused by human action. Climate change will affect every other issue: agricultural capacity, especially in the tropics; infectious disease, by altering the range and efficacy of important vectors of viruses; coastal marine ecosystems, by changing sea level.

Those who study Earth systems have long wavered between a view of change that emphasizes linear, steady progression—the uniformitarian view—and one that stresses dynamism and sudden nonlinear surprises. Indeed this contest is but one version of a struggle that is as old as human thinking about the natural world; it is the war between statics and dynamics. Once we thought Earth was stable and that the Sun revolved around it; now we find that even when standing still, we are moving in nine different directions. Once we thought that the cell membrane was a fixed skeleton, and now we know that antigens, pores, and other assemblies float around it. Once we thought that Earth's skin was solid, and now we know that buildings fall down because its great plates cruise around and crash into one another. In one case after another, we find dynamics triumphant over statics. And now, new interpretations of recent geological history have similarly damaged the relatively static, uniformitarian view of climate.

To begin to understand the problem, one must have some grasp of what has come to be called Earth systems science: the annual energy budget of Earth, primary productivity, oceanography and meteorology, the physical geography of major land masses, the principles of ecology and biological diversity, and the properties of ecosystems that determine their utility in the services of humanity. We are engaged in a giant experiment, in which Earth's climate system is being deliberately manipulated according to no planned protocol, based on no working hypothesis. Not surprisingly, we have no idea how it's going to turn out.

The Easter Islanders followed a different but similarly disastrous course: treating a rich resource of tropical forest as though it were inexhaustible. At some point, it must have been evident that the forest and seabirds were disappearing. What did the hunters and loggers think? What was the person who cut down the last tree thinking as he did it? Jobs before trees? The Easter Islanders apparently could not grasp that their accelerating ceremony-driven harvesting would eventually overtake the regeneration rate of their most precious resource. It will soon be time to shift our focus to the social sciences and to what they might tell us about human behavioral traits that will be required if we are to deal with the forthcoming environmental realities.

Some of the blame for the persistence of climate denial can be laid on the press. Not only has the number of sections and departments dedicated to science in major American metropolitan dailies fallen by half in recent years as declining newspaper economics have tightened their grip, but the journalistic tradition of objectivity is too often distorted into a kind of false balance, giving equal weight to opposing views, no matter how much or little credibility or value they possess.

A larger share of the blame falls on the handful of people exposed in Naomi Oreskes' book, *Merchants of Doubt*, documenting the fact that the very same few individuals and public relations people have been vociferously behind every major denial of scientific findings that threaten one or another vested interest for the last half century—that smoking doesn't cause cancer, that asbestos is safe, and now climate denial. Paid by the tobacco and oil companies, they have been extremely effective in casting doubt on the overwhelming scientific consensus, ironically implying that it is the scientists who are protecting self-interest.

Yet scientists as a group tend to be apolitical about their work. Most really care about the truth; it's what they signed up to uncover. Against those like Woosuk, or a few who can be bought or influenced by a need for grants, the whole enterprise of science has built-in safeguards—through peer-reviewed journals, open inquiry and debate, and results that require replication by peer researchers.

Money, however, is not the only motive behind climate denial. The most energetic deniers tend to be somewhat right of conservative, often because they sincerely believe in a libertarian position—that the result of government interference in the solution to any problem is a threat to individual freedom. But we no longer live in the nineteenth century. Society—nationally, globally—is too interdependent, if not symbiotic, and the individual too unprotected against impersonal events, natural, economic, or political, to reverse the course of history. And what is a greater threat to individual freedom than rising seas and runaway temperatures?

Climate denial rooted in ideology is perhaps even more pernicious than that engendered by scientific illiteracy. Conservatism, once the repository of a traditional wisdom that knew the connectedness of all things, has grown increasingly reactionary, fundamentalist, and antiscientific, a cynical paranoia that disposes of uncomfortable facts with conspiracy theories and simplistic psychologies. Politics has become increasingly polarized. As with all living organisms, the ills in social systems are complex, interwoven, and multilayered. But a person's opinion on one issue will usually foretell his or her stance on most other issues, and the polarization of parties widens to the point of inaction. An intelligent approach to the issues requires a balanced mind, applying the values of both left and right while adopting neither as ideological orthodoxy.

I once advised graduating seniors at commencement that, in the kind of world most of them would inhabit, "the single personal quality for which you will have the greatest need is balance. Accept the world as it is, in all its complexity, and have the patience and the courage to analyze and command that complexity rather than reducing it by simplification. Retreat to ideology is easy, and being

In 1994, Don and Stephen Schneider were already beating the drum on the peril of climate change. These guys were very early on the bandwagon trumpeting the fact that the scientific community was in near complete consensus that human-induced climate change was presenting a huge threat to the planet. That was an eye-opener, and thank goodness for the two of them. It took a sustained drumbeat to ever get it out of the academic halls into the common lexicon and public consciousness. They knew this was such a big risk that they had to figure out a way to translate very complex science in a way that could be digested by policy makers—adverse policy makers—and the general public. They really shouldered that load early on.

—*Thomas Butler*

Don was a great editor-in-chief—so generous and so much patience. His dedication and persistence in gaining recognition for the importance of climate change data must have made a significant contribution to global decision making. I was always extremely grateful for his support and supreme diplomatic talents.

—*Caroline Ash*

Birding with binoculars and wearing *Science* shirt in Don's early 80s; twenty-first century.

After completing his term as president, Don led a Carnegie study group on the relationship of environmental problems to deadly conflict, clarifying how such relations could go wrong and how violence could be prevented. It was well received, both in academic and government circles, reflecting not only his personal intellectual leadership but his wisdom in selecting outstanding biological and social scientists who worked together closely in analyzing these complex problems.

—*David Hamburg*

My first "up close and personal" encounter with *Science* came when Don Kennedy asked me to join the Senior Editorial Advisory Board. What a treat for any researcher! Don made us all a family. Thanks to my experience with Don and what I learned from him, when I was asked whether I would consider being Editor-in-Chief in 2013, I could not imagine a higher honor.

—*Marcia McNutt*

What a wonderful, wonderful man.

—*Leslie Roberts*

righteous is gratifying. Those who can boil every issue down to plain doctrine have a much easier time of it, but we have a world overloaded with doctrine."[17] The great issues in life, I suggested, are too complicated to yield easily, and we are obligated not to approach them in a lazy or wishful way.

MORE THAN MEANS: SCIENCE AS MEANING

My love of science has much to do with its mystery. In a meeting of the American Association for the Advancement of Science in 1989, I argued against the tendency to oversell science on utilitarian grounds, suggesting that its ultimate value lies less in making us richer and healthier and more in helping us grasp the true depths of the mystery. "Mystery surrounds us," wrote naturalist Chet Raymo, "it laps at our shores. It permeates the land. Scratch the surface of knowledge and mystery bubbles up like a spring." And "the larger the island of knowledge, the longer the shore of wonder."[18]

In the history of science is the message of humanism—that we must think in the limited but positive terms of fulfillment, that the true faith is a belief in the inherent potential of humanity. To believe less is to live in the shallows of what it means to be human.

I close with a quote from a great friend who shares my commitment to science:

Perhaps it had no beginning. Perhaps, being spacetime itself, it is neither where nor when. Like the scarlet ribbons of song, it came "I will never know from where." Yet here I am, awake in this vast improbability for a nanosecond of cosmic time, a mote of life on a fleck of rock afloat in the cosmic ocean. What better way to pass that waking instant than to probe its mysteries? What better ends than love and wonder, the two great gifts of consciousness? A true sense of wonder ignites an open quest for knowledge—not the idolatry born of an egocentric metaphysics, of our Paleolithic brains, our parental programming, or the need to restore childhood innocence—but a curiosity rooted in true humility, one guided by the highest of human endeavors, the enterprise of science.[19]

EPILOGUE

THE SUBJECT OF MEMORY is a sensitive one. Memories of my early family life have pained me, whereas the memory problems I deal with today are a source of stress over how they affect my loved ones.

I now find myself yearning for a conversation I was never able to conduct with my father. He passed away before it occurred to me to initiate it. The recent changes in my own cognitive health have altered my perspective on my brother Dorsey's handicap and its dominant role in my family of origin. These have been unexpected and challenging changes in how I think about my own history, as well as my present and future. The opportunity to have candid discussions with my coauthor, as well as with my wife Robin, has provided a welcome change of perspective as I have coped with a difficult decline in personal capacity. I wish I could talk to my father about it. He cared for my brother throughout his illness. He cared for my mother through Alzheimer's disease. I have no doubt he could impart wisdom and patience in my present situation.

My diagnosis involves neurological changes that entail dementia along with Parkinsonian symptoms, making it impossible for me to carry out any of the academic functions I once accomplished with ease. Because I once held prominent roles as president of a leading university, editor-in-chief of a major academic journal, and commissioner of a federal agency, I now find myself being honored and praised for what I did in the past, not what I am able to accomplish today. My roles were likely to attract public attention, but I enjoyed them all and hope that I increased the quality and sustainability of each institution. Yet my present handicap makes it impossible for me to replicate the kinds of successes I used to achieve and for which I still occasionally receive accolades. In many respects I have assumed an identity much like that of my brother Dorsey.

With this fresh perspective and a softened heart, I look back with a different kind of understanding to my parents, their history together, my handicapped brother Dorsey, and my own role in that nuclear family.

As I focused on family history, the most interesting revelations had to do with the way my career paralleled my father's. In some respects, his life was lived as a writer, editor, and publisher. Even in his military career, he wrote and published manuals covering tactics. After World War II, he signed on with the Ford Motor Company, where he and a brilliant art director took the *Ford Times*—a publication meant to help Ford dealerships make friends with their customers— and created a publication of broad national interest, drawing on new and promising writers like E. B. White and artists like Charles Harper. His staff plainly loved him. They called him "the Colonel," and I know their loyalty made the collective effort flourish. In many ways, his was an editorial career.

I thought of this often when I assumed the editorial direction of *Science*. My father's example of sensitive and encouraging leadership was a model for me, and I regret that I never had the chance to talk with him about what he had accomplished professionally under somewhat parallel but different circumstances to my own. If I could sit down with my father, I would note our common good fortune in working with people we loved and respected. I would want to ask what kinds of support he might have wanted in dealing constructively with my brother's handicap. I hope that level of support will be provided, both by friends and particularly our three daughters, to the loved one who is caring for me.

If we could have our conversation, there is something else—something deeply personal—on which I would seek his advice. That is, how does one cope with life's inevitable decline? Whether one's condition is the process of natural aging; or, as in my brother's case, the result of an unfortunate brain disorder; or, as in my case, some of each, I would want to ask my father to share the wisdom he developed both in dealing with Dorsey and graceful aging himself.

(opposite, top)
Daughter Cameron and grandchildren Leila and Joshua, *Science* farewell party, 2008..

(opposite, below)
Don and son Jamie at *Science* farewell party, 2008.

(below)
Don with Page and Julia at *Science* farewell party, 2008

During my fantasy chat with my father, would he possibly pass along parts of the wisdom he took away from his own losses and decline? My father was a realist. Thinking hard on it, I can imagine he might just remind me that times change—and sometimes form unexpected outcomes. We make plans, and God laughs.

And so, I suppose, should we, as heartily and as often as possible.

He always seemed, even at half steam, to be way ahead of the rest of us. Even now, he has a lot of reserve in him to rise to the occasion.

—Bill Stone

For me, assisting Don with the organization of his papers and the production of *The Last of Your Springs* was a course on Stanford from 1980 to 1992. As he looked back on his presidency and began the work of review-ing his personal papers, his reminiscences were long and thoughtful in their contemplation of the past. Whether talking about the impermanence of history or discussing a Stanford sports event, the time spent with him was always enlightening. It was a window into the essence of this man who had given so much of his life to Stanford and American higher education.

—Maggie Kimball

We have all seen the brilliance and good sense, the warmth of personality, the intellectual independence, and the devotion to every person and institution he served—never to himself—that have characterized Don Kennedy's incredible life.

—Jim Gaither

The qualities for which Don (whom Jamie and I call 'Pops') is renowned in his professional life—enthusiasm, curiosity, generosity, and warmth—are the same qualities that have made him a great stepfather. For ex-ample, soon after he and my mom got married, he took up tennis, in which he had never had much interest, so that he could play with Jamie and me, and he taught me how to tackle the *New York Times* crossword puzzle. During my adolescence, while he was Stanford's president, he tutored me in biology, edited essays, read drafts of college and job applications, and tried regularly (albeit unsuccessfully) to teach me the names of his favorite birds and plants. As I moved into adulthood, he helped me through bad breakups, sang to my children when they were fussy, and packed my lunch every day when I was studying for the bar exam. Pops has always made time for the unglamorous, out-of-the-limelight, day-to-day kind parenting that I needed as a teenager—and still sometimes needed as an adult. When it came to stepfathers, I hit the jackpot.

—Cameron Kennedy

One of my fondest memories of Pops, my stepfather, is his lifetime passion for collegiate athletics. When I was ten years old, he began taking me to baseball games at Stanford's Sunken Diamond and called me the team's good luck charm; Stanford won every baseball game I attended with him. We also went to Stanford basketball games, football games, and practices. When we went on my college trip (which we did as a fam-ily and while he was Stanford president!) and drove through small towns all over the United States, we played a game; almost without fail, he was able to guess the mascot of the high school in every small town before we passed it. He has been a wonderful parent to me.

—Jamie Hamill

Almost everyone at Stanford knows the Dish—a huge fifties-era radar dish in the foothills above Palo Alto, then criss-crossed with dirt paths for runners, hikers, dog walkers, and birders. Some of my best times with my Dad happened there. In 1976, I had left college after two years, knowing I was headed in the wrong direc-tion, but with no idea where I wanted to go or how to get there. My Dad started running with me, first a quar-ter mile around the track at a nearby park and eventually graduating to several miles around the Dish.

On the first Dish run, we were on a long uphill climb; I was tired and discouraged and ready to quit. My Dad said, "Just one little rise, you can definitely do one little rise." I made it to the top of that little rise, re-covered on the slight downhill, and we started up hill again. Again, my Dad said, "Just one little rise; it's not hard, just one foot in front of the other, and you can make it to the top." We made it to the top and cleared it. After that, he said, "Just one more rise, one last rise, and it will be downhill the rest of the way." We made it to the top of the last of the three rises, and then it was indeed downhill all the way the back home.

Now my Dad has a hard time finding words. When I asked him what he wanted me to write about for his memoir, he gestured toward me and family photos around us and said write about this, this is what matters to me. When I think of my Dad, I think of the Dish story. That period was a point where my life pivoted, and I began moving toward who I ultimately became. My Dad was a big part of that. He saw the best in me, even when I was not my best self. He supported and encouraged me when I was discouraged and needed a little push. And "just one more little rise" became a joke in our family for meeting any difficulties along the way, and a touchstone for me in moving forward through the next forty years. My Dad is having difficulties remembering things, but he remembers this story.

—Page Kennedy

One of the wonderful but seldom noted things about my father is his sense of humor. I remember family dinners during which we laughed until our ribs hurt—raucous, competitive, witty, and absurd; and every so often an event would fire Dad's creative/evil genius and a clever poem or song would emerge. In my early teens I kept a messy biology experiment of a bedroom; the joke was that it contained a complete ecosystem (plants, birds, various insects, reptiles, amphibians, small mammals . . .). One day my parents and sister, Page, decided to clean my room for me; the experience was so devastating that Dad memorialized it in verse:

> I'd rather suffer on the rack,
> Or cower while the rockets boom,
> Or have them tie me to the track,
> Than clean up little Julia's room.
>
> Enduring tortures medieval,
> Facing up to endless doom
> Seem a rather minor evil,
> Compared to cleaning Julia's room.
>
> But nonetheless—I wouldn't fool ya,
> Whatever rots 'neath bed or shelf,
> It beats by miles persuading Julia,
> She should clean it up herself.

There were others—one on the Watergate scandal, one from the FDA years making fun of FDA/DC politics, and my all-time favorite, his poem, "The Gut." There are also a series of "Kennedy's Laws," funny on the surface but with a deeper truth. Kennedy's Law #1: "If something is so serious that you cannot find a way to laugh at it, it's not true." I've always taken that one to heart; it implies an ability to laugh at oneself.

Personal responsibility has been a thread throughout Dad's life. I think he wrote *Academic Duty* in part as a response to what he saw as incorrect or liberal interpretations of academic freedom. His reaction to the indirect costs "scandal" is another example. I learned personal responsibility early from him, and I think it is the most important lesson he taught me—along with the ability to find humor anywhere.

—Julia Kennedy Tussing

Editor's note: I would love to have known Don at his height—the man exalted in all these sidebars. Yet the man I *have* come to know retains the marrow of those tributes—seeing the good in everyone and everything, caring for what counts, accepting the present and sparing no effort to make the best of it. Just as I felt I had lost something of myself when my fingers would no longer play the guitar, but had only lost the guitar, Don can lose the intellectual music that has defined his life, but not the deeper refrain, the contrapuntal motifs that have always defined the man. What abides, and what resounds through all these tributes, is less his brilliant mind than that humble spirit and core humanity.

—*Wyn Wachhorst*

ROBIN'S EPILOGUE

MY HUSBAND COMPLETED THE FIRST DRAFT of this memoir at the end of 2014. Although features of his dementia were by then becoming more prominent, his medium- and long-term memory were remarkably intact. He thoroughly enjoyed his sessions with his collaborator, Susan Wolfe, who continued throughout to ask him questions and elicit his stories. The result is entirely his.

In May 2015, Don experienced a serious stroke, affecting the speech and language centers of his brain and his ability to read. Since then, and characteristic of him, he has diligently pursued speech therapy and performed the homework given by his speech therapist. Meanwhile, of course, his dementia continues its relentless destruction of his mind and memory. We live—separately and together—one day at a time.

Don with Robin, Stanford Alumni Association travel study trip to Kenya, 1989.

I hope that readers of this book will recognize that it is not only a memoir but also a love story. To this day, I am deeply in love with my husband, who is also admired and beloved by thousands of others who have been the beneficiaries of his kindness, his caring, his sense of humor, his teaching genius, his farsightedness about issues that plague our society and our planet, his principles and values, and his loyalty. And I know he remains just as deeply in love with me. We are both exquisitely aware of and grateful for our ongoing romance.

What brought us together was our deep and common love of the same institution—Stanford—which so profoundly changed us both and captured our passion, enthusiasm, and commitment, and through which we found each other.

Love abides.

DONALD KENNEDY
Memberships, Boards, and Directorships

- American Academy of Arts and Sciences, *Fellow*
- American Academy for the Advancement of Science, *Fellow*
- American Bird Conservancy, *Member, Advisory Council*
- American Philosophical Society, *Member*
- Bing Professor of Environmental Science at Stanford University, *Emeritus*
- California Academy of Sciences, *Fellow*
- California Nature Conservancy, *Member, Board of Directors*
- Campus Compact, *Founding Member*
- Carnegie Commission on Preventing Deadly Conflict, *Co-Director*
- Carnegie Commission on Science, Technology and Government, *Member*
- Carnegie Endowment for International Peace, *Trustee*
- Children Now, *Founding Director and Chairman*
- Clean Sites, Inc., *Member, Board of Directors*
- Center for Environmental Science and Policy at Stanford University, *Codirector*
- CollabRx, Inc., *Chairman of Scientific Advisory Board*
- Common Sense Media, Inc., *Policy Advisor and Member, Board of Directors*
- Freeman-Spogli Institute for International Studies, *Senior Fellow*
- Harvard Board of Overseers, *Member*
- Health Effects Institute (HEI), *Founding Director*
- Inside Track, Inc., *Member, Board of Directors*
- Institute for Research in the Social Sciences (IRISS), *Member, National Advisory Board*
- Marian Koshland Science Museum of the National Academy of Sciences Committee, *Chair*

- Medical Education for South African Blacks, *Chair*
- National Academies' Project on Science, Technology and Law, *Co-chair*
- National Academy of Sciences, *Member*
- National Commission for Public Service, *Member*
- National Institute of Medicine, *Member*
- Packard Foundation, *Trustee*
- PBS News Hour, *Science Advisor*
- President of Stanford University, *Emeritus*
- Professor of Education at Stanford University, *Emeritus*
- QuestBridge, Quest Scholars Program, *Board Member*
- San Bio, Inc., *Member, Scientific Advisory Board*
- Sierra Club, *Director, Climate Recovery Partnership*
- SoAR (Supporters of Agricultural Research), *Member, Board of Directors*
- Solazyme, Inc., *Member, Scientific Advisory Board*
- Springboard Forward, *Member, Board of Directors*
- Stanford Center on Longevity, *Member, Advisory Council*
- Stanford University Board of Trustees, *Emeritus*
- Stem Cells, Inc., *Director*
- Tosk, Inc., *Member, Scientific Advisor Board*
- United States Food and Drug Administration, *Commissioner*
- Upromise, Inc., *Member, Board of Directors*
- Woods Institute, *Senior Fellow*

SIDEBAR CONTRIBUTORS

Anderson, Kai. Former graduate student. Now CEO, Cassidy & Associates.

Ash, Caroline. Senior Editor, *Science*, UK office.

Bennett, Richard. *Stanford Daily*, May 26, 1992. Former Director of Campaign Planning, Stanford Office of Development.

Biddulph, Jeff. "Stanford University's President Gets High Marks for Leadership." *Boston Globe*, April 30, 1985, p. 2.

Bok, Derek. President Emeritus, Harvard University.

Bradford, Monica. Executive Editor, *Science*.

Brest, Iris. Stanford Associate General Counsel, 1979–1995.

Brest, Paul. Dean of Stanford Law School, 1987–1999.

Bruno, Merle. Syracuse undergraduate student. Now Professor Emerita of Biology, Hampshire College.

Butler, Thomas. Stanford graduate student. Now Assistant Regional Counsel, U.S. Environmental Protection Agency.

Calabrese, Ronald. Stanford graduate student, 1969–1974. Now Senior Associate Dean for Research, Samuel Candler Dobbs Professor of Biology, Emory College of Arts and Sciences, Atlanta, GA.

Califano, Joseph A. Jr., Secretary of Health, Education, and Welfare, 1977–1979.

Camarillo, Albert. Associate Dean and Director of Undergraduates Studies in the School of Humanities and Sciences, 1991–1993; Stanford Professor of History, 1995–present.

Chase, Bill. President Emeritus, Emory University.

Chen, Josephine. Stanford undergraduate, 2016.

Chong, Lisa, Deputy Editor, *Science*.

Coontz, Robert, Deputy News Editor, *Science*

Doty, Andy. Stanford Director of Community Relations, 1972–1993.

Ehrlich, Paul. Professor of Biology, Stanford. Now President of the Center for Conservation Biology at Stanford.

Eisen, Arnold. Professor of Jewish Culture and Religion; former chairman of the Stanford Department of Religious Studies. Now Chancellor, Jewish Theological Seminary, New York.

Feldman, Edward G. "A Plea for FDA Stability." *Journal of Pharmaceutical Sciences*, 68 (July 1979).

Fields, Howard. Stanford graduate student. Now Professor of Neurology, University of California San Francisco.

Footlick, Jerrold K. "How High the Cost: Indirect Costs at Stanford University," in *Truth and Consequences: How Colleges and Universities Meet Public Crises* (Phoenix, AZ: Oryx Press, 1997).

Freelen, Bob. Stanford Vice President for Public Affairs, 1983–1993.

Fricke, Russell. Stanford graduate student in neurobiology, 1971. Now a physician.

Gaither, Jim. Chairman, Stanford Board of Trustees.

Galyan, Gohar. "Startup Finds Entry-Level Jobs, Mentors." *Stanford Daily*, April 27, 2001.

Goldsmith, Tim. Fellow graduate student, Harvard. Now Professor Emeritus, Department of Molecular, Cellular, and Developmental Biology, Yale University.

Goodman, Corey. Stanford undergraduate, 1968–1972. Now Adjunct Professor of Neuroscience, U.C. Berkeley, and Managing Partner, venBio Partners LLC (a life sciences venture capital firm).

Gough, Nancy. Editor, *Science Signaling*.

Gregorian, Vartan. President Emeritus of Brown University.

Hamburg, David. Professor and Chairman of Psychiatry and Behavioral Sciences, Stanford. Now President Emeritus, Carnegie Corporation of New York; advisor to the Nuclear Threat Initiative, Washington, D.C.

Harntha, Juthymas. "Kennedy's Style: An Asset, Liability." *Stanford Daily*, May 29, 1992, pp. 1, 6–7.

Hastorf, Albert. Chairman, Department of Psychology, Stanford, 1961–1970; Dean, Humanities and Sciences, 1970–1974; Provost, 1980–1984; one of the founding directors of Stanford's Interdisciplinary Program in Human Biology. Deceased.

Holloway, Jonathan. Stanford undergraduate, 1989.

Horton, Larry. Senior Associate Vice President and Director of Government and Community Relations, 1977–2013.

Hoy, Ronald. PhD thesis student, 1964–1968. Now David and Dorothy
Merksamer Professor of Biology; Howard Hughes Medical Institute
Professor; Department of Neurobiology and Behavior, Cornell University.

Hudnall, Mike. Stanford Deputy General Counsel, Emeritus.

Jasny, Barbara. Deputy Editor Emeritus, *Insights*.

Juilland, Alphonse. Former Chairman of the Department of French and Italian,
Stanford.

Karlin-Newman, George. Professor of Biology, Stanford. Now Senior Director,
Diagnostics Assay Development at QuantaLife, Inc.

Karlin-Newman, Patricia. Rabbi and Stanford Senior Associate Dean for
Religious Life.

Kennedy, David. Emeritus Professor of History, Stanford.

Kimball, Maggie. Stanford archivist.

LaMarco, Kelly. Senior Editor, *Science Translational Medicine*.

Lavine, Marc. Senior Editor, *Science*.

Levin, Herbert, Harvard roommate, 1948. Now U.S. Foreign Service Officer,
retired.

Lewis, Anthony. *New York Times* [clipping].

Liu, Goodwin. Stanford undergraduate. Now California Supreme Court
Associate Justice.

Lougee, Carolyn. Professor of History, Stanford.

Lyman, Richard. President of Stanford University, 1967–1970.

Mancall, Mark. Emeritus Professor of History, Stanford.

Manning, Carolyn. Vice President, Alumni Relations, *Stanford* Alumni
Association, 1998–present.

Maxmin, Jody. Stanford Associate Professor of Art and Art History and of
Classics, Stanford.

McCarthy, Colman. *Congressional Record*, July 13, 1979, quoting the *Washington
Post*.

McNutt, Marcia. Editor-in-Chief, *Science*. Now President, National Academy of
Sciences.

Mellon, DeForest. Don's first postdoctoral student at Stanford, 1961–1963. Now
Professor of Biology, University of Virginia.

Mervis, Jeff. Senior Correspondent, *Science*.

Milton, Catherine. Founder and Director of the Stanford Haas Center for Public
Service. Now Nonprofit Organization Manager, Firelight Foundation;
Philanthropic Ventures Foundation; Generations United.

Muller, Henry. Managing Editor of *Time*. Now editorial advisor for LargeNetwork.

Owen, John A. Jr. Editor-in-Chief, *Hospital Formulary*; President, U.S. Pharmacopeial Convention; now Professor of Internal Medicine, University of Virginia.

Paull, Tanya. Stanford graduate student, biology, 1991. Now Professor of Molecular Biosciences, University of Texas at Austin.

Pinholster, Ginger. Director, AAAS Office of Public Programs.

Rice, Condoleezza. Stanford provost, 1993–1999; Secretary of State and National Security Advisor under President George W. Bush; now Stanford Professor of Political Science and Director of the Global Center for Business and the Economy in the Stanford Graduate School of Business.

Richter, Ari. "Unqualified Comments." *Stanford Daily*, June 3, 1992.

Roberts, Leslie. News editor, *Science*.

Robinson, Norman. Associate and Acting Dean of Student Affairs, Stanford, Emeritus.

Rosenzweig, Robert. Stanford Vice President for Public Affairs, 1974–1983.

Rosner, Beth. *Science* publisher during the Don Kennedy years.

Roth, Richard. Don's undergraduate and postdoctoral student and research assistant. Now Professor Emeritus, Penn State University College of Medicine.

Schwartz, John. Stanford General Counsel. Now Owner, Quantum Strategies Management Co.

Shapiro, Harold. President, Princeton University, 1991.

Shultz, George P. U.S. Secretary of State, 1982–1989; Thomas W. and Susan B. Ford Distinguished Fellow at the Hoover Institution at Stanford.

Simon, Mark . "Contemplative Days for the Last Penguin off the Ice Floe." *Peninsula Times Tribune*, September 6, 1992.

Smith, Marshall. Former Dean of the Stanford School of Education, *Campus Report*, June 17, 1992, p. 8.

Stone, Bill. President Emeritus, Stanford Alumni Association.

Szuromi, Phil. Senior Editor, *Science*.

Vinson, Valda. Deputy Editor, *Science*.

Voss, David. Manager, Hoover House, 1981–1984. Now Talent Manager, Office of Development, Stanford.

Wachhorst, Wyn. Editor

Wade, Nicholas. Staff writer for the Science Times section of *The New York Times*.

Warren, Bill. Fellow student, Dublin School; Harvard roommate. Now on the Board of Directors, Saving the West Foundation.

Waxman, Hon. Henry A. Representative for California's 33rd congressional district, 1975–2015. *Congressional Record*, July 13, 1979, E3599.

Wessells, Norman. Stanford Professor of Biology and Dean of Humanities and Sciences, Emeritus.

Williams, Vaughn. Undergraduate student.

Wilson, Mark. *Boston Globe*, April 30, 1988, p. 2. Now political cartoonist, illustrator and Adirondack environmentalist.

Wolf, Howard. Director, Stanford Alumni Association.

Yeston, Jake. Deputy Editor, *Science*.

Zarin, Deborah. Stanford undergraduate, 1974. Now Director of Clinical Trials, NIH.

NOTES

INTRODUCTION

1. Donald Kennedy, *The Last of Your Springs* (Stanford, CA: Stanford Historical Society, 1998), p. 66.

CHAPTER 2

1. *The Last of Your Springs*, p. 172.

2. Donald Kennedy, *Academic Duty* (Cambridge, MA: Harvard University Press, 1977), pp. 60, 71, 95.

CHAPTER 3

1. *Academic Duty*, pp. 196, 212–213.

CHAPTER· 4

1. *Academic Duty*.

2. Herbert L. Packer, "Academic Freedom and the Franklin Case," *Commentary*, April 1972.

3. James G. March, Martin Schulz, and Xueguang Zhou, "The Dynamics of Rules: Change in Written Organizational Codes" (Stanford, CA: Stanford University Press, 2000), p. 47.

4. U.S. District Court, Fourth District of Colorado, *Franklin v. Atkins*, 409 F.Supp. 439, 443 (1976), p. 443; available at Justia.com.

5. "Decision: Advisory Board Stanford University in the Matter of Professor H. Bruce Franklin," Donald Kennedy, Chairman, January 5, 1972, p. 122.

6. "Decision: Advisory Board," pp. 141-42.

7. "H. Bruce Franklin: Tenured Radical," History News Network, January 18, 2005; available at historynewsnetwork.org/article/9654.

8. *The Last of Your Springs*, p. 12.

9. *Academic Duty*, p. 134.

CHAPTER 5

1. Donald Kennedy, "Health, Science, and Regulation: The Politics of Prevention." Messenger Lecture I, October 1980, p. 1.

2. "Laetrile," Health Education. Available at health-education.weebly.com/world-without-cancer.html.

3. Donald Kennedy, "Fixing the Drug Laws." *Science* 316 (June 22, 2007), p. 166.

4. "Report to the President on Combating Antibiotic Resistance," Executive Office of the President, President's Council of Advice on Science and Technology, September, 2014, pp. v, 1. Available at www.cdc.gov/drugresistance/pdf/report-to-the-president-on-combating-antibiotic-resistance.pdf.

5. See Nicholas Wade, "Kennedy Leaves as FDA Commissioner." *Science* 205 (July 13, 1979), p. 174.

6. *The Last of Your Springs*, p. 54.

7. *The Last of Your Springs*, p. 117.

8. Other sources for this chapter: Donald Kennedy, "Humans in the Chemical Decision Chain." *Choices* (Third Quarter, 1989), pp. 4–7; Karen J. Winkler, "Riding the Shuttle between Government and Academe." *The Chronicle of Higher Education*, October 29, 1979; PBS: Online News Hour. "NewsHour Science Reports." December 23, 2004.

CHAPTER 6

1. *The Last of Your Springs*, pp. 93–95.

2. Descriptions of these events have been adapted from *The Last of Your Springs*, pp. 75–76, 79, 85, 92–93.

3. Parts of this paragraph have been adapted from *Academic Duty*, pp. 121–122.

4. *The Last of Your Springs*, p. 78.

5. "Stanford University: The Founding Grant with Amendments, Legislation, and Court Decrees" (Stanford, CA: Stanford University Press, 1987), pp. 4, 24.

6. "John Gardner: A Salute." *Science* 295 (March 22, 2002), p. 2177; *The Last of Your Springs*, p. 71.

7. *The Last of Your Springs*, pp. 71, 99.

8. "Pete Seeger, The Power of Song." DVD (Live Nation Worldwide, Inc., 2007).

9. *Academic Duty*, p. 9.

10. *The Last of Your Springs*, pp. 142, 137.

11. *The Last of Your Springs*, p. 34.

12. *The Last of Your Springs*, p .12.

CHAPTER 7

1. Poetry Foundation. Available at www.poetryfoundation.org/poems-and-poets/poems/detail/ 44979.

CHAPTER 8

1. "'Science: The Endless Frontier,' A Report to the President by Vannevar Bush, Director of the Office of Scientific Research and Development, July 1945." (Washington, D.C.: U.S. Government Printing Office, 1945).

CHAPTER 9

1. Eugene H. Methuin, "How He Caught the Campus Chiselers," *Reader's Digest* 32 (January 1992), pp. 81–86.

2. *Academic Duty*, p. 172; *The Last of Your Springs*, p. 194.

3. The current overhead cost recovery rate for Stanford is 57 percent.

4. "Financial Infrastructure: The Indirect Cost Controversy." Available at web.Stanford.edu/dept/pres-provost/president/speeches/cares/frames/indirect .html.

CHAPTER 10

1. *The Last of Your Springs*, p. 210.

2. Available at http://patrickoverton.com/faith-poster/.

CHAPTER 11

1. David A. Sibley, "Comment on 'Ivory-Billed Woodpecker (Campephilus-principalis) Persists in Continental North America.'" *Science*, March 17, 2006, p. 1555.

2. Parts of the preceding are modified from an article I did for *Stanford Magazine* ("Everything but the Cardinal." *Stanford Magazine*, March/April 2001, pp. 60–65). The two books are Donald Kennedy and Darryl Wheye, *Humans, Nature, and Birds: Science Art from Cave Walls to Computer Screens* (New Haven, CT: Yale University Press, 2008) and *Birds of Stanford: 30 Species Seen on the Main Campus* (privately printed, 2012).

3. World Library, "Hwang Woo-suk." Available at www.worldlibrary.org /articles/Hwang _woo-suk.

4. Richard Preston, "The Genome Warrior: Craig Venter Has Grabbed the Lead in the Quest for Biology's Holy Grail." *New Yorker*, June 12, 2000.

5. Donald Kennedy, "Domestic? Forget It." *Science*, August 3, 2007, p. 571.

6. Donald Kennedy, "The Government, Secrecy, and University Research." *Science*, April 23, 1982, p. 365.

7. National Policy on the Transfer of Scientific, Technical and Engineering Information, September 21, 1985. Available at https://fas.org/irp/offdocs/nsdd /nsdd-189.htm.

8. Donald Kennedy, "Science and Secrecy," *Science*, August 4, 2000, p. 724.

9. Donald Kennedy, "A Welcome New Look." *Science*, June 16, 2006, p. 1573.

10. Donald Kennedy, "When Science and Politics Don't Mix." *Science* 296 (June 7, 2002), p. 1765.

11. "'Science for Policy Project' Final Report, 'Improving the Use of Science in Regulatory Policy.'" August 5, 2009, p. 24. Available at https://studylib.net /doc/1186612/improving-the-use-of-science-in-regulatory-policy-science.

12. Quoted in Barry Bergman, "Donald Kennedy on the Control of Scientific Knowledge." *Berkeleyan* 36 (November 8, 2007), p. 6.

13. Quoted in Cornelia Dean, "Where Science and Public Policy Intersect: Researchers Offer a Short Lesson on Basics." *New York Times*, January 31, 2006.

14. Ann Druyan, "Ann Druyan Talks about Science, Religion, Wonder, Awe . . . and Carl Sagan." *Skeptical Inquirer* 27 (November/December 2003); available at www.csicop.org/si/show/ann_druyan_talks_about_science_religion.

15. Chet Raymo, "Celebrating Creation," in Paul Kurtz, ed., *Science and Religion: Are They Compatible?* (Amherst, NY: Prometheus Books, 2003), p. 341.

16. Donald Kennedy, "POTUS and the Fish," *Science* 297 (July 26, 2002), p. 477.

17. *The Last of Your Springs*, p. 72.

18. Chet Raymo, *Skeptics and True Believers: The Exhilarating Connection between Science and Religion* (New York: Walker and Company, 1998), pp. 47–48.

19. Wyn Wachhorst, "A Case for Wonder" (unpublished paper).

DONALD KENNEDY
Bibliography

This bibliography is not complete. Unlisted, for example, are Don's many scientific publications and almost all of his editorials in Science. *Some entries are from copies and clippings with incomplete bibliographic data.*

Academic Duty. Cambridge, MA: Harvard University Press, 1997.

"Academic Health I." *Science* 305 (August 20, 2004), p. 1077.

"The American Research University." *Daedalus* 122 (Fall 1993), pp. 127–156.

"Are There Things We'd Rather Not Know?" In Marcus, Steven, *Neuroethics: Mapping the Field.* New York: Dana Press, 2002, pp. 197–211.

"Basic Research in the Universities: How Much Utility?" In National Academy of Sciences, *The Positive Sum Strategy: Harnessing Technology for Economic Growth.* Washington, DC: National Academy Press, 1986.

Behavior to Neurobiology: A Zoologist's Approach to the Study of Nervous Systems: The Collected works of Donald Kennedy, 1957–1983. 2 vols. Privately printed, 1986.

"Biology Really Matters." *BSCS Newsletter* [Biological Science Curriculum Study], Fall 2002, pp. 23–24.

"The Choice: Finding Hope in the History of Environmental Ruin." *Foreign Affairs*, 84 (March/April 2005), pp. 1–4.

"Civics 101: A Prime Export: U.S. Universities Prepare for Global Change." *Los Angeles Times*, June 10, 1989.

"Climate and Civilization: The Scientific Evidence for Climate Change, and How Our Response to It May Influence National Policy." Inaugural Lecture of the Cornell-Gladstone-Hanlon-Kaufmann Annual Series in Environmental Studies and Communications. SUNY College at Oneonta, October 4, 2000.

"Dealing with Altruism." *Journal of General Education: A Curricular Commons of the Humanities and Sciences.* 62 (2013), pp. 7–10.

"Doing Better, Feeling Worse." Rehabilitation Hospital of the Pacific Foundation, Pamphlet (Duty Free Shoppers Distinguished Lecture Series, November 12, 1990).

"Enclosing Research Commons." *Science* 294 (December 14, 2001), p. 2249.

Excellence in People: Remarks at the Democratic Issues Conference of 1987. Stanford, CA: Office of Public Affairs, 1987.

"Everything but the Cardinal." *Stanford Magazine*, March/April 2001, pp. 60–65.

"Filling a Special Place at Stanford." *Stanford Law Review* 42 (April 1990), pp. 859–861.

"The Future of Science News." *Daedalus* 139 (Spring 2010), pp. 57–65.

"Government Policies and the Cost of Doing Research." *Science* 227 (February 1, 1985), pp. 480–484.

"The Government, Secrecy, and University Research." *Science* 216 (April 23, 1982), p. 365.

"Health, Science, and Regulation: The Politics of Prevention." Messenger Lecture I, October, 1980.

"How Can We Look So Rich, Yet Feel So Poor? President Donald Kennedy's Speech at the Los Angeles Conference on March 16, 1986." *Campus Report*, March 19, 1986.

"Humans in the Chemical Decision Chain." *Choices* Third Quarter (1989), pp. 4–7.

"Investing in the Young." *Congressional Record—Senate*, August 7, 1986, S 10771–10773.

"Kennedy: Sense of Tolerance Is Weapon against Provocation." *Stanford Daily*, February 7, 1992, p. 5.

The Last of Your Springs. Stanford, CA: Stanford Historical Society, 1998.

"Life on a Human-Dominated Planet." In Donald Kennedy and the editors of *Science Magazine*, editors, *Science Magazine's State of the Planet, 2006–2007.* Washington DC: Island Press, 2006, pp. 5–12.

"Managing Our Common Inheritance." In Donald Kennedy and the editors of *Science Magazine*, editors, *Science Magazine's State of the Planet, 2006–2007.* Washington DC: Island Press, 2006, pp. 101–114.

"Of Autos and Superhighways: The Interface between Organismal and Populational Biology—I." *American Zoologist* 9 (1969), pp. 253–259.

"On Academic Authorship." Privately printed speech to Stanford Academic Council, 1985.

"Preserving the Conditions of Life." In Donald Kennedy and the editors of *Science Magazine*, editors, *Science Magazine's State of the Planet, 2006–2007*. Washington, DC: Island Press, 2006, pp. 39–48.

"Science and Its Discontents: An Evolutionary Tale." Center for Studies of Higher Education, Draft 3.10.08 Research & Occasional Paper Series. University of California Berkeley, 2008.

"Science and the Liberal Arts College." *Council on Undergraduate Research Quarterly* 22 (September 2001), 16–20.

"Science and the Media." In Donald Kennedy and Geneva Overholser, editors, *Science and the Media*. Cambridge, MA: American Academy of Arts and Sciences, 2010, pp. 1–9.

"So What If College Players Turn Pro Early?" *New York Times*, January 8, 1990, E.

"The Social Sponsorship of Innovation." *Technology and Society* 4 (1982), pp. 253–65.

"A Source of Optimism." *St. Louis Post-Dispatch*, March 25, 1979.

"Stanford in Its Second Century: An Address at the Meeting of the Academic Council." Privately printed, 1990.

"Stanford-Seeking Computer Virus Is Spotted." *New York Times*, October [?], 1991.

"Sustainability: Can Science Get Us There?" *Renewable Resources Journal*, Summer 2005, pp. 13–15.

"Studies on the Frog Electroretinogram." Dissertation Harvard University, 1956.

"A Welcome Retreat at Treasury." *Science* 304 (April 9, 2004), 171.

COAUTHOR OR COEDITOR

Adams, Amy. "Scientific Fraud Unpreventable, Donald Kennedy Warns." *Stanford Report*, January 23, 2006, pp. 7, 9.

Barnett, Bronwyn. "AAAS 'Goes Hollywood' to Show Perils when Science Meets Competitive Publishing." *Stanford Report*, February 26, 2003, p. 6.

Bipartisan Policy Center Science for Policy Project. *Improving the Use of Science in Regulatory Policy, Final Report*. Donald Kennedy and the Hon. Sherwood Boehlert, cochairs. Washington DC: Bipartisan Policy Center, 2009.

Bok, Derek C., and Donald Kennedy. *Business, Science, and the Universities: Speeding the Transfer of Technology*. Boston: Committee for Corporate Support of Private Universities, 1981.

Calabrese, Ronald L., and Donald Kennedy. "Multiple Sites of Spike Initiation in a Single Dendritic System." *Brain Research* 82 (1974), pp. 316–321.

Carnegie Commission on Deadly Conflict, *Environmental Policy and Regional Conflict.* 1998.

Fricke, Russell A., and Donald Kennedy. "Inhibition on Mechanosensory Neurons in the Crayfish." *Journal of Comparative Physiology* 153 (1983), pp. 443–453.

Goulder, Lawrence H., and Donald Kennedy. "Valuing Ecosystem Services: Philosophical Bases and Empirical Methods." In Gretchen C. Daily, editor, *Nature's Services: Societal Dependence on Natural Ecosystems.* Washington, DC: Island Press, 1997, pp. 23–47.

Kennedy, Donald, et al. "Darwin's Legacy at Stanford." *Stanford Report,* February 25, 2009, pp. 9–12.

———. "Inhibition of Mechanosensory Interneurons in the Crayfish. I. Presynaptic Inhibition from Giant Fibers." *Journal of Neurophysiology* 43 (June 1980), pp. 1495–1509.

Kennedy, Donald, and the editors of *Science Magazine,* editors. *Science Magazine's State of the Planet, 2006–2007.* Washington DC: Island Press, 2006.

Kennedy, Donald, and the editors of *Science Magazine,* editors. *Science Magazine's State of the Planet, 2008–2009.* Washington DC: Island Press, 2008.

Kennedy, Donald, Ronald L. Calabrese, and Jeffrey J. Wine. "Presynaptic Inhibition: Primary Afferent Depolarization in Crayfish Neurons." *Science* 186 (November 1, 1974), pp. 451–454.

Kennedy, Donald, and William J. Davis. "Organization of Invertebrate Motor Systems." In *Handbook of Physiology—The Nervous System I,* pp. 1023–1087.

Kennedy, Donald and Margaret L. Eaton. *Innovation in Medical Technology: Ethical Issues and Challenges.* Baltimore: Johns Hopkins University Press, 2007.

Kennedy, D., W. H. Evoy, and H. L. Fields. "The Unit Basis of Some Crustacean Reflexes." Reprinted from *Nervous and Hormonal Mechanisms of Integration, XXth Symposium of the Society for Experimental Biology* 20 (1965), pp. 75–109.

Kennedy, Donald, and Richard A. Merrill. "Science and the Law." *Issues in Science and Technology* (Summer 2000), pp. 49–51.

Kennedy, Donald, and Geneva Overholser, editors. *Science and the Media.* Cambridge, MA: American Academy of Arts and Sciences, 2010.

Kennedy, Donald, and Roger Sant. "A Global Environmental Agenda for the United States: Issues for the New Administration." *Environment* 42 (December 2000), pp. 20–24.

Lucks, Marjorie, and Donald Kennedy. "Rubber, Blight, and Mosquitoes: Biogeography Meets the Global Economy." *Environmental History* 4 (July 1999), pp. 369–383.

National Academy of Sciences Working Group on Teaching Evolution, Donald Kennedy, Chairman. *Teaching about Evolution and the Nature of Science.* Washington DC: National Academy Press, 1998.

"The New School Spirit." *New York Times*, January 5, 2002, A31.

PBS: Online News Hour. "NewsHour Science Reports." December 2004. Available at www.pbs.org/newshour/bb/science/july-dec04/year_12-23.html.

Remler, M., A. Selverston, and D. Kennedy. "Lateral Giant Fibers of Crayfish: Location of Somata by Dye Injection." *Science* 162 (October 11, 1968), pp. 281–283.

Selverston, Allen I., and Donald Kennedy. "Structure and Function of Identified Nerve Cells in the Crayfish." *Endeavor* 28 (September 1969), pp. 107–113.

Telfer, William, and Donald Kennedy. *The Biology of Organisms.* New York: John Wiley & Sons, 1965.

Wald, George, Paul K. Brown, and Donald Kennedy. "The Visual System of the Alligator." *Journal of General Physiology* 40 (May 20, 1957), pp. 703–713.

Wheye, Darryl, and Donald Kennedy. *Birds of Stanford: 30 Species Seen on the Main Campus.* Privately printed, 2012.

———. *Humans, Nature, and Birds: Science Art from Cave Walls to Computer Screens.* New Haven, CT: Yale University Press, 2008.

ABOUT

"AAAS Meeting Draws a Crowd." *Science*, January 27, 1989, p. 474.

Adams, Timothy. "FDA Chief Wins Plaudits in Perilous Job." *Atlanta Journal and Constitution*, October 8, 1978.

"Alumni Association Names Grove of Trees in Honor of Kennedy." *Campus Report*, May 13, 1992, p. 4.

Auerbach, Stuart. "Crash Program Urged on New Pest Controls." *Washington Post*, February 6, 1976, p. C4.

Bergman, Barry. "Donald Kennedy on the Control of Scientific Knowledge." *Berkeleyan* 36 (November 8, 2007), pp. 1, 6.

Bianco, David. "Kennedy Focuses on Public Service." *Stanford Daily*, September 19, 1991.

Buddulph, Jeff. "Stanford University's President Gets High Marks for Leadership." *Boston Globe*, April 30, 1985, p. 2.

Buderi, Robert. "Can Stanford Build Labs for the New Millennium?" *Business Week*, December 4, 1989, pp. 115–116.

Brody, Baruch A. "Innovation in Medical Technology: Ethical Issues and Challenges." [Review] *The New England Journal of Medicine*. 357 (October 4, 2007, pp. 1456–1457.

Califano, Joseph A. Jr. "Medical Marijuana and the Lesson of Laetrile." *Washington Post*, February 17, 1997, p. 2.

Cohen, June, and Julie Makinen. "Kennedy Had 'Vision,' Was a Brash Fund-Raiser." *Stanford Daily*, May 26, 1992, pp. 1, 3–4.

Cutler, Eric. "Activist Academe Donald Kennedy." *Vis á Vis*, July 1990, p. 76.

Dean, Cornelia. "Where Science and Public Policy Intersect: Researchers Offer a Short Lesson on Basics." *New York Times*, January 21, 2006.

De Fao, Janine. "Longevity Raises Expectations, Kennedy Says." *Stanford Daily*.

Demkovich, Linda E. "A Tough Act to Follow." *National Journal*, May 5, 1979, p. 745.

"Donald Kennedy, FDA Commissioner, to Return as Provost." *Stanford Observer*, April 1978, pp. 1, 8.

Feldmann, Edward G. "A Plea for FDA Stability." *Journal of Pharmaceutical Sciences*, 68 (July 1979).

Fenty, Leigh. "Environmentalist Donald Kennedy Says Worldwide Security Depends on Paying Attention to Climatic Changes." *San Diego Union*, July 10, 2002, Sect. F, pp. 1, 5.

Freedberg, Louis. "Stanford's Chief Farewell Talk." *San Francisco Chronicle*, June, 1992.

"Friday, Oct. 15: Just an Ordinary Day in the Life of President Donald Kennedy." *Stanford Observer*, November 1982, p. 3.

Friedly, Michael. "Changing the Face of Stanford: Kennedy Leaves Behind Legacy of Multiculturalism." *Stanford Daily*, May 27, 1992, pp. 1, 6–7.

Galyan, Gohar. "Startup Finds Entry-level Jobs, Mentors." *Stanford Daily*, April 27, 2001. Available at http://daily.stanford.edu/daily/serviet/Story?id=5560&section=News&date=04-27-2001.

Geiken, Stacy. "Head of the Class." *Runner's World*, March 1991, p. 41.

"Hail to the Chief!" *The Stanford Banner*.

Harntha, Juthymas. "Kennedy's Style: An Asset, Liability." *Stanford Daily*, May 29, 1992, pp. 1, 6–7.

Harris, Michael. "Stanford Chief Taking Time to Ponder the Future." *San Francisco Chronicle*, December 5, 1986, p. 29.

"High Marks for Stanford University President Donald Kennedy." *Congressional Record-Senate*, April 30, 1985, pp. 9844–9845.

Howland, Dave. "Kennedy: You Made Me Proud." *Peninsula Times Tribune*, June 23, 1992, pp. A1–A4.

"Kennedy: Thoughts on Past, Future." *Campus Report*, August 29, 1992, pp. 1, 5, 7.

"Kennedy Inaugural Was Stanford Family Affair." *Campus Report*, October 15, 1980, pp. 1, 11–15.

Klingler, Richard. "Kennedy to Enter Senate Race." *Stanford Daily*, April 1, 1982, p. 1.

Libit, Howard. "Controversy's Glare Scorched Kennedy." *Stanford Daily*, May 28, 1992, pp. 1, 6–8.

"Looking to the Future." *Palo Alto Weekly*, October 9, 1991, pp. 22–23.

Los Angeles Times, March 26, 2004, B12.

Madison, Mary. "Kennedy Enjoying 'Vast Change' after Life as Stanford President." *San Francisco Chronicle*, July 3, 1993, A17.

Maeroff, Gene I. "New President of Stanford." *New York Times*, June 14, 1980.

Marshall, Eliot. "AAAS Meeting Draws a Crowd." *Science* 243 (January 27, 1989), 474-75.

McCarroll, Steve. "Kennedy to Leave: Students, Educators React to Decision." *Stanford Daily*, September 19, 1991, pp. 1, 11.

Owen, John A. Jr. "Au Revoir, Dr. Kennedy." *Hospital Formulary* (August, 1979), p. 737.

"Queen Elizabeth Comes to Stanford." *Stanford Observer*, April 1983, pp. 1, 5.

"Stanford's Auspicious Choice." *Peninsula Times Tribune*, June 16, 1980, p. B-4.

Mead. Dale F. "Stanford Prof New Director for FDA." *San Jose Mercury*, March 4, 1977, p. 1+.

Miller, Marc. "Saving the Galapagos." *New York Times*, October 12, 1995 [Op-ed].

Murray, Bruce, and Bill Johnson. "Donald Kennedy: An Easy Choice for Stanford." *Palo Alto Weekly*, June 19, 1980, p. 11.

Paull, Tanya. "Donald Kennedy's First Fascination—Science." *Stanford Weekly*, July 27, 1989, p. 22.

"Picking the Next Don." *Stanford Daily*, November 5, 1991, p. 4.

"Queen Elizabeth Comes to Lunch at Stanford." *Stanford Observer*, April 1983, pp. 1, 4–5.

Rapalus, Peter. "Kennedy Thanks His Critics as Senate Bids Him a 'Fishy' Farewell." [*Stanford Daily*, 1992]

Reeve, Sara. "Renowned Environmental Scientist Sees Unfulfilled Promise in Mapped Genome." *The Weekly* [USC] 16 (February 5, 2010, pp. 1–2.

Richter, Ari. "Unqualified Comments." *Stanford Daily*, June 3, 1992.

Schwartz, Mark. "A Changing Climate, Environmentally and Politically: Donald Kennedy Outlines the Security Implications of a Shifting Environment." *Stanford Report*, June 5, 2002, pp. 1, 4.

———. "From National Security to the Human Genome: Kennedy's Full Agenda for *Science*." *Stanford Report*, October 11, 2000, pp. 1, 5.

"Science-Rich and Science-Poor: Closing the Gap." Highlights of the Summer 1989 Meeting, Business and Higher Education Forum, Berkeley, 1989.

Seawell, Mary Ann. "Kennedy Reflects on Decade at Helm." *Campus Report*, October 10, 1990, pp. 1, 9.

———. "Kennedy Waves Goodbye to/with the Class of '92." *Campus Report*, June 17, 1992, pp. 1, 8.

Shapiro, Walter. "Putting the School First." *Time*, August 12, 1991, p. 57.

Simon, Mark. "Contemplative Days for the Last Penguin off the Ice Floe." *Peninsula Times Tribune*, September 6, 1992.

———. "Donald Kennedy: Not Quite Gone, Not Quite Forgotten." *Peninsula Times Tribune*, June 18, 1992.

Singer, Brian. "A State Visit." *Stanford Daily*, April 10, 1996, pp. 1, 10.

Spector, Rosanne. "Don Kennedy's Parting Wisdom." *Peninsula Times Tribune*, July 10, 1992, pp. A1, A8.

Speich, Don F. "Donald Kennedy, Stanford Provost, Named President." *Los Angeles Times*, June 14, 1980, CC, II.

Spotlight 5 (June 1992), 1, 9.

"Stanford President Don Kennedy." *Palo Alto Weekly*, June 27, 1984, pp. 1, 13–16.

"The Step into the Unknown." *Peninsula Times Tribune*, June 23, 1992.

Stokes, Donald. "Keeping a Secret: The Queen of England Is Coming." *Stanford Observer*, April 1968, p. 4.

Stillman, Richard M. Review of *Innovation in Medical Technology: Ethical Issues and Challenges*, by Margaret L. Eaton and Donald Kennedy. *JAMA* 297 (June 13, 2007), pp. 2530–2531.

Taubman, Philip. "Donald Kennedy Dusts Up the FDA." *Stanford Magazine* 6 (Spring/Summer 1978), pp. 14–19.

"Two Hands for Donald Kennedy." *New York Times*, July 2, 1979.

"U.S. Must Be Main Funding Source for Science—Kennedy." *Stanford Observer*, April 1983, pp. 1, 10.

Vaughn, Jack. "Kennedy Rescinds Saccharine Decision." *Stanford Daily*, April 1, 1977, p. 1+.

Wade, Nicholas. "Kennedy Leaves as FDA Commissioner." *Science*, 205 (July 13, 1979), pp. 173–174.

Watson, Aleta. "Kennedy Named Chief at Stanford." *San Jose Mercury News*, June 14, 1980.

Watson, Molly. "Advancing a New Agenda." *Click: Leisure, Culture & Pleasure for the Bay Area Executive*. January 2001, p. 73.

Waxman, Hon. Henry A. "Donald Kennedy's Departure from the FDA." *Congressional Record*, July 13, 1979, E3599.

Winkler, Karen J. "Riding the Shuttle between Government and Academe." *The Chronicle of Higher Education*, October 29, 1979.

Workman, Bill. "New President Is Chosen by Stanford." *San Francisco Chronicle*, June 14, 1980, pp. 1+.

INDEX

Academic Duty, 34, 45, 109, 205

Agin, Dan: *Junk Science*, 183

Agriculture and Food Research Initiative (AFRI), 83

Alway, Robert, 184

American Association for the Advancement of Science (AAAS), 175, 180, 182. 186, 190

American Chemical Society, 85

American Civil Liberties Union (ACLU), 67

AmeriCorps, 103

Anderson, Kai, 11, 33, 39, 132, 170

Armed Services Board of Contract Appeals, 156

Ash, Caroline, 198

Bacchetti, Ray, 89

Bach, G. L., 66

Baez, Joan, 98

Bass, Anne T. and Robert M., 165–66

Baxter, Chuck, 45

Bayh, Birch, 144–45, 147

Beasley, Malcolm, 183

Beckman, Arnold, 147

Beckman Center for Molecular and Genetic Medicine, 9

Bell Laboratories, 183–84

Bement School, 18–19, 20

Bennett, Richard, 95

Bennett, William, 108, 109

Berg, Paul, 44

Beroza, Gregory, 124

Biddle, Paul, 154, 155, 156, 157

Biddulph, Jeff, 120

Big Game of 1982, 128

Bing, Peter, 105, 117, 119

Biogen, 159–150

Bipartisan Policy Center: "Improving the Use of Science in Regulatory Policy," 189

Block, Rabbi Richard, 139

Bloom, Allan: *The Closing of the American Mind*, 109

Boehlert, Sherwood, 189

Bok, Derek, 147. 149, 161

Bonestell, Chesley, 182

Booker, Cory, 128, 129

Boyer, Herbert, 145

Bradford, Monica, 176, 180

Brauman, John, 182

Brest, Iris, 121, 170

Brest, Paul, 68, 158, 170

Brin, Sergey, 4

Brown, Harold, 190

Brown, Robert McAfee, 66

Bruno, Merle, 37, 38–39

Bush, George W.: attitude regarding science, 191–92; and climate change, 192, 194; policy on stem cell research, 192

Bush, Vannevar, 116, 143, 144

Butler, Thomas, 51, 190, 198

Byer, Robert, 154

Calabrese, Ronald, 59

Califano, Joseph Jr., 73, 74, 76, 81, 84, 86

Calorie Control Council, 75–76

Camarillo, Albert, 114

Campbell, Glen, 119, 122

Carnegie Endowment for International Peace, 168

Carnegie Institution, 48

Carter, Jimmy, 86, 116

Casa Zapata, 111

Casey, William, 118

Casper, Gerhard, 10, 163, 164, 168–69, 171

Celera, 184–85

Centennial Campaign, 9, 93–94, 95, 97, 102, 134, 140, 141, 156, 160, 163

Chase, Bill, 95

Chen, Josephine, 33, 121

Chong, Lisa, 181

Christopher, Warren, 119, 141

Ciardi, John, 29

Cisco Systems, 4

Clark, William, 144

Clinton, Bill, 103, 166

Clinton, Chelsea, 126

Clinton, Hillary, 103

Coca Cola, 75

Cohen, Stanley, 145

Collins, Francis, 184

Congress, 79, 81, 82, 83, 84, 85, 91. 95, 97, 166; and antibiotics, 77; and drug reform, 78; and food additives, 80; House Energy and Commerce Committee/ Subcommittee on Oversight and Investigations, 154–59, 160, 161, 162, 163, 164; and indirect cost controversy, 7, 151–62; and Laetrile, 76; Patent and Trademark Law Amendments Act, 144; and saccharin, 75–76; and tax-supported research, 143, 152

Coontz, Robert, 180

Cooper, Rich, 81

Corn, Wanda, 108

Corson, Dale, 187

Dane, Ernest B. "Ebbie," 22–23, 28

Danforth, William, 82

David and Lucile Packard Foundation, 167–68; Board of Trustees, 12

Defense Contract Audit Agency (DCAA) and memoranda of understanding (MOUs), 152

De Forest, Lee, 1

DeLauer, Dick, 189

Department of Agriculture (USDA), 82; Agriculture and Food Research Initiative (AFRI), 83

Department of Defense, 82, 187

Department of Defense–Universities Forum, 187

Department of Energy, 82

Dershowitz, Alan, 63, 64

Dingell, John, 154–56, 157, 158, 159, 161, 162

Dish, the, 5, 10, 119, 121, 130, 131, 136, 204–5

Djerassi, Carl, 149

Doble, Jean, 45

Dole, Bob, 144–46, 147

Dornbusch, Sanford M., 52, 66

Doty, Andy, 68

Drury, Allen, 169

Drury, Bill, 31, 34

Druyan, Ann, 193

Dublin School, 22, 23, 26, 27, 29

Eastman Kodak, 3

Ehrlich, Paul, 49, 51; *The Population Bomb*, 52

Eisen, Arnold, 114

Elizabeth II, 12, 92

Elway, Jack, 128

Fairchild Semiconductor, 3, 4

Falcon, Wally, 164

False Claims Act, 157

FDA. *See* Food and Drug Administration

Federal Telegraph, 1

Feldman, Edward G., 79

Feldman, Marc, 48

Fetter, Jean, 126

Field, Chris, 48

Fields, Howard, 46, 48, 50, 136

Filo, David, 4

Fioravanti, Marc, 166

Fish & Wildlife Service, 30

Fisher, Ray, 63

Fitzpatrick, John, 178

Food, Drug, and Cosmetic Act: Delaney Clause, 75

Food and Drug Administration (FDA): and agricultural research, 81–83; and alcohol use during pregnancy, 101; and antibiotics, 77–78, 81; and drug approval process, 81; and generic drugs, 78; and ice cream, 78, 80; Donald Kennedy as Commissioner of, 9, 73–87, 154, 166, 168, 171, 205; and Laetrile, 76; lawyers at, 81; and saccharin, 75–76, 85

Footlick, Jerrold K., 158

Ford, John, 94

Ford, Tom, 93

Ford Foundation, 53

Ford Times, 202

Franklin, H. Bruce, 34, 61–71; *The Most Important Fish in the Sea*, 69

Freedom of Information Act, 154

Freelen, Bob, 10, 95, 104, 137, 158

Freelen, Sally, 64
Fricke, Russell, 121
Friedman, Milton, 118

Gaither, Jim, 10, 73, 132, 142, 172, 204;
    relationship with Donald Kennedy, 117,
    155, 161, 168
Galyan, Gohar, 105
Gardner, John W., 102, 105, 140
Gardner, Sherwin, 75
Geiger, Andy, 128
General Accounting Office, 154
General Electric, 3
Gerberding, Julie: on climate change, 192
Gilbert, Walter, 149–50
Glen Alpine Creek, 57
Goldsmith, Tim, 33, 40, 57, 137
Goldstone, David, 191
Goodall, Jane: kidnapping of Stanford
    students with, 56
Goodman, Corey, 38, 59
Goodman, Ellen, 109
Google, 4
Gorbachev, Mikhail, 12, 141, 142, 156
Gore, Al, 167
Gottlieb, Jeff, 154
Gough, Nancy, 190
Gould, Stephen J., 175
Greenberg, Daniel, 192
Gregorian, Vartan, 114
Griffin, Don, 30–31, 32–33
Grobstein, Clifford, 49
Grumbly, Tom, 81–82, 83
Gwynne, Ed, 29

Haas, Mimi, 102
Haas, Peter, 102, 105
Haas Center for Public Service, 8, 102–3, 105
Hamburg, David, 46, 52, 56, 66, 73, 78, 114,
    171, 180, 198
Hamburg, Margaret, 78
Hamill, Jamie, 204
Hampshire College, 37, 80, 86
Hargadon, Fred, 126
Harntha, Juthymas, 136
Hart-Rudman Commission Report (2001),
    193
Harvard University, 3, 5, 24, 37, 38, 115,
    149, 150, 152, 175; Board of Overseers,
    99; Donald Kennedy at, 22–23, 28–31,
    32, 34, 35, 40, 43, 54, 56; Porcellian Club,
    22–23; vs. Stanford, 54–55, 156
Hastorf, Albert, 10, 52–53, 131, 172

Healy, Pat, 80
Healy, Timothy, 103
Heller, Craig, 48, 52
Heller, Tom, 164
Hennessy, John, 10
Herrington, Marvin, 137
Hewlett, William, 2
Hewlett-Packard, 2, 3, 4, 45
Holloway, Jonathan, 38
Holtz, George, 37
Horner, Henry, 28
Horton, Larry, 60, 78, 136, 158, 159, 181,
    190
Howard Hughes Medical Institute, 145, 146
Hoy, Ron, 38, 46, 51, 132
Huang, Alice, 175
Hudnall, Mike, 11
Hunter, Carrie Jane, 56
Hwang Woo-suk, 182–83

Inman, Bobby, 188
Institute of Medicine, 73, 80
Intel, 3

Jackson, Michael, 110
Jackson, Rev. Jesse, 109
Jaffe, Rona, 29
Jasny, Barbara, 185, 190
Jasper Ridge Biological Preserve, 5, 172, 173
Johnson, Pitch, 131, 133
Jordan, David Starr, 1, 115
Juilland, Alphonse, 39
Justice Department, 157

Kabila, Laurent, 56
Kaplan, John, 97
Karlin-Neumann, George, 50, 58, 132
Katchadourian, Herant, 53
Kaufman, Bill, 56, 131
Kennedy, Barbara Bean, 15, 17–18, 22, 25,
    26, 32, 203; relationship with Donald, 19,
    20, 21, 60
Kennedy, Cameron, 103, 203, 204
Kennedy, David, 118, 119, 131, 136
Kennedy, Donald: *Academic Duty*, 34, 45,
    47, 109, 207; *Birds of Stanford*, 181, 184;
    as chairman of Biological Sciences Dept.,
    48–49, 51, 52, 58; as chairman of Faculty
    Advisory Board of the Academic Council,
    61, 62, 63–71; early life, 15–26, 203; as
    editor-in-chief of *Science*, 12, 77–78,
    146, 171, 173, 177–201, 204; as FDA
    Commissioner, 9, 73–87, 101, 156, 170;

Kennedy, Donald (*continued*)
   at Harvard, 22–23, 28–31, 32, 34, 40, 54,
   58; health condition, 12–13, 203, 207,
   208, 209; *Humans, Nature, and Birds*, 181,
   184; and indirect cost controversy, 7,
   12, 14, 131, 142, 153–62, 170, 177, 207;
   during kidnapping of Stanford students,
   56, 58; *The Last of Your Springs*, 206;
   photographs of, 11, 16, 25, 39, 44, 47,
   48, 49, 55, 68, 74, 81, 91, 92, 94, 101,
   102, 104, 108, 112, 114, 116, 117, 120,
   125, 127, 133, 134, 139, 143, 151, 166,
   173, 174, 200, 204, 205; as president of
   Stanford, 8–9, 10, 11, 12, 51, 69–70, 85,
   91–121, 123–44, 145–52, 153–64, 170,
   173, 174, 206; as provost of Stanford,
   89–91, 137, 170; relationship with Peter
   Bing, 117–18; relationship with Cory
   Booker, 129, 130–31; relationship with
   Merle Bruno, 37, 38–39; relationship
   with Earnest Dane, 22–23, 28;
   relationship with Dorsey, 15, 18, 19, 21,
   22, 23, 26, 203; relationship with Bill
   Drury, 31, 34; relationship with Ehrlich,
   49, 52; relationship with father, 22, 23,
   26, 27, 29, 134, 203–5; relationship with
   Howard Fields, 48; relationship with Jim
   Gaither, 117, 157, 163, 170; relationship
   with John Gardner, 141; relationship
   with Don Griffin, 30–31, 32–33;
   relationship with Tom Grumbly, 81–82,
   83; relationship with George Holtz, 37,
   40; relationship with Jeanne, 26, 28,
   32–33, 35–36, 40–41, 56, 59, 67, 73, 86,
   135–36, 140–41, 162, 168; relationship
   with Julia, 56, 59, 135–36, 140, 204, 207;
   relationship with Catherine Milton,
   100–101, 104–5; relationship with
   mother, 19, 20, 21, 60; relationship with
   Page, 35–36, 56, 59, 60, 135–36, 140, 204,
   206–7; relationship with James Preston,
   36–37, 40, 44; relationship with Robin,
   26, 40, 59, 125, 133, 136–37, 140–43, 158,
   162, 167, 177, 203, 209–10; relationship
   with Joel Smith, 90; relationship with
   students, 9, 10, 11, 12, 31, 33, 34–35, 37,
   38–39, 45, 46, 48, 50, 51, 53, 57, 58, 100,
   105, 115, 120, 125–27, 129, 130–31, 132,
   133, 135, 138, 139, 163, 165–66, 168–69,
   172; relationship with George Wald,
   30; relationship with Werner Wulff,
   37; relationship with Yanofsky, 49, 52;
   research interests, 36–37, 38, 43, 44–45,

   46, 47–48, 81–83; resignation, 12, 153,
   165, 166; running the Dish, 10, 129, 133,
   138, 163, 206–7; at Syracuse, 35–36, 38,
   40–41, 43, 44, 58, 134; views on academic
   freedom, 44, 61, 70–71, 93, 207; views on
   antiapartheid divestment, 96–97; views
   on climate change denial, 196–200; views
   on complementary authorship, 45, 47;
   views on government secrecy, 188–91,
   193–94; views on multiculturalism, 113,
   114; views on public service, 8, 57, 83,
   85–86, 100–103, 105, 106, 129; views on
   teaching and research, 113, 115–17; views
   on Western Culture program, 109
Kennedy, Dorsey, 16–18, 23, 25, 202;
   relationship with Donald, 1, 15, 18, 19,
   21, 22, 23, 26, 201
Kennedy, Jeanne Dewey, 20, 46, 51, 67,
   73–74, 80, 104; relationship with Donald,
   28, 32–33, 35–36, 40–41, 57, 58, 60, 73,
   86, 135, 139
Kennedy, Julia, 20, 40, 41, 56, 57, 58, 60,
   74, 80, 86; relationship with father, 56,
   202, 205
Kennedy, Page, 4, 20, 37, 41, 60, 74, 80, 86,
   202; relationship with father, 35–36, 57,
   58, 60, 135–36, 140, 204–205
Kennedy, Robin Hamill, 12, 13, 53–54, 131,
   138–39, 163–64, 165–66; relationship
   with Donald, 26, 123, 125, 133, 135–36,
   140–43, 158, 167, 175, 201, 207–8
Kennedy, Ted, 75, 80, 81, 138
Kennedy, William, 23–24, 32, 43; at
   Harvard, 24; photographs of, 24, 25;
   relationship with Donald, 26, 27, 29, 134,
   203–5; relationship with Dorsey, 23, 203,
   204
Kihara, Sylvia, 176
Kimball, Maggie, 204
Kimball, William, 118
Klein, Joel, 63, 65
Kornberg, Arthur, 43–44
Kornberg, Roger, 44
Krauthammer, Charles, 109
Kretchmer, Norm, 52
Kyoto campus, 9

LaMarco, Kelly, 180
Lavine, Marc, 181
Lederberg, Josh, 52
Levin, Herbert, 56, 58, 121
Levine, Jon, 48
Levitsky, Rob, 131

Lewis, Anthony, 159
Lewis, Meriwether, 144
Lieberman, Gerald, 89, 172
Litton Industries, 2
Liu, Goodwin, 10
Lockheed, 3
Loma Prieta earthquake, 7, 53–54, 123–24
Los Angeles Times, 158, 178
Lougee, Carolyn, 110, 114
Luce, Henry, 24
Lyman, Richard, 62, 66, 69, 89, 90, 91, 95, 171
Lyons, Jim, 110, 113

Malik, Pratap, 123
Mancall, Mark, 68
Manning, Carolyn, 95, 136
Marquis, Don: *New York Sun* columns, 186
Mason, David M., 66
Massy, William, 89
Maxmin, Jody, 120, 121, 163
Mazza, Annie-Marie, 168
McBride, Tom, 101
McCarthy, Colman, 84
McCoy, William, 172
McCune, Michael, 145
McEuen, Paul, 183
McNutt, Marcia, 198
Meese, Edwin, 118
Mellon, DeForest, 46
Merrill, Richard, 81, 168
Mervis, Jeff, 190
Milkman, Roger, 35
Milton, Catherine, 100–101, 102, 103, 105, 170
Mitchell, Ted, 163
Morales, Pablo, 127
Morell, Frank, 184
Muller, Henry, 159
Myers-Briggs Type Indicator, 110

National Academy of Sciences, 81, 168, 180, 182, 187, 191
National Aeronautics and Space Administration (NASA), 82
National Audubon Society, 179
National Cancer Institute (NCI), 76
National Institute of Food and Agriculture (NIFA), 82
National Institutes of Health (NIH), 82, 144, 145, 184
National Milk Producers Federation, 80
National Science Foundation (NSF), 82

National Security Defense Directive (NSDD) 187–88
Nature, 175, 183, 184, 185, 186, 191
Newman, Frank, 103
New York Times, 79, 80, 84, 118, 147, 148, 159, 178, 194, 204
Nierenberg, William, 73
North, William, 29

O'Connor, Sandra Day, 117, 172
Office of Foreign Assets (OFAC), 189
Office of Management and Budget, A-21, 152
Office of Naval Research (ONR), and memoranda of Understanding (MOUs), 152, 154
Oreskes, Naomi: *Merchants of Doubt*, 197
Orr, Lynn, 167
Orr, Susan Packard, 167
Overton, Patrick: "Faith," 164
Owen, John A. Jr., 79
Oxford University, 10, 23, 54, 130; Stanford Oxford campus, 9

Packard, David, 2, 3, 167–68
Packard, Lucille, 167–68
Packer, Herbert L., 62–63
Page, Larry, 4
Pajaro Dunes Conference, 147–48, 149
Panofsky, Wolfgang K. H. "Pief," 66
Pape, Stuart, 81
Patent and Trademark Law Amendments Act, 144
Paull, Tanya, 121
Pepsi Cola, 26, 75
Perle, Richard, 187
Pinholster, Ginger, 190
Pittendrigh, Colin, 53–54, 130
Planck, Max, 162
Plumer, PattiSue, 131
President's Council of Advisors on Science and Technology, 78
Preston, James, 36–37, 44
Program in Human Biology, 5, 12, 44, 52, 54, 58, 67, 131
Proxmire, William, 192

Raymo, Chet, 194, 199
Reader's Digest: "How He Caught the Campus Chiselers," 154
Reagan, Nancy, 122
Reagan Presidential Library, 118–19, 122
Reagan Rule, 187–88

Regnery, David, 45, 46
Reilly, Bill, 167
Resor, Stanley, 27
Rice, Condoleeza, 137, 168–69, 188
Richter, Ari, 132
Riggs, Henry, 94, 136
Roberts, Leslie, 298
Robinson, Edwin Arlington: "Mr. Flood's Party," 133
Robinson, Norm, 110, 114, 161
Rocky Mountain Biological Laboratory, 52
Rogers, Paul, 81
Rosenzweig, Robert, 89–90, 104, 159, 161
Rosner, Beth, 181
Ross, Peter, 105
Rosse, Jim, 140, 172
Roster, Michael, 164
Roth, Richard, 50

Saccharin Safety and Labeling Act, 75
Sandoz, 146
San Francisco Chronicle, 109, 113
San Jose Mercury News, 154, 160
Sant, Roger, 166, 179
Sant, Victoria, 166, 179
Schlesinger, James, 79
Schneider, Stephen, 198
Schön, J. Hendrik, 183–84
Schwartz, Amy, 109
Schwartz, John, 89, 132
Science, 79, 82; and climate change denial, 196–200; and dual use science, 188; and government secrecy, 188–91, 193–94; and human genome project, 184–85, 190; Donald Kennedy as editor-in-chief, 12, 77–78, 144, 169, 171, 175–199, 201; vs. *Nature*, 177, 186, 187, 188; news staff vs. editorial staff, 178; peer review for, 177–78, 186; and regulatory policy, 191; and religion, 194–95; and science illiteracy, 194–96; and scientific fraud, 182–84; and sighting of ivory-billed woodpecker, 178–79
Science and Government Report, 192
Search for Extraterrestrial Intelligence (SETI), 192
Seeger, Pete, 106
Segal, George, 96
Seoul National University (SNU), 182–83
Shapiro, Harold, 10
Shockley, William, 3
Shockley Transistor Laboratory, 3
Shultz, George, 95, 118, 142

Sibley, David, 179
Silicon Valley, 2, 3, 4, 10, 131, 146, 187
Simon, Mark, 172
Smith, Joel, 89, 90, 94, 135
Smith, Kenneth Stephen, 56
Smith, Marshall, 114
Smith College, 28
Smuts, Barbara, 56
Sohn, Lydia, 183
South Africa: antiapartheid movement, 7–8, 96–99
Springboard, 105
Stanford, Jane Lathrop, 1, 100, 115, 126
Stanford, Leland, 1, 115, 126
Stanford Challenge, 6
Stanford Daily, 8, 105, 112, 128, 132, 136
Stanford in Washington campus, 9, 12, 103, 117, 140, 165–67, 170
Stanford Review, 109
Stanford Sierra Camp, 57, 93
Stanford University: Academic Senate, 55, 109; antiapartheid movement at, 7–8, 96–100; Backman Center for Molecular and Genetic Medicine, 9; Bing Concert Hall, 117; Bing Nursery School, 117; Bing Overseas Studies Program, 117; Black Student Union, 107; Board of Trustees, 54, 73, 90, 93, 97–98, 100, 106, 113, 114, 117–19, 142, 155, 157, 158, 162, 170; Campus Compact, 103, 105, 106; Cardinal Service, 103; Centennial Campaign, 9, 93–94, 95, 96–97, 102, 136, 158, 162, 165; Center for Integrated Systems, 9; Center for Public Service at Owen House, 101–2; Center for the Advanced Study of the Behavioral Sciences, 93; Center for the Study of Language and Information, 9; Committee on Graduate Studies, 149; Committee on Minority Issues, 112; Controller's Office, 156; Department of Biological Sciences, 40, 48–49, 51, 52, 58; Department of Physics, 112; the Dish at, 5, 10, 119, 129, 133, 138, 163, 206–7; diversity at, 107, 110–13; endowment funds, 162; Faculty Advisory Board, 61, 62, 63–71; Faculty Senate, 108, 119; Founding Grant, 100; Fundamental Standard, 112; Graduate School of Business, 5, 103; Green Library, 7, 123–24; growth, 5–6, 9, 115–16; Haas Center for Public Service, 8, 102–3, 105; vs. Harvard, 54–55, 158; Honors Cooperative Program, 3; Hoover House, 53, 92, 104,

124, 129, 133, 136, 139, 142, 154–55; Hoover Institution Archives, 118–19; Hopkins Marine Station, 5, 45, 53, 175; Humanities Center, 5, 9, 115; indirect cost controversy, 7, 12, 14, 131, 142, 153–62, 170, 177, 207; Institute for International Studies, 5, 9; interdisciplinary programs, 5, 9, 44–45, 52–55, 171; Introduction to the Humanities (IHUM) program, 110; Jewish Studies program, 114; Marching Band, 126, 128, 129, 133; Men's Swim Team, 127; Office of the General Council, 166–67; overseas campuses, 9; Program in Earth Systems, 5, 54; Program in Human Biology, 5, 12, 44, 52, 58, 67, 134, 166, 167, 171; Residential Education program, 110–11, 114; role in digital revolution, 1, 2–4; School of Medicine, 9, 44, 46, 52, 53, 94, 147; Special Committee on Investment Responsibility (SCIR)/ Advisory Panel on Investment and Licensing (APIRL), 98–100; Stanford Industrial Park/Stanford Research Park, 3; Stanford Institute for Economic Policy Research (SIEPR), 5, 93; Stanford Linear Accelerator, 5, 44; Stanford Medical Center, 5–6; Statement of Faculty Discipline (1972), 70; stem cell research at, 6; student aid, 6; transition in 1960s, 1, 40, 43; tuition, 162, 164; Vietnam War protests at, 61–71; Western Culture program, 8, 107–10. *See also* Casper, Gerhard; Kennedy, Donald; Lyman, Richard; Stanford-in-Washington campus; Sterling, J. E. Wallace; Terman, Frederick
State University of New York (SUNY): School of Forestry, 36
Sterling, J. E. Wallace, 3, 44, 91, 116
Stever, Guyford, 73
Stone, Bill, 137, 204
Sullivan, Rev. Leon, 98
Summers, Larry, 55
Sun Microsystems, 4
Supporters of Agriculture Research (SoAR), 82–83
Supton, Alice, 110
Syntex, 3
Syracuse University: Department of Zoology, 36, 37; Donald Kennedy at, 35–37, 38, 40–41, 43, 44, 56, 131
Systemix, 145–46
Szuromi, Phil, 180

Tanzania, 56
Tatum, Sandy, 118
Taylor, Mike, 81
Tektronix, 45
Terman, Frederick, 2, 3, 43–44, 52, 116
The Play, 128–29
Time magazine, 24
Tocqueville, Alexis de, 102
Trudeau, Michelle, 56
Turing Awards, 4
Tutu, Desmond, 99
Twitty, Victor, 40, 48–49, 55

Ujamaa, 8, 111–13
Union of Concerned Scientists, 192
University of California, Berkeley, 38, 55, 126, 128, 131, 192; Big Game of 1982, 128–29
University of California, San Diego, 49
University of California, San Francisco, 48, 145
University of California Board of Regents, 99
Unterman, David, 139
U.S. Office of Scientific Research and Development, 116, 143

Van Zinnicq Bergmann, Emilie, 56
Varian Associates, 2, 3
Varian, Russell and Sigurd, 2
Venter, Craig, 184–85
Vetter, Jan, 63, 65–66
Victoria, 153
Vietnam War protest, 61–70
Vinson, Valda, 181
Vodra, William, 81
Voss, David, 104

Wachhorst, Wyn, 206
Wade, Nicholas, 79
Wald, George, 30
Wall Street Journal, 146
Warner, Tim, 89
Warren, Bill, 28, 32
Washington Post, 80, 84
Washington University, 44, 82
Waxman, Henry A., 79, 84
Weissman, Irving, 145–46, 149
Welsh, John, 30
Wessells, Norm, 38, 58, 112, 131, 172, 174
Wheye, Darryl: *Birds of Stanford*, 179; *Humans, Nature, and Birds*, 179
W. H. Freeman Company, 56–57

Wiley, Harvey, 85
Will, George, 109
Williams, Vaughn, 59
Wilson, Don, 48, 55
Wilson, Mark, 95
Wolf, Howard, 171
Wolfe, Susan, 207
Woods, Ward, 167
Woods Hole Oceanographic Institution, 30–31
Worcester tornado, 28
Writer, The, 24
Wulff, Verner, 37

Xerox, 3

Yahoo, 4
Yang, Jerry, 4
Yanofsky, Charles, 49, 52
Yates, Margaret, 57
Yeston, Jake, 190
Young, Charles, 106

Zaire: kidnapped Stanford students in, 56, 58; People's Revolutionary Party (PRP), 56
Zarin, Deborah, 33, 51, 132